The Politics of the Draft Common Frame of Reference

Private Law in European Context Series

VOLUME 16

Series Editors:
Martijn Hesselink
Ugo Mattei
Horatia Muir Watt

A list of previous titles in the series may be found at the end of this volume.

KLUWER LAW INTERNATIONAL

The Politics of the Draft Common Frame of Reference

Edited by

Alessandro Somma

Wolters Kluwer
Law & Business

AUSTIN BOSTON CHICAGO NEW YORK THE NETHERLANDS

Published by:
Kluwer Law International
PO Box 316
2400 AH Alphen aan den Rijn
The Netherlands
Website: www.kluwerlaw.com

Sold and distributed in North, Central and South America by:
Aspen Publishers, Inc.
7201 McKinney Circle
Frederick, MD 21704
United States of America
Email: customer.care@aspenpubl.com

Sold and distributed in all other countries by:
Turpin Distribution Services Ltd.
Stratton Business Park
Pegasus Drive, Biggleswade
Bedfordshire SG18 8TQ
United Kingdom
Email: kluwerlaw@turpin-distribution.com

Printed on acid-free paper.

ISBN 978-90-411-3141-6

Printed in Great Britain.

List of Contributors

Guido Alpa
Professor of Civil Law, University La Sapienza, Rome.
President of the Italian Bar Council.

Gert Brüggemeier
Professor of Private Law and Comparative Law, University of Bremen.
Former Director of ZERP – Centre of European Law and Politics,
University of Bremen.

Aurelia Colombi Ciacchi
Lecturer in Comparative Law and Fellow,
ZERP – Centre of European Law and Politics,
University of Bremen.

Stefan Grundmann
Professor of German, European and International Private and Business Law,
Humboldt University, Berlin.
President of SECOLA – Society of European Contract Law.

Martijn Hesselink
Professor of European Private Law, University of Amsterdam.
Director of the Centre for the Study of European Contract Law,
University of Amsterdam.

Brigitta Lurger
Professor of Civil, Commercial and European Law, University of Graz.

Marisa Meli
Professor of Private Law and Comparative Law, University of Catania.

Peter Rott
Junior Professor of Private Law with a focus on European Private Law, University of Bremen.

Jacobien W. Rutgers
Senior Lecturer, Free University, Amsterdam.

Arthur F. Salomons
Professor of Private Law, Centre for the Study of European Contract Law, University of Amsterdam.

Ruth Sefton-Green
Maître de conférences, UMR de droit comparé de Paris, Université Paris 1 (Panthéon-Sorbonne).

Alessandro Somma
Professor of Private Comparative Law and European Private Law, University of Ferrara.
Director of CeStInt – Center for Foreign and International Law, University of Ferrara.

Summary of Contents

Table of Contents

Preface

The Draft Common Frame of Reference and the Social Justice Study Group

In 2001, the European Commission called for a reflection on the traditional Community approach to contract law: the adoption of 'directives on specific contracts or specific marketing techniques where a particular need for harmonization was identified'.[1] This approach has been held to be the cause for excessive diversity at a national level and, therefore, as the cause for creating unnecessary obstacles to the internal market. Hence, it had to be revised, and, to that end, a few – potentially cumulative – options were developed:

(i) *The development of common contract law principles leading to more convergence of national laws.* 'One solution would be for the Commission to promote comparative law research and co-operation between, amongst others, academics and legal practitioners (including judges and experts). This co-operation could aim to find common principles in relevant areas of national contract law. The existing work in this area could be used and developed, including the results of academic studies and conclusions drawn in international academic forums. The framework for this research and co-operation could be a kind of partnership, in which the EC institutions, and more particularly the Commission, could play a co-ordination role'.[2]

(ii) *The improvement of the quality of legislation already in place.* 'Improving the quality of legislation already in place implies first modernizing existing instruments. The Commission intends to build on action already undertaken on consolidating, codifying and recasting existing instruments centred on transparency and clarity. Quality of drafting could also be reviewed; presentation and terminology could become more coherent.

1. COM (2001) 398 final.
2. *Ibid.*, at 52.

Apart from those changes regarding the presentation of legal texts, efforts should moreover be systematically focused on simplifying and clarifying the content of existing legislation'.[3]

(iii) *The adoption of a new comprehensive legislation at EC level.* 'Another option would be an overall text comprising provisions on general questions of contract law as well as specific contracts. For this option, the choice of instrument and the binding nature of the measures need to be discussed'.[4]

The Commission's call for reflection on these options has been picked up by a number of governments and stakeholders, including businesses, legal practitioners, academics and consumer organizations. Their reactions have been summarized in a document by the Commission which states that the differing national laws create 'obstacles and disincentives to cross-border transactions'.[5] In that document a majority holds that the sectorial approach, as such, is not problematic, but that it would be helpful to develop 'common principles of European contract law' and, in particular, to improve the 'existing EC law in the area of contract law'. Only a minority of the interventions was in favour of the idea of developing 'a new instrument on European contract law', while 'an important number of contributors suggested that further thought might be given to this'.[6]

This has inspired the formulation of an Action Plan which is supposed to lead to 'a more coherent European contract law', particularly in two ways:

(i) *Improving the existing* acquis *by developing a Common Frame of Reference (CFR).* 'A CFR, establishing common principles and terminology in the area of European contract law is seen by the Commission as an important step towards the improvement of the contract law *acquis*. This CFR will be a publicly accessible document which should help the Community institutions in ensuring greater coherence of existing and future *acquis* in the area of European contract law. This frame of reference should meet the needs and expectations of the economic operators in an internal market which envisages becoming the world's most dynamic economy'. The CFR 'should provide for best solutions in terms of common terminology and rules, i.e., the definition of fundamental concepts and abstract terms such as contract or damage and of the rules which apply, for example, in the case of the non-performance of contracts. In this context contractual freedom should be the guiding principle; restrictions should only be foreseen where this could be justified with good reasons'.[7]

(ii) *Reflecting on the opportuneness of non-sector-specific measures such as an optional instrument in the area of European contract law.* 'Some

---

3. *Ibid.*, at 58.
4. *Ibid.*, at 61.
5. COM (2003) 68 final, at 25.
6. *Ibid.*, at 7.
7. *Ibid.*, at 59 and 62.

> arguments have been made in favour of an optional instrument, which would provide parties to a contract with a modern body of rules particularly adapted to cross-border contracts in the internal market. Consequently, parties would not need to cover every detail in contracts specifically drafted or negotiated for this purpose, but could simply refer to this instrument as the applicable law. It would provide both parties, the economically stronger and weaker, with an acceptable and adequate solution without insisting on the necessity to apply one party's national law, thereby also facilitating negotiations'.[8]

The Action Plan has provoked varied reactions. Amongst the most detailed, one should mention that of the Study Group on Social Justice in European Contract Law (Social Justice Study Group), founded in 2003 following the initiative by Hugh Collins and Martijn Hesselink. Its main ideas have been defined in the Manifesto on social justice in European contract law, drafted during a series of meetings which took place in Amsterdam, London, and Paris.[9]

The ideas developed in the Manifesto focus on the political character of the different forms of intervention in European Contract Law, which the Commission does not acknowledge, on the basis that the principle of contractual freedom is widely diffused and recognized. In fact, on the one hand, contract law necessarily reflects the fundamental principles of social justice and strongly influences the satisfaction of citizens' primary needs, especially when viewed in connection with the beginning privatization of the Welfare State. On the other hand, the development of the CFR, on which the different Community interventions in contract law are based, is seen as a technocratic process exposed to the influence of strong economic forces.

To remedy the democratic deficit that characterizes the Commission's approach, one would need to develop participatory procedures, especially by an increased inclusion of the European Parliament, and to clarify in advance the model of social justice on which to build a European contract law. Obviously, this presupposes an overhaul of the idea that the limits to contractual freedom, like those relating to consumer protection, are simply a way of solving market failures. Moreover, it requires a re-evaluation of the diversity of national laws. The latter may represent an obstacle to the development of the internal market, but it is not an obstacle to the development of a European identity. On the contrary, diversity is its core.

This set of ideas, as highlighted by the Manifesto, may foster a link between the European contract law in the making and the system of EC-fundamental rights,

---

8. *Ibid.*, at 90.
9. The Manifesto was published in *European Law Journal* 10 (2004): 653 et seq., and was signed by Gert Brüggemeier, Mauro Bussani, Hugh Collins, Aurelia Colombi Ciacchi, Giovanni Comandé, Muriel Fabre-Magnan, Stefan Grundmann, Martijn Hesselink, Christian Joerges, Brigitta Lurger, Ugo Mattei, Marisa Meli, Jacobien Rutgers, Christoph Schmidt, Lesley Jane Smith, Ruth Sefton-Green, Horatia Muir Watt, and Thomas Wilhelmsson. The following have asked to be associated with the content of the Manifesto: Guido Alpa, Mario Barcellona, Duncan Kennedy, Marisaria Maugeri, and Gunther Teubner.

codified in the Nice Charter of Fundamental Rights of the European Union.[10] In fact, this document indicates which model of social justice underpins the European Union – the model summarised in the formula 'social market economy'. This is to be implemented preferably without using hard law such as a European Civil Code, which the Commission probably has in mind when it mentions the elaboration of an 'optional instrument'.

Especially this last aspect has been highlighted during the presentation of the Manifesto. If understood in the indicated way, the optional instrument 'would amount to a kind of mass destruction – that is, destruction of the national private law traditions of every Member State'.[11] This does not mean that the utility of measures directed at fostering European integration should be denied. Rather, it stresses that these measures do not have only technical significance, and that their political importance needs to be highlighted as well and to be discussed within the democratic framework: 'a European civil code will represent a statement of the political values that will govern the basic principles of social justice in the market economy. Such a statement of the ideals of a social market economy requires both democratic endorsement and regulatory legitimacy. The institutions of the European Union, with their unique constellation of multilevel systems of governance, are not designed, and were never intended to be competent, to engage in the construction of such a political statement'.[12]

Thanks also to the French[13] and Italian[14] translations, the Manifesto immediately provoked a number of reactions and has sparked interventions concerning European private law, in which the diverging cultural and political profiles of the different authors have come to play a central role. This was especially the case when the Manifesto was presented to the Italian scientific community in a meeting which took place at the University of Ferrara in 2005.[15]

---

10. Article 6 of the EU Treaty now attributes 'the same legal value as the Treaties' to this Charter, as adapted at Strasbourg, on 12.12.2007.
11. H. Collins, 'The Future of European Private Law: An Introduction', *European Law Journal* 10 (2004): 649.
12. *Ibid.*, 650. This starting point has been developed in specific contributions of some authors and subscribers of the Manifesto: Guido Alpa (734 et seq.), Hugh Collins (787 et seq.), Stefan Grundmann (698 et seq.), Martijn Hesselink (675 et seq.) and Thomas Wilhelmsson (712 et seq.). *See also* the contributions of Daniela Caruso (751 et seq.), and Oliver Gerstenberg (766 et seq.).
13. *Revue trimestrielle de droit civil* (2005): 713 et seq.
14. *Rivista critica del diritto privato* (2005): 99 et seq. In that occasion the number of people signing the Manifesto has increased to include: Cristina Amato, Claudia Amodio, Elena Bargelli, Joerg Benedict, Odavia Bueno Diaz, Anthony Chamboredon, Giuseppe Conte, Lucilla Gatt, Ivo Giesen, Axel Halfmeier, Geraint Howells, Christophe Jamin, Bertram Keller, Johanna Kemper, Ilka Klöckner, Matthias Leistner, Marco Loos, Maria Rosaria Marella, Giovanni Marini, Pier Giuseppe Monateri, Emanuela Navarretta, Elizabeth Oikonomidou-Poulou, Tomasz Pajor, Salvatore Patti, Kristina Riedl, Arthur Salomons, Elena Sanchez, Alessandro Somma, Mark Van Hoecke, Albert Verheij, Giuseppe Vettori, and Jan Vranken.
15. *See* A. Somma (ed), *Giustizia sociale e mercato nel diritto europeo dei contatti* (Torino: Giappichelli, 2007), with contributions of Guido Alpa (33 et seq.), Cristina Amato (55 et seq.), Mario Barcellona (67 et seq.), Hugh Collins (83 et seq.), Stefan Grundmann (107 et seq.),

The Social Justice Group then organized two further meetings in which the reflections contained in the Manifesto were further developed. The first meeting was hosted by the University of Paris I in 2005 and dealt with political, philosophical, and cultural aspects of social justice, with social justice from a constitutional point of view, with social justice in contract law, and with social market economy.[16] The second meeting was hosted by the University of Helsinki within an international seminar dedicated to the 'substantive consequences for private law of the fact that the society to which it is applied is multicultural and multilingual'.[17]

Meanwhile, the Community initiatives intending to develop a European private law have multiplied. A communication by the Commission has provided some specifications on the role and on the nature of the CFR, and the communication emphasizes that the CFR will contribute to 'improving the quality and consistency of the *acquis* in the area of contract law' and that, to this end, it 'will provide clear definitions of legal terms, fundamental principles, and coherent model rules of contract law, drawing on the EC *acquis* and on best solutions found in Member States' legal orders'. Moreover, other functions of the CFR have been identified: 'national legislators could use the CFR when transposing EU directives in the area of contract law into national legislation. They could also draw on the CFR when enacting legislation on areas of contract law which are not regulated at Community level. Another role, suggested by the European Parliament, is the possible use of the CFR in arbitration... The CFR would be likely to serve as the basis for the development of a possible optional instrument... Finally the CFR, based on the EC *acquis* and on best solutions identified as common to Member States contract laws, could inspire the European Court of Justice when interpreting the *acquis* on contract law'. As to the legal nature of the CFR, it is said that 'the Commission considers at this stage that the CFR would be a non-binding instrument. However, the Commission will consult extensively all interested parties when elaborating the CFR. In that context this question might be raised again'.[18]

The same communication then mentions the 'optional instrument', specifying that it is 'neither the Commission's intention to propose a European civil code which would harmonize contract laws of Member States, nor should the reflections

---

Brigitta Lurger (141 et seq.), Marisa Meli (167 et seq.), Pier Giuseppe Monateri (175 et seq.), Baldassare Pastore (187 et seq.), Stefano Rodotà (193 et seq.), Ruth Sefton-Green (205 et seq.), Alessandro Somma (227 et seq.), Giuseppe Vettori (249 et seq.), and Thomas Wilhelmsson (267 et seq.).

16. *See* R. Sefton-Green, 'Introduction', *European Review of Contract Law* 2 (2006): 131 et seq. This volume contains contributions of Hugh Collins (213 et seq.), Aurelia Colombi Ciacchi (167 et seq.), Maria Rosaria Marella (257 et seq.), Maria Rosaria Maugeri (250 et seq.), Marisa Meli (159 et seq.), Jacobien Rutgers (199 et seq.), Lesley Jane Smith (227 et seq.), Ruth Sefton-Green (275 et seq.), Alessandro Somma (181 et seq.), and Stephen Weatherill (136 et seq.).
17. Th. Wilhelmsson, E. Paunio & A. Pohjolainen, 'Preface', in *Private Law and the Many Cultures of Europe*, eds Th. Wilhelmsson, E. Paunio & A. Pohjolainen (Alphen aan den Rijn: Kluwer), xxi. *See* the contributions of Hugh Collins (155 et seq.), Brigitta Lurger (177 et seq.), Ruth Sefton-Green (837 et seq.), Alessandro Somma (201 et seq.), and Thomas Wilhelmsson (3 et seq. and 243 et seq.).
18. COM (2004) 651 final, 2 et seq.

be seen as in any way calling into question the current approaches to promoting free circulation on the basis of flexible and efficient solutions'.[19]

Regarding the achievement of the project, it is said that, 'in order to ensure that the CFR is of high quality, the Commission will finance three years of research under the Sixth Framework Programme for research and technological development'.[20] In fact, in 2005, the Joint Network on European Private Law was instructed to elaborate a CFR on European contractual law, to be presented in the form of a draft (DCFR). In particular, 'the Network will deliver a proposal for the CFR for European contract law as described in the Commission's Action Plan (COM 2003 68 final) and the Communication of 11 October 2004. The proposal will be presented in the form of principles (Common Principles of European Contract Law – CoPECL), including definitions, general concepts and legal rules. They will be supplemented by comments, comparative information and by evaluative analysis . . . On the one hand, the researchers will take into account national laws, including case-law of national courts and established contractual practice. On the other hand, they will consider the existing EC *acquis* and relevant international instruments'.[21]

The Joint Network consists of two drafting groups and of a number of supportive groups, all called upon to contribute to the development of the DCFR. The drafting groups are the Study Group on a European Civil Code (Study Group) and the Research Group on the Existing EC Private Law (Acquis Group). The former is the successor to the Commission on European Contract Law, the so called Lando Commission, which had proposed the famous Principles of European Contract Law (PECL). It has the task of reconstructing European law starting with the analysis of national laws and of developing Principles of European Law (PEL) from that point of view. The latter instead is charged with the reconstruction of the fragmented existing Community law and with formulating the Principles of the Existing EC Contract Law (Acquis Principles).[22]

Amongst the supportive groups, the Association Henri Capitant, the Société de Législation Comparée and the Conseil Supérieur du Notariat 'will concentrate on cultural and philosophical underpinnings and different notions of law'. The Research Group on the Economic Assessment of Contract Law Rules 'will undertake a broad assessment of economic implications of the rules, taking into consideration the needs of the economic operators in the internal market'. The Common Core of European Private Law Group 'will carry out a case law assessment focusing on the applicability and practicability of results elaborated by the Principle drafting groups'.[23]

---

19. *Ibid.*, 10.
20. *Ibid.*, 11.
21. Contract n. 513351 within the sixth Framework Programme of the European Union (Priority 7 – Research topic 5.1.3. Towards a European Contract Law).
22. A third drafting group, the Project Group Restatement of European Insurance Law (Insurance Group), is charged with the drafting of Principles of European Insurance Law, which will be organised separately from the DCFR.
23. Contract n. 513351, n. 21 above.

One should note that the drafting of the DCFR is not only an academic activity. A primary role has been assigned to a commission of stakeholders, representing the world of companies and the legal professions and, albeit in a small part, of consumer associations (CFR-net).[24] This commission has to provide input, 'firstly at the beginning of the research, through the identification of the main problems which need to be addressed. Subsequently, this input will be provided in the course of the research, through detailed practical comments on the research works and the documents which will be submitted for observations to the CFR-net experts . . . In order to ensure that the research focuses on actual problems in the area of contractual practice and that the proposed solutions can effectively solve these problems, CFR-net experts are expected to discuss any problems, proposed solutions, and related comments within the stakeholder group to which they belong'.[25]

The fundamental role of CFR-net within the Joint Network is emphasized in the First annual progress report on European contract law and the *acquis* review, which specifies that 'throughout the research process, it will provide input through comments on the research papers, to be discussed in workshops and via a dedicated website'. More specifically: 'Before workshops, the research drafts are posted on the dedicated website. Those CFR-net members who have registered an interest in the specific topic are invited to examine the drafts and comment. After workshops, CFR-net experts are invited to summarise their contribution to the discussion in writing. The Commission prepares a report which reflects the comments raised by CFR-net members in the workshop, their written contributions and the reactions of researchers. The reports specifically identify policy issues, in particular those relevant to the consumer contract law *acquis*, as well as horizontal questions. The researchers have six months to react to the CFR-net comments summarised in the Commission report, by taking them on board in their revised drafts, or, in case of disagreement, by explaining the reasons'. Moreover, 'policy decisions should be clearly identified and explained, in particular in the researchers' outline and in the comments linked to the draft rules' and 'the principle of freedom of contract needs to be emphasised as crucial for the process'.[26]

The role of the European Parliament is, however, clearly marginal. In fact, it has complained about this on various occasions,[27] and it specifically highlights the political character of the development of a European contract law: 'even though the Commission denies that this is its objective, it is clear that many of the researchers and stakeholders working on the project believe that the ultimate long-term outcome will be a European code of obligations or even a full-blown European Civil Code . . . The decision to work towards and on such a Code must be taken by the political authorities, since the very decision to opt for a Code is political and its

24. The members of the CFR-net are listed in <www.ec.europa.eu/consumers/cons_int/safe_shop/fair_bus_pract/cont_law/cfr_net_members_en.pdf>.
25. Call for expression of interest with a view to setting up a network of stakeholder experts on the Common Frame of Reference in the area of European contract law (CFR-net), in *Official Journal of the European Union* S 148 of 31.07.2004.
26. COM (2005) 456 final, 3 and 5.
27. E.g., P6_TA (2005) 0053 and P6_TA (2005) 0615.

content, albeit legal, is predicated on social and political objectives'. Not only does a European contract law have to take 'into account the European social model', it also has to respect the 'differing legal traditions'.[28]

The Joint Network presented the first results at the beginning of 2008, with the publication of the Interim Outline Edition of the DCFR.[29] Apart from the introduction, which lists some of the 'core aims and values'[30] as well as an annex of definitions,[31] it contains the following books: 1. General provisions 2. Contracts and other juridical acts 3. Obligations and corresponding rights 4. Specific contracts and the rights and obligations arising from them 5. Benevolent intervention in another's affairs 6. Non-contractual liability arising out of damage caused to another and 7. Unjustified enrichment.

Recently, the Outline Edition of the DCFR was published. It contains a few revisions to already published books and the addition of three new ones: 8. Acquisition and loss of ownership of goods, 9. Proprietary security rights in movable assets, and 10. Trust.[32] Regarding the Interim Outline Edition, the Outline Edition of the DCFR, pays more attention to the 'underlying principles', albeit not formulated as black letter rules, so as to take the work done by the Association Henri Capitant and by the Société de Législation Comparée into account.[33] A Full Edition with comments and notes will follow, thus achieving the work commissioned by the Joint Network of the European Commission.

This volume collects the contributions of the Social Justice Group to the Interim Outline Edition of the DCFR. These are contributions in which the normative policy perspective is being privileged. They refer equally to the Outline Edition of the DCFR, which has been taken directly into account in the analysis of some more specific issues as well.

It is of note that the chosen perspective is the common thread running through the different contributions. They all intend to critically identify and evaluate the model of social justice underlying the DCFR. This is an aspect which the introduction to the Draft treats insufficiently even in its most recent version, in line with the Commission's tendency to present the creation of a European private law as a purely technical matter.

Nevertheless, the different contributions are not comparable as far as the solutions proposed by the authors are concerned. On the contrary, they make sure to stress their different political and cultural views on the topic, something which has always distinguished the work of the Social Justice Group. Indeed, during the years, its members have developed different approaches towards the many themes evidenced in the Manifesto. Not everyone considers the creation of a

28. P6_TA (2006) 0109. *See also* P6_TA (2006) 0352.
29. C. von Bar, E. Clive & H. Schulte-Nölke (eds), *Principles, Definitions and Model Rules of European Private Law* (München: Sellier, 2008).
30. C. von Bar, et al., 'Introduction', in *Principles, Definitions and Model Rules of European Private Law*, n. 29 above, 1 et seq.
31. Annex 1, ibid., 327 et seq.
32. von Bar, Clive & Schulte-Nölke (n. 29 above).
33. *Principes contractuels communs* (Paris: Société de Législation Comparée, 2008).

European civil code as a threat to national traditions. Some agree with the approach of limiting contractual freedom only in the case of market failures. Others instead criticize the model of social justice referred to by the formula of 'social market economy' and, with it, the system of fundamental Community rights. However, the demand for an involvement of democratic institutions and civil society in the construction of a European private law is common to all and is in line with the confirmation of the political character of an undertaking, which cannot be reduced to a mere technical exercise.

A first group of contributions is dedicated to the legal instruments with which a European private law is to be created. *Aurelia Colombi Ciacchi* reflects on the recent trend of the Commission, trying to reduce the role of the CFR and to predispose only sector-specific binding measures in consumer related matters. It is said, on the contrary, that a comprehensive optional instrument on contract law has to be enacted, whose application will not be prevented by the Rome I Regulation and therefore by conflicting domestic mandatory rules. Such an optional instrument should refer to both cross-border and domestic contracts, be adopted as a Regulation and have the same characteristics as the unified Contract Acts of the Nordic countries: a pragmatic approach, flexible remedies, and weaker-party-friendly orientation.

Stefan Grundmann focuses on the absence of a political consensus surrounding the publication of the CFR. The reasons for this absence are various: the DCFR has too many general clauses and thus undermines legal certainty; it allows for excessive intervention into private autonomy, it suffers from highly formal thinking, and it deals with too many subjects. In other words, the DCFR is a comparative law synthesis of traditional codes with a certain German bias. Therefore, it tends to lose sight of the fact that modern contract law is both party autonomy and policy regulations, and it does not pay enough attention to the latter. Moreover, there is a lack of awareness that long-term relationships form a second pillar besides traditional exchange contracts and that in business it is difficult to see whether contract or organization is at stake. Ultimately, it would have been helpful to coordinate the regulatory framework for contracts in general and the regulatory framework for consumer contracts by elaborating a general theory of weak contracting parties based on the disclosure mechanism.

Ruth Sefton-Green analyzes the political character of the DCFR, which is academic in its mode of elaboration, but certainly not in its value: in this sense, there is no dichotomy between an academic DCFR and a political CFR. There are many indications of the political character of the DCFR: the choice to implicitly adopt the Commission's market-functionalist approach is political, the attempt to strike a balance between the different national laws is political, and the choice of creating a common market through harmonization is political. At the same time, there are some doubts about the possibility of improving the quality, coherence, transparency, and accessibility of European contract law through harmonization. These results are impeded by the fact that the CFR is an instrument of soft law and by the use of overly general or broad standards, which are able to lead to uniformity only if a coherent European civil society develops.

The topic of soft law is at the heart of *Alessandro Somma*'s contribution. Soft law is the privileged instrument at a Community level to develop rules in which solidarity is diluted by economic efficiency considerations. This is in line with the ordoliberal theory of the social market economy and of the private law society. For the DCFR, the reference to soft law concerns the formation of the optional instrument and the selection of the rules which are supposed to become mandatory. The optional instrument is packaged according to a neo-corporatist scheme, destined to create an artificial environment, called upon to reproduce an artificial European civil society made of producers and consumers, and thus to suffocate social conflict. The selection of mandatory rules is inspired by the intent to use the competition mechanism as an instrument of State intervention and, in particular, to transform producers into efficient multipliers and consumers into rational selectors of goods.

A second group of contributions deals with party autonomy and social justice. *Guido Alpa* looks at the public dimension of the relationship created by the parties and thus at the relative significance of contractual freedom and party autonomy. This would force to see the contract not only as an instrument of commutative justice but also of distributive justice. On merit, however, the DCFR, as well as the concept of mandatory rules to which it refers to, is ambiguous. The same can be said about the link with the system of fundamental Community rights, from which some more precise indications on the role of solidarity amongst private parties could have been deduced, as opposed to those set out in the DCFR.

Martijn Hesselink reflects on the model of social justice to which the DCFR refers. When compared to the PECL the latter may be seen as more liberal, for instance with respect to the control of unfair terms and to the role of good faith. Yet the DCFR is less liberal than many national codes, especially regarding the rules on pre-contractual information duties, on unfair exploitation or change of circumstances. Above all, the Draft remains based on party autonomy, mentioned in black letter rules, and not on solidarity, which is mentioned only in the introduction. Moreover, the notion of contractual weakness is not satisfactory because it has no link to fundamental Community rights and because it ignores small businesses, employees, and tenants. In this sense, the DCFR looks like a classical nineteenth Century pre-Welfare State Civil Code. At the same time, it would be an exaggeration to view it as a law for big business or as a source of massive reduction of private autonomy.

Jacobien Rutgers looks at the relationship between the DCFR and national public policies. This relationship is complicated by the missing coordination of the Draft with the Rome I Regulation and by the fact that the contracts are contrary to fundamental principles only if these are principles recognized in the European Union. This is a step backwards compared to the discretion which the European Court of Justice allows the Member States with respect to the concept of public policy to justify an impediment of free movement. In particular, it determines a direct influence of European contract law on the organization of the Welfare State. In fact, even though the Welfare State still belongs to the competence of the Member

States, its organization is highly dependant on the possibility of affirming the mandatory character of its regulatory framework.

A third group of contributions develops the theme of consumer protection. *Brigitte Lurger*'s analysis starts from the criticism of the recent proposal for a directive on consumer rights, which as a maximum harmonization instrument will determine a decrease of consumer protection in some Member States. The insertion of consumer protection in the DCFR is positive, but it is only partial and is not linked to the protection of other weak parties. More generally, the DCFR does not develop references to solidarity, even though they are present in its introduction. This is due to the unresolved issue of Community competences but also to the narrow market-oriented approach at a Community level, which is the expression of a market access justice. With regards to this approach, the continental private legal orders seem to be inspired by a model of social justice that also includes aspects of distributive justice.

A different evaluation of the proposal for a directive on consumer rights can be found in *Marisa Meli*'s contribution. Indeed, it is held that the proposal deals with the unfairness test of consumer contract clauses in a much more incisive and innovative way than the approach chosen by the DCFR. Moreover, the DCFR does not consider aspects regulated by important directives such as the one on unfair commercial practices. More generally, the DCFR does not go beyond private enforcement for the removal of unfair terms: in this sector, a form of market regulation is needed, which includes forms of public implementation entrusted to an independent authority.

Peter Rott looks at the right of withdrawal, which is viewed as an example of bad law-making. The DCFR gave in to a formalistic wish for coherence and consistency of the law and has therefore integrated the right of withdrawal into the set of the other available remedies. This has led to a neglect of the differences between the various rights of withdrawal in consumer contract law and between the latter and the general contract law right of termination. Hence, a reduction of consumer protection – in particular, in doorstep selling – harmonization concerns have prevailed over social justice considerations, or the former has become an alibi for reducing the level of protection previously guaranteed.

The volume ends with two contributions dedicated to other specific issues dealt with in the DCFR. *Gert Brüggemeier* analyzes tort law and denounces its traditional policy structure: the Draft does not regard fault and strict liability as equivalent modes of accountability. Moreover, some rules on central aspects are missing: for example, rules on general enterprise liability for organizational fault or on employee liability. One should also note the terminological confusion and conceptual inconsistency of the DCFR, caused by its intention to mediate between the different legal cultures. Here, however, mediation hardly seems possible: the harmonization of liability law should be achieved by convergence in substance on parallel paths within the different legal traditions.

Finally, the contribution by *Arthur Salomon* looks at the new elements of the Outline Edition of the DCFR and in particular at the good faith acquisition protection. He analyzes it from a law and economics perspective, which is interested in safeguarding commerce against the disruptive effects of the reclaiming of property by dispossessed owners from *bona fide* acquirers. With specific reference to stolen property, the DCFR grants protection only to the acquirer who acted in the ordinary course of business. U.S. scholars tend to consider this rule as inefficient. However, it is in line with the market overt rule, firmly rooted in European legal tradition both in civil law countries and in common law countries.

ALESSANDRO SOMMA

List of Abbreviations

ACQP	Acquis Principles
BW	Burgerlijk Wetboek
CFR	Common Frame of Reference
CISG	International Sale of Goods
CoPECL	Common Principles of European Contract Law
DC	Draft Code
DCFR	Draft Common Frame of Reference
DG SANCO	Directorate General for Health and Consumer Affairs
EC	European Community
ECJ	European Court of Justice
EEC	European Economic Community
EMU	Economic and Monetary Union
EU	European Union
FAZ	Frankfurter Allgemeine Zeitung
IBM	International Business Machines Corporation
IIA	Inter-Institutional Agreement
MiFID	Markets in Financial Instruments Directive
MEPs	Members of the European Parliament
MPs	Members of Parliament
PECL	Principles of European Contract Law
PEL	Principles of European Law
PELS	Principles of European Law Sales
PETL	Principles of European Tort Law
PICC	Principles of International Commercial Contracts
SMEs	Small and Medium Enterprises
SGECC	Study Group on a European Civil Code
UCC	Uniform Commercial Code
UNIDROIT	International Institute for the Unification of Private Law

Part One

The Shaping of a European Private Law

Chapter 1

An Optional Instrument for Consumer Contracts in the EU: Conflict of Laws and Conflict of Policies

Aurelia Colombi Ciacchi

1. FROM THE EUROPEAN CIVIL CODE TO THE OPTIONAL INSTRUMENT: A BRIEF HISTORY

The discussion on a possible future European Civil Code began in the early 1970s. During that period, the topic was closely connected to the unification of the European rules of private international law. In 1974, at a conference dinner, the European Commission official Hauschild agreed with Ole Lando that uniform rules of private international law would not suffice, since a common European market would require a uniform substantive law. Hauschild said: 'We need a European Code of Obligations'.[1]

In 1976, Lando proposed the creation of a 'European Uniform Commercial Code'. In the years thereafter, he joined with many supporters and partners in this project, which came to embrace the entire area of contract law. However, not all

1. Cf. the Preface and Introduction to Parts I and II of the PECL: O. Lando & H. Beale (eds), *Principles of European Contract Law, Parts I and II* (The Hague: Kluwer, 2000), xi.

Alessandro Somma, *The Politics of the Draft Common Frame of Reference*, pp. 3-18.

participants in Lando's network agreed on the desirability of a Code.[2] So the 'Principles of European Contract Law' (PECL) were born.[3]

In Lando's view, the main purpose of the PECL was to serve as first draft of a part of a European Civil Code.[4] As from 1989, the European Parliament has shared the same view and requested that the Commission proceed toward the preparation of a European Civil Code. However, as is well known, neither the Commission nor the Council agreed on this proposed direction.

Pragmatic supporters of the idea of a future European Civil Code (or Code of Obligations, or Code of Contracts) are fully aware that in the short and medium term, only few European countries, if any, will allow their domestic laws be replaced by a binding European set of rules. The most realistic alternative seems to be the creation of a model Code, open to voluntary adoption by Member States or contracting parties. Thus the contemporary discourse revolving around a European Civil Code has to a great extent been canalized towards an Optional Code.[5] However, just as Lando's Code needed to be called 'Principles', the Optional Code had to be referred to as 'Optional Instrument' in order to become more politically correct.

The idea of an optional instrument for contract law was first presented by the Commission in its Communication on European contract law of 2001.[6] Herein, three alternatives for a 'new comprehensive legislation at EC level' (Option IV) were proposed:

(a) a purely optional model, enshrined in a Recommendation or Regulation, which applies when the parties agree that their contract is to be governed by it ('opt-in' model);

---

2. O. Lando, 'My Life as a Lawyer', *Zeitschrift für Europäisches Privatrecht* (2002): 520; H. Beale, 'The Future of the Common Frame of Reference', *European Review of Contract Law* 3 (2007): 259 et seq.
3. Lando & Beale (eds) (n. 1 above); O. Lando et al. (eds), *Principles of European Contract Law, Part III* (The Hague: Kluwer, 2003).
4. Lando (n. 2 above), 521.
5. *See* amongst others, S. Grundmann & W. Kerber, 'European System of Contract Laws – A Map for Combining the Advantages of Centralised and Decentralised Rule-Making', in *An Academic Green Paper on European Contract Law*, eds S. Grundmann & J. Stuyck (The Hague et al.: Kluwer Law International, 2002), 295 et seq.; C. Kirchner, 'An Optional European Civil Code (OECC): Initiating a Learning Process', id., 399 et seq.; S. Grundmann, 'The Optional European Code on the Basis of the *Acquis Communautaire* – Starting Point and Trends', *European Law Journal* 10 (2004): 698 et seq.; B. Lurger, 'The Common Frame of Reference/Optional Code and the Various Understandings of Social Justice in Europe', in *Private Law and the Many Cultures of Europe*, eds T. Wilhelmsson, E. Paunio & A. Pohjolainen (Alphen aan den Rijn: Kluwer Law International, 2007), 177 et seq.
6. COM (2001) 398 final (hereinafter: '2001 Communication'). Beforehand, the idea had been proposed in academic literature: *see* J. Basedow, 'A Common Contract Law for the Common Market', *Common Market Law Review* 33 (1996): 1181 et seq. (opt-out model); O. Lando, 'Optional or Mandatory Europeanisation of Contract Law', *European Review of Private Law* 8 (2000): 59 et seq.

(b) a set of rules which would apply unless their application was excluded by the contract ('opt-out' model);
(c) a set of rules whose application cannot be excluded by the contract.

In the Commission's Action Plan 'A more coherent European contract law' of 2003,[7] a 'Common Frame of Reference' (CFR) was envisaged in order to realize Options II, III, and possibly also Option IV of the 2001 Communication. Option IV was referred to in the Action Plan as 'non-sector-specific measures',[8] and the above-mentioned alternatives a) and b) of Option IV merged into the concept of 'Optional Instrument'.

Thus, one could say that since 2003, the phantom of 'The Thing', which the European Parliament once dared to call Code, has been concealed behind a four-layered terminological veil, in the hope of making it appear less scary.[9] No one can exclude that in the future, after having been accustomed to terms such as 'principles',[10] 'common frame of reference', 'non-sector-specific measures', and 'optional instrument', new euphemisms which indicate the same 'Thing' will be required. This search for the best euphemism reveals the struggle of Community institutions and transnational research groups to sell to the Member States, including the common law countries, measures of harmonization which in fact consist in a 'continentalization' of their private laws.

2. CFR AND OPTIONAL INSTRUMENT: THE SAME OR DIFFERENT BODIES OF RULES?

In the Action Plan and in the Commission's Communication 'European Contract Law and the revision of the *acquis*: the way forward' of 2004,[11] the CFR and the 'non-sector-specific measures' appear as separate entities. The optional instrument

7. COM (2003) 68 final (hereinafter: 'Action Plan'). For a critical analysis *see* M. Kenny, 'The 2003 action plan on European contract law: is the Commission running wild?', *European Law Review* 28 (2003): 538 et seq.
8. For a critique of the use of this euphemism to indicate a European Code *see* H. Collins, 'Editorial: The Future of European Private Law: An Introduction', *European Law Journal* 10 (2004): 649 et seq.
9. On the fears generated by the ghost 'European Contract Law' *see* S. Vogenauer, 'The Spectre of a European Contract Law', in *The Harmonisation of European Contract Law: Implications for European Private Laws, Business and Legal Practice*, eds S. Vogenauer & S. Weatherill (Oxford: Hart, 2006), 2; the metaphor, 'ghost' was used by N. Reich, 'A European Contract Law – Ghost or host for integration?', *Wisconsin International Law Journal* 24 (2006): 425 et seq.; and ZERP Discussion Paper 7/2006 (updated version).
10. 'Principles' is actually an incorrect word to indicate a code-like text: cf. H. Eidenmüller, et al., 'Der Gemeinsame Referenzrahmen für das europäische Privatrecht – Wertungsfragen und Kodifikationsprobleme', *Juristenzeitung* (2008): 533.
11. COM (2004) 651 final (hereinafter: Way Forward). For a critical analysis *see* M. Kenny, 'The 2004 Communication on European Contract Law: those magnificent men in their unifying machines', *European Law Review* 11 (2005): 724 et seq.

is presented as a body of optional contract law rules to be enacted on the basis of the CFR.

A first possibility is that the 'political' CFR and the optional instrument will be enacted consecutively as two separate sets of provisions regulating contracts.[12] In this case, the rules of the optional instrument need to be harmonious with the CFR, although they would not need to reproduce its wording. Moreover, the optional instrument could cover a narrower area of law than the CFR. This appears to be a very possible scenario, should the 'political' CFR, like the Draft Common Frame of Reference (DCFR),[13] regulate torts, restitutions, and other non-contractual matters. The optional instrument could then concentrate on general contract law, and/or specific contract types.[14]

Today, the idea of a comprehensive Optional Civil Code, or Code of Obligations, no longer seems to be supported at the EU level. Not even the European Parliament pleads for such a Code nowadays. In its Resolution of 3 September 2008, the Parliament stated that an optional instrument 'should confine itself to those areas where the Community legislature has been active or is likely to be active in the near future, or which are closely linked to contract law'.[15]

In the same Resolution, the European Parliament explicitly confirmed that the selection of parts of the DCFR, which are to be integrated into a forthcoming EC document, e.g., a Commission White Paper on a Common Frame of Reference, 'is a highly political exercise'.[16] If the CFR and the optional instrument were to be enacted as two separate bodies of rules, one may argue that the political dimension of the optional instrument would be even more crucial than that of the CFR. Indeed, the CFR would probably be issued as an instrument which is not directly binding for Member States and their citizens. On the contrary, an optional instrument would be directly binding for the citizens who choose it as the law applicable to their contracts.

On 18 April 2008, the Council took a clear position in this regard: the CFR should only serve as 'a set of non-binding guidelines to be used by lawmakers at Community level on a voluntary basis as a common source of inspiration or reference in the lawmaking process'.[17] If this position on the CFR as

12. *See* Grundmann, ''(n. 5 above), 700; R. Schulze, 'Gemeinsamer Referenzrahmen und *acquis communautaire*', *Zeitschrift für Europäisches Privatrecht* (2007): 136 et seq.
13. C. von Bar, et al. (eds), *Principles, Definition and Model Rules of European Private Law: Draft Common Frame of Reference (DCFR)*, Interim Outline Edition (München: Sellier, 2008).
14. Cf. Beale (n. 2 above), 273; C. von Bar & H. Schulte-Nölke, 'Gemeinsamer Referenzrahmen für ein europäisches Schuld- und Sachenrecht', *Zeitschrift für Rechtspolitik* (2005): 168.
15. European Parliament Resolution of 3.9.2008 on the CFR for European contract law, B6-0374/ 2008 /P6_TA-PROV(2008)0397, para. 12.
16. *See* n. 15 above. This evidences the strength of the points made by the Social Justice Manifesto: Study Group on Social Justice in European Private Law, 'Social Justice in European Contract Law: a Manifesto', *European Law Journal* 10 (2004): 653 et seq.
17. Council of European Union, 2863rd Council meeting, Justice and Home affairs, Luxembourg, 18.4.2008, Press release 8397/08 (Presse 96), <www.eu2008.si/en/News_and_Documents/ Council_Conclusions/April/0418_JHA.pdf>.

'toolbox'[18] were to prevail, the CFR would become clearly different from a future optional instrument.

Nevertheless, the optional instrument and the CFR would not necessarily constitute two separate sets of rules.[19] This has been acknowledged by the European Parliament in its Resolution of September 2008: the future format of the CFR could be that of an optional instrument.[20] Theoretically, an optional regime could be enacted by a single EC law provision, which enabled contracting parties to select the CFR instead of the otherwise applicable national law. In this case, there would be no substantive difference between the CFR and optional instrument, or between their political dimensions. However, this scenario seems rather unlikely.

3. AN OPTIONAL INSTRUMENT FOR CONSUMER CONTRACTS

The possible content, form, and coverage of a future optional instrument for European contract law is still unclear. Should it address both consumer and commercial contracts or just one of these two categories? Should it only cover cross-border contracts or also domestic transactions? Should it regulate general contract law, specific types of contracts, or both? Should there be one optional instrument for contract law as a whole, or should there be several instruments for different specific matters?[21]

In the 2001 Communication, a combination of the alternatives b) and c) of Option IV was proposed for the regulation of consumer contracts: 'a general and automatically applicable set of fall-back provisions' (an opt-out model), along with 'some mandatory provisions which cannot be waived by the contracting parties'. In the Action Plan, the Commission continued to envisage an optional set of contract law rules for both consumer and commercial contracts. It presented a purely optional (opt-in) model to be chosen by the parties through a choice of law clause, and an opt-out model based on that of the International Sale of Goods (CISG).

In the 'Way Forward' Communication, the Commission acknowledged that the majority of responses to the Action Plan concerning the optional instrument favoured an opt-in model. Nevertheless, the opt-out model was not excluded.

---

18. Cf. C. von Bar, 'Coverage and Structure of the Academic Common Frame of Reference', *European Review of Contract Law* 3 (2007): 351 et seq.: 'with all due respect one wonders a bit whether the toolbox model is nothing but a synonym for a first class funeral to some more important aspects of the CFR idea'.
19. A. Flessner, 'Der Gemeinsame Referenzrahmen im Verhältnis zu anderen Regelwerken', *Zeitschrift für Europäisches Privatrecht* (2007): 112 et seq.
20. *See* n. 15 above, paras 11-12.
21. On the advantages and disadvantages of having several separate optional instruments, *see* M.W. Hesselink, J.W. Rutgers & T.Q. de Booys, *The legal basis for an optional instrument on European contract law*, Study for the European Parliament, Final Report (8.2.2008), 2.8.

In both the Action Plan and the 'Way Forward' Communication, the rules of the optional instrument were conceived as freely modifiable by the parties, with the exception of few mandatory rules protecting the consumer. Thus one may say that the Commission expressed a clear preference for an optional instrument which also applies to consumer contracts. The majority of responses obtained from public and private actors to the Action Plan appear to indicate no opposition to this preference.

From 2001 until 2004, the Commission arguably favoured approaches which envisaged the widest possible scope for a future body of European contract law, be it either a binding or optional instrument. The optional instrument was conceived as a single measure, covering both general contract law and a number of specific contracts. This instrument would have corresponded to a comprehensive Optional Contract Code, enshrining general principles first and then regulating individual contract types.

The picture dramatically changed after the 'Way Forward' Communication. The picture probably changed because the Commission realized that there was insufficient time to complete both the CFR and the *acquis* review by 2009, thus it gave priority to the latter. Since then, the design of an optional instrument as a comprehensive contract law regulation seems to have taken a much lower priority on the Commission's agenda.[22] In its 'First Annual Progress Report on European Contract Law and the Acquis Review' of 2005,[23] the Commission detailed concrete proposals for a plurality of optional instruments in the fields of insurance contract,[24] savings products, retail products, and mortgage contracts. These optional instruments were conceived as '26th regimes' (as there were twenty-five EU Member States at that time), 'sitting alongside, but without replacing, national rules'.[25]

The Commission's Second Progress Report on the Common Frame of Reference[26] of 2007 did not refer to any optional instrument. In its Resolution of 12 December 2007, the European Parliament reported that, according to the Commission, evidence from existing workshops did 'not suggest support for a horizontal optional instrument going beyond specific contracts'. Nevertheless, the Commission affirmed that when deciding on the scope of the CFR, it will take into account the European Parliament's position (which is still in favour of a broader optional instrument based on the CFR).[27]

22. Cf. H. Beale, 'The European Commission's Common Frame of Reference Project: a progress report', *European Review of Contract Law* 2 (2006): 307 et seq.; id. (n. 2 above), 256, 273; M.W. Hesselink 'Common Frame of Reference & Social Justice', *European Review of Contract Law* 4 (2008): 249.
23. COM (2005) 456 final (hereinafter: First Progress Report).
24. Cf. J. Basedow, 'Insurance Contract Law as Part of an Optional European Contract Act', *ERA-Forum* no. 2 (2003): 56 et seq.; D. Weber-Rey, 'Harmonisation of European Insurance Contract Law', in *The Harmonisation of European Contract Law* (n. 9 above), 207 et seq.
25. First Progress Report, 4.2.
26. COM (2007) 0447 final.
27. European Parliament Resolution on European Contract Law, B6-0513/2007/P6-TA-PROV(2007)0615, 6.

To summarize: until 2004, the optional instrument envisaged by the Commission resembled a single, comprehensive, non-sector-specific code of contracts. Since then, this vision has been re-defined and downgraded to a few sector-specific optional regulatory models for individual contract types only.[28]

One could argue that there is a clear link between this new restrictive Commission's approach to the optional instrument, and the Commission's recent plans to adopt a fully binding (non-optional!) instrument in the field of general consumer contract law. In October 2008, the Commission presented a proposal for a Directive on consumer contractual rights.[29] This proposal combines a non-sector-specific, horizontal approach with the full harmonization approach pursued in recent years by the Commission.[30] Would the enactment of such a Directive deprive a comprehensive optional instrument on contract law of the reason for its existence?[31]

In my opinion, this would not be the case, for three reasons. Firstly, the proposed Directive is embedded in the process of revision of the *acquis*,[32] which has been carried out by the Community separately, parallel to the discussion on the content of the CFR and a future optional instrument. Neither the 2007 Green Paper on the review of the consumer *acquis* nor the 2008 proposal for a horizontal Directive contain any reference to the CFR. Evidently, the revision of the consumer *acquis* on one hand and the CFR and a possible optional instrument for consumer contract law on the other are now regarded by the Commission as two completely different projects. If an optional instrument were be enacted on the basis of the CFR, this would not occur before 2010.[33] Between now and then, the Commission could change its position several times. Thus all the alternative scenarios concerning the optional instrument remain possible.

---

28. Cf. D. Staudenmayer, 'European Contract Law – What Does It Mean and What Does It Not Mean?', in *The Harmonisation of European Contract Law* (n. 9 above), 237; H. Schulte-Nölke, 'EC Law on the Formation of Contract – from the Common Frame of Reference to the "Blue Button" ', *European Review of Contract Law* 3 (2007): 348 et seq.: envisaging a plurality of optional instruments for the sale of goods, for services like music and software downloads, for the financial sector covering insurances, consumer credits or mortgages, and for product guarantees.
29. Proposal for a Directive of the European Parliament and of the Council on consumer rights, COM (2008) 614 final.
30. For a recent critical comment *see* T. Wilhelmsson, 'Full Harmonisation of Consumer Contract Law?', *Zeitschrift für Europäisches Privatrecht* (2008): 225 et seq.
31. In this sense Hesselink, Rutgers & de Booys (n. 21 above), 2.4.2.; S. Hähnchen, 'Die Rechtsform des CFR und die Frage nach der Kompetenz', in *Der gemeinsame Referenzrahmen: Entstehung, Inhalte, Anwendung*, ed. M. Schmidt-Kessel (München: Sellier, 2008), 153; N. Reich, 'Der Common Frame of Reference und Sonderprivatrechte im "Europäischen Vertragsrecht" ', *Zeitschrift für Europäisches Privatrecht* (2007): 178; P. Huber, 'European Private International Law, Uniform Law and the Optional Instrument', *ERA-Forum* 2 (2003): 97.
32. On this *see* R. Schulze (ed.), *Common Frame of Reference and Existing EC Contract Law* (München: Sellier, 2008); M.B.M. Loos, *Review of the European Consumer Acquis* (München: Sellier, 2008); C.C. Wendehorst, 'The CFR and the Review of the Acquis Communautaire', in *Der gemeinsame Referenzrahmen* (n. 31 above), 323 et seq.
33. The adoption of the CFR by the Commission is envisaged for 2009: *see* Way Forward, 3.2.4.

Secondly, as Schulte-Nölke has convincingly demonstrated,[34] there is a characteristic pattern of regulatory density in the EC contract law *acquis*, which will also remain stable for the foreseeable future. The highest density can be found at the pre-contractual stage. The moment of conclusion of the contract is almost not regulated at all, and the post-contractual phase is only partly regulated. Most EC Directives on consumer contracts, including the proposed Directive on consumer contractual rights, focus on the pre-contractual phase,[35] and leave very important aspects such as requirements for the validity of contracts, or remedies for breach of contract totally or partially to national law. Large parts of the regulation on the contractual relationship between a business and a consumer still are, and it will also remain present in the near future, outside the scope of EC secondary law. Here, an optional instrument that reduces barriers to trade might be helpful. Even after the enactment of the proposed Directive, there would still be enough space for the operation of one or more optional instruments concerning aspects of consumer contract law which are not regulated by the Directive.

Thirdly, the independent business survey conducted by Clifford Chance in 2005 under the academic supervision of Vogenauer and Weatherill (without any involvement of the Commission)[36] has provided strong empirical evidence for the usefulness of an optional instrument on general contract law. Eighty-two percent of the respondent businesses indicated that they would 'likely' or 'very likely' use an optional European contract law, if this were established. Fifty-seven percent were of the opinion that the optional instrument should regulate general issues concerning all contracts. Only eighteen percent were in favour of an optional instrument containing rules on specific contracts as well.[37]

Therefore, the recent narrowing of the Commission's focus to a few optional instruments for specific contracts only can hardly be motivated by a clear position of the majority of business operators. The main reason of the new restrictive Commission's approach is likely the limited timeframe to which the Commission committed itself for completing the *acquis* revision. It is highly unlikely that the Health and Consumer Protection Directorate General (DG SANCO) will find the time and resources before 2010 to develop an optional instrument on general (consumer) contract law.[38]

---

34. Schulte-Nölke (n. 28 above), 332 et seq.
35. *See* S. Grundmann, W. Kerber & S. Weatherill (eds), *Party Autonomy and the Role of Information in the Internal Market* (Berlin: de Gruyter, 2001); T. Wilhelmsson & C. Twigg-Flesner, 'Pre-contractual Information Duties in the Acquis Communautaire', *European Review of Contract Law* 2 (2006): 33 et seq.
36. Clifford Chance had reacted with strong scepticism about the Commission's Action Plan in 2003: *see* <http://europa.eu.int/comm/consumers/cons_int/safe_shop/fair_bus_pract/cont_law/stakeholders/4-5.pdf>.
37. S. Vogenauer & S. Weatherill, 'The European Community's Competence to Pursue the Harmonisation of Contract Law – an Empirical Contribution to the Debate', in *The Harmonisation of European Contract Law* (n. 9 above), 134-136.
38. *See* M.W. Hesselink, *The Values Underlying the DCFR: What Role for Fairness and 'Social Justice'?* (München: Sellier, 2008), 10: 'Maybe the project is simply on hold, also within Commission, until content of final CFR is known'.

4. NO DISCRIMINATION BETWEEN DOMESTIC AND CROSS-BORDER CONSUMER CONTRACTS

Should an optional body of European consumer contract law only regulate cross-border contracts or also domestic transactions? The Community institutions left this question open. In the 2001 Communication, optional measures were explicitly taken into account for consumer contract law without distinguishing between domestic and cross-border transactions. By contrast, the Action Plan seemed to focus specifically on cross-border trade. However, the 'Way Forward' Communication returned to a more general approach, under which no distinction between domestic and cross-border contracts is made. This is revealed inter alia by the list of specific contracts which, according to the Commission's summary of the responses to the Action Plan, could be regulated by an optional instrument: 'sale, exchange, donation, lease, cross-border financial transactions and contracts of insurance'. As the specification 'cross border' only referred to financial transactions, the other categories arguably covered both domestic and cross-border contracts. Moreover, no mention was made of cross-border contracts by the Commission in its First Progress Report of 2005, where it envisaged an optional '26th regime' for insurance contracts, mortgages, contracts on saving, and retail products.

A possible future optional instrument in the field of e-commerce has been conceived by Schulte-Nölke as a 'blue button'. Businesses which market their goods over the Internet could use the blue flag logo of the EU to represent their choice of law clause for a European optional contract law regime. The blue button could be labelled with an inscription such as 'Sale under EU Law'. By simply clicking on this button, consumers or commercial actors would be able to choose the optional instrument instead of the otherwise applicable national law.[39]

Arguably, it would make little sense to adopt a blue-button model for cross-border contracts only. Why should enterprises which market their products online throughout Europe be compelled to distinguish between domestic and cross-border transactions? Why should they be obliged to provide two different sets of contract terms, depending on whether the client's country of habitual residence is the same as that where the enterprise is based or different?[40] Would it not be simpler, more effective, and less costly to offer the blue-button option to all potential clients, independent of their nationality? Moreover, if the optional European regulation were more consumer-friendly than the law of the country where the enterprise is based, why should clients living in that country be excluded from enjoying such a preferred option?

The validity of these arguments is not limited to the relatively narrow field of e-commerce, but rather it also extends to the widest possible field of consumer contracts in general. There would be less discrimination between different

---

39. Schulte-Nölke (n. 28 above); id., 'Europäisches Vertragsrecht als blauer Button im Internet-Shop', *Zeitschrift für das gesamte Schuldrecht* (2007): 81 et seq.; Beale (n. 2 above), 271 et seq.
40. Cf. Hesselink, Rutgers & de Booys (n. 21 above), 2.6.; C. Hertel, 'Preventive Consumer Protection in an Optional Instrument – A Practitioner's View', *ERA-Forum* 2 (2003): 78.

categories of consumers,[41] transaction costs would be reduced, and the Internal Market would function more efficiently if an optional instrument were available for both domestic and cross-border contracts.[42]

5. THE OPTIONAL INSTRUMENT AND THE ROME I REGULATION

The 'Way Forward' Communication considered three possible different relationships[43] between the optional instrument and the EC Regulation on the law applicable to contractual obligations (Rome I).[44] Firstly, the optional instrument could be adopted as international uniform law, like the CISG. Thus, Rome I would only apply to matters not regulated by the optional instrument. Secondly, besides substantive rules, the optional instrument could also contain special conflict of law rules relating to its application. Also in this case, Rome I would not apply to matters regulated by the optional instrument. Thirdly, Rome I could provide private parties with the possibility of selecting the optional instrument as the law applicable to their contract. Then the optional instrument would not contain any scope clause but only provisions of substantive law.

This third scenario is no longer an option today. The original Commission's proposal of 2005 for a Rome I Regulation[45] included a provision (Article 3(2)) which allowed parties 'to choose as the applicable law the principles and rules of the substantive law of contract recognized internationally or in the Community'. However, no political agreement on this was found. Article 3(2) was repealed from the text of the Rome I Regulation, which was then finally approved on 17 June 2008.

---

41. Cf. Reich (n. 31 above), 178: consumers concluding cross-border contracts would be privileged compared to consumers concluding domestic contracts.
42. In favour of an optional instrument applicable to domestic contracts: J. Smits, 'Toward a Multi-Layered Contract Law for Europe', in *An Academic Green Paper on European Contract Law* (n. 5 above), 397 et seq.; Basedow (n. 24 above), 64 et seq.; id., 'Ein optionales Europäisches Vertragsgesetz – opt-in, opt-out, wozu überhaupt?', *Zeitschrift für Europäisches Privatrecht* (2004): 3; Hertel (n. 40 above), 78; Grundmann ''(n. 5 above), 709; K. Richter, 'Privatautonomie und Verbraucherschutz im Lichte der Pläne zur Schaffung eines Europäischen Zivilgesetzbuches', *Archiv für die civilistische Praxis* 206 (2006): 19 et seq.; S. Leible, 'Auswirkungen des CFR auf eine gemeinschaftsrechtskonforme Auslegung', in *Der gemeinsame Referenzrahmen* (n. 31 above), 227; G.P. Calliess, 'Coherence and Consistency in European Consumer Contract Law: a Progress Report', *German Law Journal* 4, no. 4 (2003): 357. Cf. also G. Wagner, 'The Economics of Harmonization: The Case of Contract Law', *Common Market Law Review* 39 (2002): 1018.
43. On these *see* Staudenmayer (n. 28 above), 238 et seq.; id.; 'The Place of Consumer Contract Law within the Process of European Contract Law', *Journal of Consumer Policy* 27 (2004): 282 et seq.; J. Rutgers, 'An Optional Instrument and Social Dumping', *European Review of Contract Law* 2 (2006): 209 et seq.
44. OJ L 177/6, 4.7.2008.
45. COM (2005) 650 final.

Thus, before and after the entry into force of the Rome I Regulation, a contract must be governed by at least one national law. Contractual parties can only incorporate soft-law models such as the PECL, the DCFR, and a future CFR or optional instrument into their contracts,[46] to replace national default provisions. Once a domestic law is contractually chosen or otherwise confirmed as governing a contract, the parties cannot circumvent an application of the mandatory rules of that law.[47]

The Rome I Regulation itself does not allow for a choice of law in favour of an optional instrument, but it obviously does not preclude this choice from being otherwise permitted by EC law. The considerandum (14) explicitly provides for the possible future enactment of a Community instrument on contract law, which can be chosen by the parties. If a future optional instrument contained conflict of law rules relating to its application, these as *lex specialis* would prevail over the Rome I provisions.[48]

Thus when the Community envisages the adoption of an optional instrument, it will need to specifically regulate the right of contracting parties to choose it as the applicable law. Although the substantive rules of the optional instrument could theoretically be enacted as soft law (e.g., through a recommendation), the conflict of law rule enabling contracting parties to choose the optional instrument as the law which governs their contract instead of a national law, can only be 'hard law'.[49] A new EC Regulation would be best suited to this purpose. Its legal basis could either be Article 95 EC Treaty,[50] provided that the optional instrument was considered to be an optional measure of harmonization of the Member States' contract laws,[51] or Article 308 EC Treaty.

Optional instruments in the field of commercial law have already been introduced on the basis of Article 308: the Societas Europaea, the European Cooperative Society and the Community Trade Mark. Therefore, Article 308 seems to be the most appropriate legal basis for an optional instrument in the field of contract law.[52]

---

46. *See* considerandum (13) of the Rome I Regulation. Eidenmüller envisages an optional instrument which, in cross-border contracts, can be selected by the parties as the applicable law under a conflict of laws model, while in domestic transactions it would have to be incorporated into the contract: H. Eidenmüller, 'Obligatorisches *versus* optionales europäisches Vertragsgesetzbuch', in *Vereinheitlichung und Diversität des Zivilrechts in transnationalen Wirtschaftsräumen*, eds C. Ott & H.-B. Schäfer (Tübingen: Mohr Siebeck, 2002), 240.
47. Cf. P. Mankowski, 'CFR und Rechtswahl', in *Der gemeinsame Referenzrahmen* (n. 31 above), 396 et seq.
48. Cf. Art. 23 Rome I.
49. Cf. Reich (n. 31 above), 177.
50. D. Staudenmayer, 'The Way Forward in European Contract Law', *European Review of Private Law* 13 (2005): 95 et seq.; Rutgers (n. 43 above), 205 et seq.
51. This is denied by Reich (n. 9 above), 40; Hesselink, Rutgers & de Booys (n. 21 above), 5.3.2. *See also* Vogenauer & Weatherill (n. 37 above), 113; Hähnchen (n. 31 above), 167.
52. *See* Basedow (n. 24 above), 65; Reich (n. 9 above), 40; U.G. Schroeter, 'Europäischer Verfassungsvertrag und Europäisches Privatrecht', *Zeitschrift für Europäisches Privatrecht* (2006): 527 et seq.; Hesselink, Rutgers & de Booys (n. 21 above); Hähnchen (n. 31 above), 168; Leible (n. 42 above), 227.

6. CONFLICT OF LAWS AND CONFLICT OF POLICIES

If an optional instrument for consumer contract law included mandatory substantive rules, a question that is politically very important would arise: to what extent would the application of the optional instrument exclude the application of conflicting national mandatory consumer protection standards? Would consumers be allowed, by simply clicking on a 'blue button' while surfing the Internet, to renounce the perhaps stricter mandatory rules of their respective countries of habitual residence?

In order to deal properly with this question, a distinction should be made according to whether the optional instrument is envisaged for cross-border transactions only or also for domestic contracts. In fact, cross-border transactions are governed by private international law, while domestic transactions are not. The parties to a domestic transaction cannot select a different law of contracts instead of their national law. They can only incorporate rules of foreign law or non-state bodies of law into their contract as contract terms. Those terms are valid only as far as they do not conflict with the mandatory national law applicable to the contract.

If an optional instrument were only applicable to cross-border contracts, the most important question would be whether the parties' choice of the optional instrument would be subject to the limitations governing the choice of law in cross-border consumer contracts as provided for in Article 6 Rome I. Under the latter article, if a contract is concluded between a consumer and a business which directs its activity (also) to the consumer's country of habitual residence, a choice of law clause cannot have the effect of excluding the application of the mandatory provisions of the law of the country of the consumer's habitual residence, insofar as they are more favourable to the consumer when compared to the correspondent provisions of the contractually chosen legal system.

If the choice for the optional instrument were subject to this limitation, contractual parties would not be able to straightforwardly replace the otherwise applicable national law with the optional instrument. The mandatory domestic provisions which were more favourable to the consumer would prevail over the correspondent provisions of the optional instrument. The latter would become just an optional measure of minimum harmonization.[53]

If the Community wished to adopt an optional measure of full harmonization,[54] which, if chosen by the parties, excludes the application of conflicting

53. On optional harmonization *see* J. Currall, 'Some Aspects of the Relation between Arts 30-36 and Art. 100 of the EEC Treaty, with a Closer Look at Optional Harmonization', in *Yearbook of European Law* 4 (1985): 169 et seq.; P. Oliver & M.A. Jarvis, *Free Movement of Goods in the European Community* (London: Sweet & Maxwell, 2003), 478 et seq.; C. Barnard, *The Substantive Law of the EU. The Four Freedoms* (Oxford: Oxford University Press, 2004), 515. Cf. Rutgers (n. 43 above), 208 et seq.

54. Reich (n. 31 above), 175: speaks of 'full harmonisation through the back door'; id., 'Die Stellung des Verbraucherrechts im "Gemeinsamen Referenzrahmen" und im "optionellen Instrument" – Trojanisches Pferd oder Kinderschreck?', in *Liber Amicorum Bernd Stauder*, eds L. Thévenoz & N. Reich (Genève et al.: Schulthess, 2006), 378, 382: the optional instrument would be a Trojan horse for the maximum harmonization approach. *See also* R. Sefton-Green,

domestic mandatory rules,[55] it would theoretically have three possibilities. The first possibility would be to enact a regulation that in principle embeds the optional instrument in the Rome I system[56] but that expressly derogates from Article 6.[57] In this case, one could argue that mandatory national consumer protection standards, as *lois de police* or national *ordre public*, could still prevail over the optional instrument.[58] However, in my opinion, the European Court of Justice (ECJ) would never agree on this view.[59] The second possibility would be to introduce a separate conflict of law rule for the optional instrument, which as *lex specialis* prevails over Rome I, so that Article 6 would not apply.[60] The third possibility would be to enact an optional instrument that operates outside the field of private international law altogether.

If the optional instrument regulated both cross-border and domestic transactions, only the third possibility would come into consideration. The Community institutions might decide to introduce an optional measure of full harmonization, which remains outside the scope of conflict of laws. This could be realized through a binding regulation which enables contracting parties to opt for the optional instrument as a body of directly applicable EC law. In this case, as soon as the parties choose the optional instrument, its provision will prevail on all domestic provisions by virtue of the primacy of Community law.[61] Thus the question of which rules are more favourable to the consumer would no longer be of importance. Contracting parties would be able to opt out of their domestic consumer contract laws completely and select the optional instrument instead.

If the rules of the optional instrument prevailed over domestic mandatory rules by virtue of the primacy of EC law, conflict of laws in the strict sense would no longer play a role. The parties' choice for the optional instrument would be the choice for an optional body of domestic law, introduced into the national legal system through a binding EC Regulation.[62]

'Sense and Sensibilities: The DCFR and the Preservation of Cultural and Linguistic Plurality', *European Review of Contract Law* 4 (2008): 290: '(O)nce the parties elect for the CFR to apply, it will have the effect of maximal harmonisation or even unification'.

55. This is envisaged by von Bar & Schulte Nölke (n. 14 above), 167; Staudenmayer (n. 28 above), 241; Beale (n. 2 above), 271 et seq.; Mankowski (n. 47 above), 422 et seq.; D. Martiny, 'Common Frame of Reference und Internationales Vertragsrecht', *Zeitschrift fur Europäisches Privatrecht* (2007): 227. *See also*, for insurance contracts, Basedow (n. 24 above), 61.
56. *See*, against this option, Martiny (n. 55 above), 220.
57. Cf. H. Heiss & N. Downes, 'Non-Optional Elements in an Optional European Contract Law. Reflections from a Private International Law Perspective', *European Review of Private Law* 5 (2005): 701 et seq.
58. Rutgers (n. 43 above), 204 et seq. For the opposite view, *see* Mankowski (n. 47 above), 422. Cf. also S. Leible, 'Rechtswahl', in *Ein neues Internationales Vertragsrecht für Europa*, eds F. Ferrari & S. Leible (Jena: Jeaner Wissenschaftlicher Verlagsgesellschaft, 2007), 50.
59. A. Colombi Ciacchi, 'Internationales Privatrecht', *ordre public européen und Europäische Grundrechte*, ZERP Discussion Paper 1/2008.
60. *See* Hesselink, Rutgers & de Booys (n. 21 above), 2.4.3.
61. Cf. Mankowski (n. 47 above), 422; Martiny (n. 55 above), 218.
62. Mankowski (n. 47 above), 414 et seq.; P. Jung, 'Der Gemeinsame Referenzrahmen und die Frage einer differenzierter Integration im Gemeinschaftsprivatrecht', in *Der gemeinsame Referenzrahmen* (n. 31 above), 273.

In any case, the enactment of an optional measure of full harmonization in the field of consumer contract law would not only give rise to conflicts of laws in a broad sense,[63] but it would also give rise to serious conflicts of policies.[64] Indeed, in national legal systems which provide higher standards of consumer protection compared to the optional instrument, this instrument would enable businesses to systematically avoid the application of those higher standards. In Jacobien Rutgers' words: the optional instrument could result in social dumping.[65]

Even leading members of the Study Group on the European Civil Code, who are in favour of an optional instrument excluding the application of possibly higher national consumer protection standards, acknowledge that the rules of the optional instrument would not be a purely technical matter. Parties would frequently opt in without knowing exactly, or even approximately, what rules would then apply to their transaction and the degree of protection that they would be afforded, and they might not have the bargaining power to avoid the optional instrument.[66] So private powers could easily eliminate mandatory national consumer protection law just by using standard contract terms, without any political discussion on the subject at an EU or at a national level.[67]

However, this scenario would not be fair. If the Community envisages such an optional instrument which provides for maximum harmonization, thorough political discussions should take place, both in the European Parliament and in the national parliaments.[68] The conflicting policy interests should be addressed very openly and debated.[69]

---

63. On EC law as conflict of laws, *see* C. Joerges, 'Rethinking European Law's Supremacy: A Plea for a Supranational Conflict of Laws', in *Debating the Democratic Legitimacy of the European Union*, eds B. Kohler-Koch & B. Rittberger (Lahnham, MD et al.: Rowman & Littlefield, 2007), 311 et seq.; R. Michaels, 'EU Law as Private International Law? Re-conceptualising the Country-of-Origin Principle as Vested Rights Theory', ZERP Discussion Paper 5/2006.
64. On the risk that inclusion of consumer law in an optional set of principles may lead to emphasizing freedom of contract at the expense of consumer protection, *see* W. van Gerven, 'Codifying European private law? Yes, if . . . !', *European Law Review* 27 (2002): 170; R. Sefton-Green, 'Cultural Diversity and the Idea of a European Civil Code', in *The Politics of a European Civil Code*, ed. M.W. Hesselink (Alphen aan den Rijn: Kluwer Law International, 2006), 74.
65. Rutgers (n. 43 above); *see also* Lurger (n. 5 above); id., 'The Future of European Contract Law between Freedom of Contract, Social Justice, and Market Rationality', *European Review of Contract Law* 4 (2005): 445 et seq.
66. So Beale (n. 2 above), 272: the optional instrument 'would involve political choices of the kind that concerns the Social Justice Group'. Cf. also Hesselink (n. 38 above), 11; Sefton-Green (n. 64 above), 74.
67. Cf. Reich (n. 31 above), 176 et seq.; id. (n. 54 above), 382; Lurger (n. 5 above).
68. On the crucial role of the national parliaments, which should be involved in the debate on European contract law, *see* van Gerven (n. 64 above); id., 'Codifying European Contract Law: Top Down and Bottom Up', in *An Academic Green Paper on European Contract Law* (n. 5 above), 424 et seq.; the Social Justice Manifesto (n. 16 above); A. Somma, 'Social Justice and the Market in European Contract Law', *European Review of Contract Law* 2 (2006): 181 et seq.; Hesselink (n. 22 above), 255.
69. Cf. R. Schulze & T. Wilhelmsson, 'From the Draft Common Frame of Reference Towards European Contract Law Rules', *European Review of Contract Law* 4 (2008): 168; Beale (n. 2 above), 272: 'Some means of ensuring both a reasonable degree of social justice in the provision

7. AN OPTIONAL CONTRACT ACT FOLLOWING THE NORDIC MODEL?

It is very improbable that the Member States will agree on the enactment of an optional instrument which, if chosen by contracting parties, excludes the application of conflicting national mandatory law.[70] Should the Member States surprisingly agree on this, the optional regulation should provide for a very high level of consumer protection.[71] This level should not fall below the national protection standards of the North-Western European countries, which are actually higher than the standards of the *acquis communautaire*.[72] It is submitted that an optional EC consumer contract law should embody the most consumer-friendly solutions found in the Member States.

As Martijn Hesselink pointed out, 'businesses could save so much in terms of transaction costs by using the optional instrument, that they could accept a somewhat higher level of consumer protection than they would otherwise be prepared to accept, and still be better off.' This would create a win-win situation, where both businesses and consumers would benefit from the optional instrument.[73]

An optional 'twenty-eight' (or, more correctly, thirtieth)[74] regime could be enacted, which embraces the entire scope of contract law,[75] including consumer contracts, and which is also applicable to domestic transactions. It could be called the European Contract Act,[76] and it could be based on the model of the unified

---

of the instrument and a modicum of democratic input would both be essential'. Cf. also A. Colombi Ciacchi, 'Der Aktionsplan der Europäischen Kommission für ein kohärenteres Vertragsrecht: Wo bleibt die Rückbindung an die Europäische Verfassung?', *Jahrbuch Junger Zivilrechtswissenschaftler* (2004): 162 et seq.; C. Schmid, 'On the Legitimacy of a European Civil Code', *Maastricht Journal of Comparative Law* 8 (2001): 277 et seq.

70. Cf. Eidenmüller (n. 46 above), 241 et seq.
71. Cf. Schulte-Nölke (n. 28 above), 342; Beale (n. 22 above), 312: 'if the Commission is to pursue its stated aim of full rather than minimum harmonisation, the *acquis* may need to be strengthened so that consumers who currently have better rights under national law do not lose out to the lowest common denominator'; Staudenmayer (n. 28 above), 241; Heiss & Downes (n. 57 above), 699. Cf. also J. Basedow, 'Der Gemeinsame Referenzrahmen und das Versicherungsvertragsrecht', *Zeitschrift für Europäisches Privatrecht* (2007): 286; Martiny (n. 55 above), 226.
72. Cf. inter alia G. Howells & T. Wilhelmsson, 'EC Consumer Law: Has it Come of Age?', *European Law Review* 28 (2003): 370 et seq.; G. Monti, 'The Revision of the Consumer Acquis from a Competition Law Perspective', *European Review of Contract Law* 3 (2007): 299: 'the consumer might suffer if stricter national laws are forbidden.'
73. Hesselink (n. 22 above), 249. Also the outcomes of the Clifford Chance business survey *seem* to point in this direction; *see* Vogenauer & Weatherill (n. 37 above); Weber-Rey (n. 24 above), 225.
74. Because of the autonomy of the Scottish and Catalan private law systems: cf. Eidenmüller, et al. (n. 10 above), 530.
75. Cf. Wilhelmsson (n. 30 above), 227: full harmonization of important parts of consumer contract law, connected with an unharmonized general contract law, would create a 'complete legal mess'.
76. For this terminology, *see* Basedow (n. 24 above); id., 'The Case for a European Contract Act', in *An Academic Green Paper on European Contract Law* (n. 5 above), 147 et seq.

Contract Acts of the Nordic countries. It would be desirable for this optional instrument to adopt not only the name of the Nordic Contract Acts but to also adopt their pragmatic approach, their flexible remedies, and their weaker-party-friendly orientation.

However, whether the DCFR provisions would be fit for such a European Contract Act is questionable. On one hand, in several cases the DCFR extended consumer protection beyond the minimum required by the Directives.[77] On the other hand, when the draft of the Study Group on a European Civil Code merged with the Acquis Principles, some of the latter seem to have been amended to become more business-friendly.[78]

In any case, the DCFR does not seem to reflect the most consumer-friendly solutions which can be found in the Member States. Some commentators have criticized the DCFR for being even less 'social' than the PECL.[79] A plurality of academics, including not only the contributors to the present volume, but also the grandfather of the DCFR, Ole Lando, have called for amendments to be made to the DCFR so as to better address concerns for social justice and weaker-party protection.[80]

If the solution proposed here, i.e. an optional instrument embodying the most consumer-friendly solutions found in the Member States, is not ultimately realisable politically, one could consider the following second-best scenario: the optional measure adopted by the Community should at least incorporate additional information duties concerning the effect of excluding conflicting national mandatory law. If the optional instrument allowed consumers to contractually renounce the possibly higher standards of consumer protection of their country of habitual residence, then the optional instrument itself would have to ensure that consumers really know what they are doing – not only when they surf the Internet and eventually click on a 'blue button'.

77. Cf. Hesselink (n. 22 above), 262 et seq.
78. Cf. O. Lando, 'The Structure and the Legal Values of the Common Frame of Reference (CFR)', *European Review of Contract Law* 3 (2007): 256: 'The Study Group may have thought that if the rules of the CFR will consider the interests of the customers too much, suppliers will not offer this option to their customers.'
79. Lando (n. 78 above), 251 et seq.; Schulze & Wilhelmsson (n. 69 above), 167 et seq.; Hesselink (n. 22 above), 257. For a critique of the PECL as not sufficiently 'social'; *see* T. Wilhelmsson, 'Private Law in the EU: Harmonised or Fragmented Europeanisation?', *European Review of Private Law* 10 (2002): 86 et seq.; Lurger (n. 65 above), 447.
80. Lando (n. 78 above), 256: the CFR should be 'more intelligible and socially orientated'. *See also* Schulze & Wilhelmsson (n. 69 above), 167 et seq.: 'It is desirable that the discussion concerning the DCFR (. . .) will also lead to improvements with regard to social justice.'

Chapter 2

Grand European Code Napoléon or Concise Uniform Contract Law? Defining the Scope of a Common Frame of Reference

Stefan Grundmann

1. THE DCFR AS A STEP TOWARD A EUROPEAN CODE?

The DCFR[1] – more precisely: the prospect of a CFR – arouses high interest also on the political level. Last year, the leading German newspaper, the Frankfurter Allgemeine Zeitung (FAZ) discussed the DCFR in its section on national and international politics ('Staat und Recht').[2] Based on the views of six outstanding German Private Law scholars[3] – from established to young and dynamic, from interdisciplinary in approach to dogmatically oriented, from classical contract lawyers to company, tort, and general private law scholars – the article draws a very outspoken conclusion: on the basis of this DCFR, 'the moment is far from being reached for a politically legitimized text'. If this is representative at least for German academia – and it would seem to be – in the country where the DCFR

1. C. von Bar et al. (eds), *Principles, Definition and Model Rules of European Private Law: Draft Common Frame of Reference (DCFR)*, Interim Outline Edition (München: Sellier, 2008).
2. R. Müller, 'Ungesteuerte Richtermacht', *Frankfurter Allgemeine Zeitung*, 5.6.2008: 8.
3. H. Eidenmüller et al., 'Der Gemeinsame Referenzrahmen für das Europäische Privatrecht – Wertungsfragen und Kodifikationsprobleme', *Juristenzeitung* 63 (2008): 529-550.

Alessandro Somma, *The Politics of the Draft Common Frame of Reference*, pp. 19-37.

process was mostly guided, there is the rather generalized feeling that taking this DCFR as a model for codification would mean that 'the' chance for a convincing European Private – or Contract – Law structure is lost. This is an important statement.

Two points are particularly interesting in this *prise de position*: while the CFR is not at all aimed exclusively at serving as a model for a European Code,[4] the article in the FAZ deals, albeit implicitly, almost exclusively with this prospect, although the EC Commission never dared to be so outspoken and primarily speaks of a toolbox for further (rather restricted) legislation, potentially as well as a frame of reference for scientific and political debate.[5] This lack of clarity about the scope of the text makes it difficult to assess the process, both with respect to questions of Community competence and with respect to fields of law, included substance and coherence.[6] Many have criticized the openly opaque way of proceeding. It does, however, not seem impossible that also important players in the political scene could see the DCFR as a model for an Optional – perhaps later on even for an Exclusive – 'instrument' (again a traitorously 'neutral' term). Therefore: 'let's consider it as if it was a Code!' . . . or a model for it, because this was the intention of many of its authors. Therefore, let's discuss whether the structure is one for a modern and convincing contract law codification.

The second interesting point the criticism made by many authors, even German ones. In the authors' view, there are far too many general clauses, and, as a consequence, there will be little legal certainty, and even democratic

4. The most important steps are the decision taken by the Council on the Tampere summit: European Council of Tampere 1999, *SI* (1999), 800, n. 39; and then three 'communications' by the EC Commission: Communication of the Commission to the Council and the European Parliament on European Contract Law, COM (2001) 398 final – *EC OJ* C 255/1 (2001); the international discussion can be found in: S. Grundmann & J. Stuyck (eds), *An Academic Green Paper on European Contract Law* (The Hague et al.: Kluwer Law International, 2002); Communication of the Commission to the Council and the European Parliament – a more coherent European Contract Law, Action Plan of 12.2.2003, COM (2003) 68 final – *EC OJ* C 63/1 (2003); Communication of the Commission, European Contract Law and the revision of the acquis: the way forward, COM (2004) 651 final. Then the First Progress Report on the Common Frame of Reference, COM (2005) 456 final; and Second Progress Report on the Common Frame of Reference, COM (2007) 447 final. The European Parliament had already taken resolutions, at that time still of little political relevance: Resolution of the European Parliament of 26.5.1989 on the Endeavours to Harmonize Private Law in the Member States, *EC OJ* C 158/400 (1989); Resolution of the European Parliament of 6.5.1994 on Harmonization of Certain Areas of Private Law in the Member States, *EC OJ* C 205/518 (1994). And it answered to the first communication by the Commission in Decision on the Approximation of Civil and Commercial Laws of the Member States, *EC OJ* C 140E/538 (2001).
5. Much more outspoken, for the vision as a Code, *see*, for instance: H. Collins, 'The "Common Frame of Reference" for EC Contract Law: A Common Lawyer's Perspective', in *L'armonizazzione del diritto privato europeo*, eds M. Meli & M. Maugeri (Milano: Giuffrè, 2004), 107-124, at 107: ' "Let's call it a Code" '.
6. *See*, in detail, on this dilemma: W. Ernst, 'Der "Common Frame of Reference" aus juristischer Sicht', *Archiv für die civilistische Praxis* 208 (2008): 248-282, at 258-266.

legitimacy will be lacking ('ungesteuerte Richtermacht'). In the following, it will be argued that general clauses also constitute a failure to decide core issues and to find solutions for demanding questions of modern contract law. The second criticism is that the DCFR contains too many inroads into party autonomy, and the third is that it limits itself too much to just reproducing the existing European Contract Law (*acquis communautaire*) and does not add a lot to the development of the law on the basis of the *acquis communautaire.* In the following, it will be argued that indeed the whole endeavour should primarily aim at developing the potential for law reform and a modern, convincing contract law (codification) within the *acquis communautaire* and elsewhere.

2. HOW BIG A CODE? OR 'DO CONTRACTS WELL!'

2.1. Which Fields to Include?

The first phrase of the DCFR reads as follows: 'these rules are intended to be used primarily in relation to contractual and non-contractual rights and obligations and related property law matters.' (Article I.-I:101 paragraph 1). This is a lot, even if one limits it to the areas named explicitly and even if one disregards the word 'primarily'. The Study Group works 'on a European Civil Code', the (Acquis) Research Group 'on EC Private Law'. Potentially, this could include even company and capital market law, perhaps as well competition law, all this without involving any of the leading scholars in these fields who are not really interested in the CFR process. This already shows: even if, more likely, 'only' a traditional Civil Code is at stake, including obligations and property law, perhaps also some family law or wills and estates (although it is far from evident for many of these areas why Europe should unify them) and the first question is that of size.

The 'Draft Code' (DC) contains seven books: 1. General Provisions; 2. (General Part on) Contracts and other Juridical Acts; 3. Obligations and corresponding rights; 4. Specific contracts; 5. Benevolent intervention in another's affairs; 6. Non-contractual liability (arising namely from torts); and 7. Unjustified enrichment. It is clear from the statements made by members of the Study group and from Article I.-I:101 paragraph 1 that an eighth book on (some or most) property law is intended to be added.

If one changes the order between 6 and 7, it is evident that this is exactly the order adopted by the German Civil Code (first three books).[7] The prominence of the concept of 'juridical act' – an invention of the drafters of the German Civil

7. Books 4. to 7., corresponding to the specific part(s) of the Law on obligations which form the second large part in the second book in the German Civil Code (after the general law of contracts and obligations 2. [in part] and 3. in the DCFR). For this order, its importance in the evolution of Codes – and also on some ideas developed in this section – see more in detail S. Grundmann, 'Structural Elements in the Contract Law Parts of the German Civil Code', in *The Architecture of*

Code which has now found its way even into the title of Book 2 of the DCFR[8] and the inclusion of a specific book on benevolent intervention strongly add to this impression.

Regardless, however, of how 'Germanic' the DCFR is, the core question is how much it really adds to the development of a good contract law to draft a big Code and what the disadvantages are. More concisely: if contract law is the vehicle to promote the Europeanization of areas where Europeanization would not be justified on its own merits, imperative reasons should be shown to combine the areas nevertheless.

2.2. Do Contracts Need Torts or Vice Versa?

The DCFR, because of the inclusion of obligations generally, has a somewhat strange order in the first three larger books. They contain: contract law (general part); the law of obligations (general part); then again contract law (now specific contracts). This formal disruption within the law of contracts may be seen as being rather one in name than in substance, because in fact this section also contains general contract law. One can even go further and say that it contains mostly rules which, practically, matter *only* in contracts, although theoretically they could apply as well to an obligation arising out of torts, unjust enrichment, or other sources.

Looking at Book 3 (on obligations), inserted between the general contract and the specific contract law, one finds the following subject matters which, of course, all matter for contract law: 1. General; 2. Performance; 3. Remedies for non-performance (including rescission, reduction of price, damages, termination); 4. Plurality of debtors and creditors; 5. Transfer of rights and obligations; 6. Set-off and merger; 7. Prescription.

The question, however, arises as to how meaningful it really is to apply these rules to all obligations. In other words: how much common ground there really is between contracts and, for instance, torts. Is it really worth disrupting contract law (Books 2 and 4) to insert a law of obligations which is mostly a book on contract law again? Would it not be more meaningful to find a convincing system and order for contract law? The answer depends largely on how telling the category of obligation really is, i.e., on how much of Book 3 does matter also beyond contract law, i.e., in how many questions generalization is really meaningful in the sense that a rule applies to contracts, torts, and perhaps even to other obligations.

If one considers the *substance of Book 3*, rules which practically matter also outside contract law are scarce. It is already difficult to imagine cases where the

---

European Codes and Contract Law, eds S. Grundmann & M. Schauer (Alphen: Kluwer Law International, 2006), 57-80.

8. For a common law scholar's perspective and, at the same time, a French law scholar's perspective on juridical act, *see* the contribution by R. Sefton Green, 'Sense and Sensibilities: The DCFR and the Preservation of Cultural and Linguistic Plurality', *European Review of Contract Law* 4 (2008): 282-305, at 292-294.

rules contained in Chapter 1 – mainly good-faith, non-discrimination and variation or termination of the obligation – really matter for torts as well. Similarly, the rules on performance in Chapter 2 may matter as well for torts as far as a few rules also dealing with monetary obligations, but are these problematic at all?

Among the remedies for non-performance (Chapter 3) about one half, again, is completely irrelevant for torts, namely the remedy of withholding (own) performance (Chapter 3, Section 4), termination, including rescission (Chapter 3, Section 5, *see* explicitly Article III.-3:501), and price-reduction (Chapter 3, Section 6). In others, such as the debtor's (right to) cure (Chapter 3, Section 2) the involved parties' interests clearly differ from contract to tort: does the victim of a tort desire at all that the tort-feature performs in kind? Does he want the tort-feature, be it a car-driver or even a doctor who has treated him poorly, to give him the necessary medical treatment? The answer would seem to be negative (in this sense indeed § 249 paragraph 2 of the German Civil Code). No 'second chance' is the normal answer, while in contract law the contrary is true. The DCFR, in its longing for generalization, does not really differentiate. One can of course apply Article III.-3:203 lit. d allowing the creditor to pursue monetary compensation without setting an additional period of time whenever 'cure [in kind] would be inappropriate in the circumstances'. The question is, however, why the draft does not have the strength to decide typical cases and instead postpones decisions and creates legal uncertainty by choosing a general clause ('inappropriate') for whole areas of the law (i.e., for the question: is there the right to a second chance in torts?). For the same reasons, the question whether and when the creditor can ask for specific performance (Chapter 3, Section 3) is one for contracts only. Therefore, what really matters for torts in the chapter on remedies is (solely) Section 7 on damages.[9] Also in the German Civil Code, which has developed the idea of a general law of obligations it is this part on (the amount of) damages – the so-called *Schadensrecht* in §§ 249-254 *Bürgerliches Gesetzbuch* – where contracts really meet torts. The DCFR deals with these problems in Article III.-3:701 et seq. The two problems which most acutely raise the question whether the regime should be the same for both contracts and torts are immaterial damages and the limitation to foreseeable damages. The DCFR regulates these questions in Article III.-3:701 paragraph 3 ('loss includes... non-economic loss' which 'includes pain and suffering and impairment of the quality of life') and Article III.-3:703 (which limits damages in contracts – and only in contracts – to foreseeable damages, unless the debtor acted in a grossly negligent way, recklessly or intentionally). Analyzing these two rules, the following conclusions can be drawn: the one rule opts for a contractual regime only and thus shows that it does *not* want to be considered as a rule on obligations (for whatever reason will hopefully be explained in the comments). The other rule leaves the core question open: when should non-economic loss be

9. Of course, the question of cumulation of remedies, the only one in Section 1 ('General') which is important for the relationship to torts, has to be decided, but it is a question again of contract law: whether it is exclusive or not.

compensated outside the (rather simple) cases of pain and suffering? It leaves this question open by awarding non-economic loss on the basis of 'impairment of the quality of life'. This criterion really begs the question,[10] is having to go to court for several years – and potentially in a case which is existential for the contract partner concerned – not more of an 'impairment of the quality of life' than trouble in a journey? It is much too open or does it not help at all in the differentiations which need to be made? There are a great many cases in torts, namely in the area of privacy, legal protection of the personality, inroads into the life of couples and families (including similar natural status), and immaterial loss, where material loss is difficult to prove, namely in environmental questions. A modern regulation of the law of torts would have to deal with these issues, a contract law much less. In any case, the need where it exists would not be satisfied by the rule chosen – so even a good regime on torts would probably add little to the regime in contract law, and the regime chosen is of even less help (in both areas). In contracts, package holidays as one disputed case,[11] could, for instance, easily be understood as commercialization of leisure time and therefore be special: in fact, workers pay for their holidays by working before for them and earning proportionally less while they work. The question is, however, which kind of inconvenience in contracts should really be compensated. In a law on obligations, apparently, neither part, contracts or torts, really gets guidance in the truly vital issues which are of importance and which are disputed here *or* there. Neither part gets much guidance from the cases which are important in the other part.

Apart from prescription (Chapter 7) for which a general regime – applying to all obligations in a mostly uniform way – seems appropriate indeed,[12] all the *rest of the book* (plurality of debtors and creditors, transfer of rights and obligations, set-off and merger) is relevant in torts only in very exceptional cases, with the exception of insurance law, or has to be regulated in a different way in torts (namely plurality of tort-features where certainly the question whether they 'collaborated' in creating the obligation is a completely different one from that in contracts).

Summarizing these few remarks, one can say three things: (i) that most of the book is primarily contract law which in the very rare situations where they matter also for torts can easily be applied by analogy – so why not just say this; (ii) that a substantial body of the book, about one third, perhaps nearly a half, is not applicable to torts even theoretically; and (iii) that in this 'ocean of rules', the few cases have been regulated sloppily where the question really arises in practice whether a rule should apply to contracts only or to torts and other obligations as well and whether, on the contrary, one should differentiate: the question has not been given real attention, for instance, in Article III.-3:203 lit. d or in Article III.-3:701

10. In this sense as well (and far too open): Eidenmüller et al. (n. 3 above), 539-541.
11. Decided, as is known, by the ECJ which awarded damages for non-economic loss in case of considerable impairment of a package journey: ECJ of 12.3.2002 – case C-168/00 *Simone Leitner/TUI* [ECR] 2002, I-2631.
12. *See*, for instance, R. Zimmermann, *Comparative Foundations of a European Law of Set-Off and Prescription* (Cambridge: Cambridge University Press, 2002), 62 et seq.

paragraph 3, which does not solve the question of non-economic loss for contracts or for torts.

2.3. How to Deal with Little Common Ground and Intersections?

From the above, it follows that about half of the questions dealt with in Book 3, even formally, cannot arise outside the realm of contracts. Most other questions, while potentially arising also in the realm of torts, practically matter only for contracts, and they are mainly regulated so that the regime for contracts applies as well by analogy to torts or other obligations. The remaining few questions where the relationship between contracts on the one hand and torts or other obligations on the other really does matter are treated in a highly unspecific way in the DCFR. The advantages from creating a book on obligations would therefore seem minimal. Conversely, two considerable disadvantages can be seen: (i) regulating too much seems to distract the attention from the few questions where really the relationship between contracts on the one hand and torts or other obligations on the other does matter; (ii) moreover, the drafters are no longer free to follow a simple order which would have taken into consideration, only the 'life' of a contract. They have to split up general contract law into two books – in a rather artificial way. Not being able to consider only the life of contract also has the consequence that the links between related issues in contract law, the value judgments, the differentiations within contract law, cannot be the sole concerns. Therefore, these relationships cannot be developed in an optimal way. Deploring the lack of time after about one decade of work and nevertheless including many fields of law which do not add considerably to the regulation of contract shows that the optimal contract law was not the prime aim.

The disadvantage named first (above (i)) is even more striking when one considers what has not been regulated in the book on obligations (or elsewhere): interestingly, some, perhaps even most, situations where the relationship between contract and tort really is tricky, are not dealt with or at least not in detail. The DCFR does not contain a section on networks of contracts – despite their high practical importance (*see* below Section IV. 2.); therefore it remains very vague about the question which is the role of direct claims between partners to the network which, however, are not linked by contract themselves – and in national laws, these claims are seen as being based on torts where they are accepted.[13] A second major field where torts and contracts are considered in parallel and which

13. Namely in France, *see* M. Fabre-Magnan, *Les obligations* (Paris: Presses Universitaires de France, 2004), 465-472 and the (now a bit more restrictive lead decision of the Senate of the Cour de Cassation (Supreme Court)), Bulletin Assemblée plénière, *Dalloz* 5 (1991): 549; and on the European level: H. Beale & G. Howells, 'EC Harmonisation of Consumer Sales Law – A Missed Opportunity?', *Journal of Contract Law* 12 (1997): 21-46; M. Bridge, 'Part of Introduction' and 'Article 4 and the Right of Redress', in *EU Sales Directive – Commentary*, eds C. M. Bianca & S. Grundmann (Antwerp, Oxford: Intersentia, 2002), 78-87 and 179-210;

is of high practical importance is liability of third parties involved in the negotiation process, namely representatives and intermediaries; the question is whether there is liability also of this third party, although the contract is formed between the two partners to the contract. This question arises, for instance, with respect to prospectus liability of intermediaries or liability for advice given, for example, in expert opinions: in a considerable number of cases, this opinion is given to one contract partner only, for instance, a bank which wants to place a mortgage on an immovable and therefore has its value checked, but it nevertheless also interests the other contract partner, here the client of the bank, typically the purchaser who borrows money. Again, the DCFR does not give advice on these questions, namely not in the section devoted to the pre-contractual phase (Chapter 3 of Book 2, Articles II.-3:101 et seq.). There are not many intersections of similar importance between contracts and torts, but it is meaningful that the DCFR does not deal with them because it is too focused on generalizing and transforming what mainly is contract law into a law of obligations. A good contract law would concentrate on an adequate structure for contract law and then define and deal with the (few) intersections which really matter – not more.

The question is why regulate obligations in general if in most cases this is not really meaningful for other obligations, but yet not regulate or scarcely regulate those questions where the relationship between contracts and torts is really problematic? Thus the DCFR in this first core decision – going for a big Code, regulating all obligations *together* – rather opts for a formal and all-embracing system than for a convincing contract law structure and dealing in depth with the rather restricted number of intersections which are important in practice and where good policy reasons should justify one solution or the other.

This has repercussions not only in Book 3, but as well in *all other parts on specific obligations.* Reserving a specific Book 5 for such a marginal question as benevolent intervention in another's affairs, may still be 'justified' by the fact that this is the contribution of the co-ordinator of the Study Group to the series of books prepared by the Study Group[14] and therefore it 'had' to be in the DCFR. Much more importantly, however, had the DCFR limited itself to first drafting a convincing contract law, one could have approached the old unconvincing 'heritage' of the *Bürgerliches Recht* which has to do with the other most important 'non-contractual' obligation: unjust enrichment. This is a heritage that both courts and scholars and, in 2002, also the legislature, had to struggle with, and all parties tried to bring contractual rules on restitution and rules on restitution based on unjust enrichment closer to one another.[15] Had one had the courage to think first of contracts, a coherent system of restitution could have been designed where

F. Gomez, 'The European Directive of Consumer Sales: An Economic Perspective', *ibid*, 127 et seq.

14. C. von Bar, *Benevolent Intervention in Another's Affairs* (München: Sellier, 2006).

15. *See* in detail P. Sirena, 'The DCFR – Restitution, Unjust Enrichment and Related Issues', *European Review of Contract Law* 4 (2008): 450-460. Sirena raises as well the question, why, if, at all, one includes benevolent intervention, one excludes the certainly not less puzzling phenomenon of malevolent intervention into another's affairs.

differences in dealing with void contracts, contracts avoided for instance via withdrawal rights and contracts 'terminated' for breach of contract could have been discussed, upheld only where they really were justified and in any case made explicit. The relevant rules would not have had to be split into two bodies of the law (Articles III.-3:511 et seq. and VII.-1:101 et seq.) which are separated from one another by about 400 rules. Careful coordination could have been the prime aim.

The alternative to the DCFR is a contract law (including rules on restitution) and – separately – a tort law (with some part on restitutionary damages as well). If Europeanization is not about making a grand symbolic step, a grand Code, it is advisable rather to go for a good and modern contract law – and perhaps one day as well a good tort law where tort law is indeed market related or a good law of securities in movables or covered bonds. There is too much energy needed for a good contract law to 'spoil' it on a general law of obligations. To give just one example, the intersections between market regulation and contracts are much more important . . . and, as will be shown, are not really considered in the DCFR. Therefore, the alternative would be to regulate contracts completely and not design abstract categories for all obligations (and potentially all traditional Civil Law matters). The latter is still the heritage of a highly formal thinking: all obligations have one – formal – characteristic in common: that they bind two parties (and even this, as will be seen, is to be questioned in today's practical life). Conversely, a convincing, modern contract law would have to be pragmatic in that it puts the structure of real markets at the forefront.

3. FOR WHICH PRIVATE LAW SUBJECTS?

No less important is a second decision taken with respect to the 'size' of the codification, now with respect to the persons included as potential contract partners. As the core policy arguments have, however, been developed elsewhere (footnote 19), they need only be summarized very briefly here – as a basis for an evaluation of the approach adopted by the DCFR.

3.1. Traditional Approaches to the Question of Different Contract Types of Contract Partners

Civil Law was not split up into several sets of rules when it still was *ius commune*, and this was so despite the fact that, of course, also at that time there were 'commercial' transactions as well. One can speak of an old unitary approach in this respect.[16]

16. *See* only R. Zimmermann, *The Law of Obligations – Roman Foundations of the Civilian Tradition* (South Africa: Juta & Co., 1990 and Oxford: OUP, 1996).

With the French Commercial Code of 1807, the long history of private law fragmentation ratione personae started. Countries such as Germany and Austria followed the example and adopted both a Civil and a Commercial Code, but they have increasingly reduced the importance of the separate commercial law as far as contractual transactions are at stake. Today most contract law rules in the German Commercial Code apply to all private law transactions by analogy – beyond commercial transactions – and therefore can be seen as private law generally;[17] thus the law for commercial becomes general private law, and only a few specific types of contract still form an exception, namely sale by commission and contracts in the area of transportation. Moreover, the German Commercial Code owes its existence also to the fact that commercial law could be harmonized at a time shortly after the middle of the nineteenth century when this was not yet possible for civil law in the politically fragmented landscape of Germany. Conversely, countries such as Switzerland and Italy – in its codification of 1942 – completely departed from this approach and opted for a unitary contract law. In Spain, there are currently similar projects discussed. Therefore the split into 'civil' and 'commercial' contract law seems to be on a more general retreat.

However, the same cannot be said of a more recent split ratione personae and this is the split between 'consumer' contract law and 'general' contract law – now general with respect to the contract partners included. This split can be seen somehow in the tradition of the split introduced by the French Commercial Code, both being motivated by peculiarities of professional contract partners. The difference is only that in the nineteenth century, the ease of contractual transactions was seen as being particularly worth fostering on the side of professional – or commercial – partners, while in the last decades of the twentieth century, the dangers stemming from a stronger bargaining position on the side of the professional partner (mainly his stronger informational basis) was seen as a problem which required regulation beyond 'general' or 'civil' contract law.[18] Moreover, consumer law – or more precisely, contract law for b2c-transactions – is of course the largest part of European Contract Law, though by no means the only one (*see* again footnote 18). In European Contract Law, however, the limitation ratione personae can easily be explained by questions of Community competence. On national levels, the trend is not uniform. While there is a certain trend to introduce Consumer Codes – namely in France, Austria, Greece, then Italy and now probably Portugal – some countries have gone in the opposite direction – namely Germany in 2002 when it first integrated consumer law into the Civil Code (*Bürgerliches Gesetzbuch*) and some new Member States. Therefore, while the split between general

---

17. *See*, for instance, S. Grundmann, 'Generalreferat – Internationalisierung und Reform des deutschen Kaufrechts', in *Europäisches Kaufgewährleistungsrecht – Reform und Internationalisierung des deutschen Schuldrechts*, eds S. Grundmann, D. Medicus & W. Rolland (Cologne: Heymanns, 2000), 281-321. (Survey on the German literature and case law in this sense.)
18. *See* S. Grundmann, 'Europäisches Handelsrecht – vom Handelsrecht des laissez faire im Kodex des 19. Jahrhunderts zum Handelsrecht der sozialen Verantwortung', *Zeitschrift für das gesamte Handelsrecht* 163 (1999): 635-678.

contract law and consumer contract law on the EC level may well be due mainly to reasons of competence and while some laws tend to integration, this can nevertheless not be seen as the dominating trend on the national level.

3.2. Modern Integration Approaches: Policy Considerations

Regardless of what trend may be seen as dominating today, for a European Contract Law to come about, integration would seem to be the more desirable solution – at least if the approach to consumer protection should not be fundamentally changed. The reason for this is threefold:[19] putting 'consumer contract law' and 'general contract law' side by side forces the legislature always to rethink – and thereby justify – why and where it really wants to differentiate; neither a European Contract Law limited to general contract law (with the exception of 'consumer contracts') nor a European 'Consumer Contract Law' only could help to reach one, if not *the*, core aim of codification, i.e., fostering cross-border trade by providing a level playing field; and finally, if the main instrument of 'consumer contract law' is seen in information rules – as is the case today in European Consumer Contract Law (*see* below footnote 20) – the difference between 'consumer contract law' and 'general contract law' is rather one of grade than of fundamental character: information rules are paramount for the whole of contract law, even if they are more important in b2c-transactions. In this case, moreover, both bodies of the law share most rules.

For these reasons, the starting point taken by the DCFR is laudable. The DCFR adopted an integrative approach, regulating all contracts, b2c, b2b and as well p2p. The question is, however, whether this approach was rather taken because the DCFR opted for an all-encompassing Code anyhow and this just required covering all types of contract partners or because particular policy reasons like those named spoke in favour of the integrated approach. The question why integration was chosen also has, of course, repercussions on the question of how to approach the relationship between 'consumer' and 'general' contract law.

The first impression is, for whatever reason, that the part on pre-contractual information duties is not really linked to other rules which deal with the informational basis of the contract, namely on mistakes (*see* more in detail below

---

19. J. Drexl, 'Verbraucherrecht – Allgemeines Privatrecht – Handelsrecht', in *Wandlungen des Schuldrechts*, ed. P. Schlechtriem (Baden-Baden: Nomos, 2002), 97-151; S. Grundmann, 'Consumer Law, Commercial Law, Private Law – how can the Sales Directive and the Sales Convention be so similar?', *European Business Law Review* 14 (2003): 237-257; E. Hondius, 'Consumer Law and Private Law – The Case for Integration', in *Neues Europäisches Vertragsrecht und Verbraucherschutz – Regelungskonzepte der Europäischen Union und ihre Auswirkungen auf die nationalen Zivilrechtsordnungen – New European Contract Law and Consumer Protection – The Concepts Involved in Community Regulations and Their Consequences for Domestic Civil Law – Le nouveau droit des contrats et la protection des consommateurs – concepts de la réglementation communautaire et leurs conséquences pour le droit civil national*, ed. W. Heusel (Cologne: Bundesanzeiger, 1999), 1-19.

Section IV.1.). What is very clear is that the theory of a consumer law was not developed into a general theory of a weaker party – a step which would have been quite logical if the driving factor in drafting was not so much the role of the party protected ('consumer') but the definition of what weaknesses have to be cured and by which type of specific rule this can be accomplished. The latter approach would have started out from the reasons which require a deviation from the general regime (for instance 'structural asymmetry of information'). Again, the DCFR would seem to opt rather for a formal approach and not focus on the policy considerations and shape the law accordingly – always on the basis of the *acquis communautaire.* All this can best be shown by scrutinizing the body of law which forms the core of consumer law. This is information rules in the process of formation of contracts, because it is (only) in this set of rules that a substantial part – and even the largest part – applies only to b2c transactions ('consumer law').

4. CORE SUBSTANTIVE CONTRACT LAW QUESTIONS IN TOO GRAND A CODE

4.1. Building a Consistent Information Model and Questions of Power within the Formation of Contracts

Of particular importance today is private party power based on (superior) information (information asymmetries). This area is currently the subject of intensive research.[20] At the end of the twentieth century, the informational basis of the contract would seem to be even more important in the contract laws than the will basis of contracts. From Kantian and Savigny's will theory to a modern knowledge theory! Binding force is mainly based on (the chance to act on) the relevant information. Real will becomes less important. Accordingly, the rules on a meeting of the minds would seem to decrease in importance if compared with the rules on the informational basis of consent.

At first sight, this is as well reflected in the DCFR in the fact that it contains a whole section on information duties in Articles II.-3:101 through II.-3:107 (Section 1 of Chapter 3 – marketing and pre-contractual duties – of Book 2; for the other contents of this chapter *see* below Section 2). The rules contained in this section are

---

20. Path breaking G. Stigler, 'The Economics of Information', *Journal of Political Economy* 3 (1961): 213-225; and the broad survey (legal and on economics) in H. Fleischer, *Informationsasymmetrie im Vertragsrecht* (Tübingen: Mohr-Siebeck, 2001); *see also* W. Magat, 'Information regulation', in *The New Palgrave Dictionary of Economics*, ed. P. Newman, vol. 2 (Basingstoke, New York: Palgrave & Macmillan, 1998), 307-310; and focusing on European private and business law in particular: S. Grundmann, W. Kerber & S. Weatherill (eds), *Party Autonomy and the Role of Information in the Internal Market* (Berlin, New York: de Gruyter, 2001); S. Grundmann, 'Information, Party Autonomy and Economic Agents in European Contract Law', *Common Market Law Review* 39 (2002): 269-293; R. Schulze, M. Ebers & H. Grigoleit (eds), *Informationspflichten und Vertragsschluss im Acquis Communautaire* (Tübingen: Mohr-Siebeck, 2003).

basically an ordered transcript of what can be found in the directives, combined with a generalization of their content: the generalization is that information is owed insofar 'as the other person can reasonably expect', in commercial transactions when it is required by 'good commercial practice', and in b2c-transactions the content is specified as all information that 'the average consumer needs' (*see* Articles II.-3:101 and 3:102 respectively). Whether this is much more than begging the question again can remain open. Certainly, more subtle information mechanisms have not been developed. It does not seem as if solutions such as standardization and application on the basis of a comply-or-explain have been considered.[21] Nor does it seem that, outside those contracts where the *acquis* already contains more specific rules, a systematic effort has been made to develop coherently, for all types of contracts regulated, a set of items which are so important that information on them should be due: in the words of the DCFR information which 'can be reasonably expected' or which would constitute 'good commercial practice' or – probably the best description – which 'the average consumer needs'. If, of course, one feared an information overkill, a useful endeavour would also have been to cut down on the information due and to summarize what is most needed. Altogether, if the informational basis is really as important as submitted here, what could have been expected is a more thorough endeavour than transcribing the *acquis* and adding a general clause which does not really add a lot.

Information is the issue not only in the Section 1 of Chapter 3 considered so far. The regime of mistake has to do with the informational basis as well. Moreover, if the remedies are regulated in the same section (namely Article II.-3:107), including binding effect of information, the question of the binding effect of advertising also, of course, belongs to this body of law. Therefore, the question can be asked why, already systematically, the rules on the informational basis could not be brought together and why they had to be scattered. The reader has to find them in at least three different places in the general contract law (Articles II.-3:101 et seq., Article II.-7:201 et seq. and Article II.-9:102 paragraph 4). One has the impression that the DCFR did not have the courage really to merge these three bodies of the law: the law of mistake derived from old national codifications (Article II.-7:201 et seq. on mistake), information duties contained in more recent consumer directives (Articles II.-3:101 et seq.), and hidden information rules (based on Article 2 paragraph 2 lit. d of the Sales Directive). Based on a coherent information model, this would have been a typical task of system building – and this in the core area of recent progress in the pre-contractual phase. While placing the rules at different places may be seen as mere formality, this has repercussions as well in content. Thus, for instance, if the chance to act on the basis of the relevant information is the requirement of binding effect, it cannot easily be explained any longer why – outside the cases of *falsa demonstratio* – a mistake should really matter only because the other side made the same mistake. This is, in fact, a rule

21. *See* for such solutions, for instance, the strong case of O. Ben-Shahar, 'The Myth of the "Opportunity to Read" in Contract Law', *European Review of Contract Law* 5 (2009): 1-28.

based on the old will theory.[22] The DCFR did not seize the chance to bring the old body of law on mistake in line with a coherent theory of information rules. If information is paramount in the formation process and if these are the two major bodies of law in this respect, albeit of considerably different character, finding coherence between them would seem to be the challenge which a coherent and modern contract law has to face.

Apart from information, the negotiation process as such is regulated in four norms: the duty to prevent input errors (Article II.-3:201);[23] the lack of binding effect of all reactions but express consent to the unsolicited delivery of goods and services (Article II.-3:401);[24] the duty of confidentiality (Article II.-3:302); and the duty not to break-off negotiations in bad faith, a duty which of course mainly concerns complex commercial contracts (Article II.-3:301).[25] Two of these rules are largely transpositions of some rules in the *acquis*, one is scrutinized (and criticized) elsewhere in this special issue (*see* last three footnotes). The duty of confidentiality is indeed helpful to regulate, although commercial contracts typically do regulate it already themselves.

The negotiation process is, however, much more than this. The really demanding question in system building would have been to integrate what the EC Commission denies to be contract law, but what in substance, of course, is at least related to contract law: the regime of unfair competition or large parts of this regime which found its way, to a considerable extent, into the Unfair Commercial Practices Directive.[26] This is meaningful in a more general way: it is no concern for the DCFR how and whether the regime on formation of contract (and pre-contractual negotiation) is changed by modern phenomena such as publicity, aggressive marketing techniques, and so forth unless the Community

22. *See*, for instance, E. Kramer, 'Bausteine für einen "Common Frame of Reference" des Europäischen Irrtumsrechts', *Zeitschrift für Europäisches Privatrecht* 15 (2007): 247-259.
23. Reproducing Art. 11 para. 2 of the Directive 2000/31/EC of the European Parliament and of the Council of 8.6.2000 on certain legal aspects of information society services, in particular electronic commerce, in the Internal Market ('Directive on electronic commerce'), *EC OJ* L 178/1 (2000); *see also* Directive 1999/93/EC of the European Parliament and of the Council of 13.12.1999 on a Community framework for electronic signatures, *EC OJ* L 13/12 (2000).
24. Developed on the basis of Art. 9 Directive 97/7/EC of the European Parliament and of the Council of 20.5.1997 on the protection in respect of distance contracts, *EC OJ* L 144/19 (1997).
25. *See* B. Fages, 'Pre-contractual Duties in the Common Frame of Reference – What Relevance for the Negotiation of Commercial Contracts?', *European Review of Contract Law* 4 (2008): 306-318: not regulating those cases which really happen.
26. Directive 2005/29/EC of the European Parliament and of the Council of 11.5.2005 concerning unfair business-to-consumer commercial practices in the internal market and amending Council Directive 84/450/EEC, Directives 97/7/EC, 98/27/EC and 2002/65/EC of the European Parliament and of the Council and Regulation (EC) No. 2006/2004 of the European Parliament and of the Council '("Unfair Commercial Practices Directive" '), *EC OJ* L 149/22 (2005); on this directive *see*, for instance, H. Collins (ed.), *The Forthcoming EC Directive on Unfair Commercial Practices – Contract, Consumer and Competition Law Implications* (The Hague: Kluwer International Law, 2004); F. Gomez, 'The Unfair Commercial Practices Directive: A Law and Economics Perspective', *European Review of Contract Law* 2 (2006): 4-34.

legislature itself has already 'translated' the problems into contract law language. It does not seem to be a concern of the drafters to base their rules on a theory of how to deal with the power of one party in the formation process, to define problematic situations, to give them a contract law regulation and define remedies. Space does not permit presenting details and discussion of, for instance, hold-up situations and other typical situations in which asymmetric power (apart from information asymmetries) influences the formation of contracts.

4.2. System Building: Long-Term Service Contracts and Networks Just a Variant of Traditional Exchange Contracts?

Turning from formation to contents of contracts and the phase of performance, one may take as an example service contracts which in many, if not most cases, are long-term contracts. In a service society where the contribution of services to the gross income of many, if not most, countries is higher or (almost) as high as that of (production and distribution of) goods, service contracts would seem to ask for similar attention; and even more so if service and namely long-term contracts have played a less prominent, if not even a rather marginal role at a time when the most important and indeed paradigmatic piece of international contract law unification, the Vienna Convention on the CISG of 1980,[27] was drafted and negotiated. If this Convention still dominates all principles,[28] included the DCFR, this is problematic. It can dominate them with respect to content (which has been described by others). Such domination becomes, however, perhaps even more evident by merely looking at the external system and process.

What strikes the reader from the beginning is that the DCFR does not seem to be of the opinion that service and long-term contracts is more than one variant of specific contract types. In other words, in its general contract law, it does not differentiate between exchange contracts, types of contracts where interests are pooled (joint-venture, syndicates, partnerships), and types of contracts where the

27. (Vienna) UN Convention on Contracts for the International Sale of Goods of 11.4.1980, United Nations, *Official Records* (1981), 178; for the States which have ratified the convention (altogether 71 in 8/2008) *see* <www.uncitral.org/uncitral/en/uncitral_text/sale-goods/1980CISG_status.htm> and annex B to (German) *Bundesgesetzblatt* 2 (2007): 690 et seq.; *see also* J. Honnold, *Documentary History of the Uniform Law of International Sales* (Boston: Kluwer, 1989).
28. On their role as a general model, *see*, for the Directive, Emma Bonino, the responsible Commissioner, cited, for instance, by Trochu, *Dalloz* (2000), Chron. 119, 119; in this sense also for the UN Convention: Communication of the Commission to the Council and the European Parliament on European Contract Law, COM (2001) 398 final, 9. For the two sets of principles: Unidroit, *Principles of International Commercial Contracts* (Rome: Unidroit, 1994), viii et seq.; O. Lando & H. Beale (eds), *Principles of European Contract Law, Part I* (Dordrecht et al.: Martinus Nijhoff, 1995); id., *Part II* (1999); and O. Lando et al. (eds), *Principles of European Contract Law, Part III* (The Hague et al.: Kluwer Law International, 2003), XIX et seq.

interests of one party is the guide-line which the other has to follow (being separately compensated for this). These are three sets of types of contract which in their mechanisms diverge fundamentally.

Of course, one can say that the former is company law and therefore can be disregarded in a 'Civil Law' Codification. This, however, ignores the manifold phenomena in business where it is difficult to see whether contract or organization is at stake, where both types are mixed, and even more importantly, where some degree of pooling of interests is combined with some degree of exchange. Both production and distribution are often unthinkable without this. A codification which just takes the old 'civilian' combination of fields of law as granted does not ask the question whether the ties and intersections between different types of obligations, or the ties between contract and organization, are stronger. In the modern contract law world, it is submitted, the latter is the case.

More theoretically, one has to stress the fundamental difference between contracts dealing with types of performance which really can be defined already when drafting the contract – the typical case of exchange contracts – and contracts where this is not possible because the basic object of the contract will come into being or change only in the future and do so constantly. The DCFR, in its general part, does not distinguish between definition, in the contract, of a quality owed and a defining of governance mechanisms on how to reach decisions within the ongoing (long-term) relationship – instead of defining the quality of the good or service owed.[29] It does not seem that such basic models as those developed in the principal-agent theory played a role.[30] This, however, implies that the basic models on long-term relationships were seen as being irrelevant. This, however, is not acceptable as an approach to today's contract law. It may be that it is more advisable to disregard organization in the CFR or a codification. In this case, however, excluding company law may not have the consequence to ignore the manifold intersections between contracts and organization or those 'company law theories' which are clearly relevant also for long-term contracts. Indeed, not including

29. O. Williamson, 'Transaction-Cost Economics: The Governance of Contractual Relations', *Journal of Law & Economics* 22 (1979): 233-261; id., *The Economic Institutions of Capitalism* (New York: Free Pr. [et al.], 1985), 43-63 and 68-84.

30. Path breaking M. Jensen & W. Meckling, 'Theory of the Firm: Managerial Behavior, Agency Costs and Ownership Structure', *Journal of Financial Economics* 3 (1976): 305-360; M. Jensen & W. Meckling, 'Separation of Ownership and Control', *Journal of Law and Economics* 26 (1983): 301-325; today M. Roe, *Strong Managers and Weak Owners – The Political Roots of American Corporate Finance* (Princeton: Princeton University Press, 1994); A. Shleifer & R. Vishny, 'A Survey of Corporate Governance', *Journal of Finance* 52 (1997): 737-783; beautiful description also in P. Behrens, 'Corporate Governance', in *Festschrift für Ulrich Drobnig zum siebzigsten Geburtstag*, eds J. Basedow, K. J. Hopt & H. Kötz (Tübingen: Mohr-Siebeck, 1998), 491-506; and M. Ruffner, *Die ökonomischen Grundlagen eines Rechts der Publikumsgesellschaft – ein Beitrag zur Theorie der Corporate Governance* (Zurich: Schulthess, 2000), 131 et seq.; summarized in S. Grundmann, *European Company Law – Organization, Finance and Capital Markets* (Antwerp, Oxford: Internsentia, 2007), paras 82-84. For an additional, concisely contract-based perspective of the problems, *see also* U. Schweizer, *Vertragstheorie* (Tübingen: Mohr-Siebeck, 1999), 33-85 and 230-238.

organization may not have the consequence that theories and models which are more discussed in company law – because companies are always or mostly long-term relationships – can just be ignored in a contract law world only because traditional contract law may have had little to deal with long-term relationships. This is no longer the state of the practice today.

Similar arguments can be made with respect to contracts in the interest of the other contract partner, namely where professional services are at stake. One can, of course, limit oneself in this huge area of the law – with directives elaborated like the Markets in Financial Instruments Directive (MiFID)[31] – to the few rules which have been developed with the mandate in Roman Law. The question is, however, whether they represent the complexity of today's business world.

Accepting that long-term relationships form a second pillar aside from traditional exchange contracts – from exchange to cooperation[32] – has several implications. To name just two dimensions which, again, cannot really be sensed in the DCFR – and certainly not as a constitutive element of the general part.

When dealing with long-term contracts, in many cases, perhaps even in most, one has to deal as well with networks of contracts. While it is true that the discussion of this phenomenon is still in its infancy,[33] it is also true that virtually no relationship in the chain of values added can be imagined nowadays outside a network context: not production (with the range of supply relationships around the producer); not distribution (with its chains); not franchise networks (again a range of contracts around the franchisor) nor syndicates; not in payment

31. Directive 2004/39/EC of the European Parliament and of the Council of 21.4.2004 on markets in financial instruments amending Council Directives 85/611/EEC and 93/6/EEC and Directive 2000/12/EC of the European Parliament and of the Council and repealing Council Directive 93/22/EEC, *EC OJ* L 145/1 (2004); for this measure see G. Ferrarini, 'Contract Standards and the Markets in Financial Instruments Directive (MiFID): An Assessment of the Lamfalussy Regulatory Architecture', *European Review of Contract Law* 1 (2005): 19-43; A. Knight, 'The Investment Services Directive – Route Map or Obstacle Course', *Journal of Financial Regulation and Compliance* 11 (2003): 219-224; C. Chance, 'EU Legal and Regulatory Developments: Safeguarding of Client Assets: CESR's Technical Advice in Relation to Directive 2004/39/EC on Markets in Financial Instruments (MiFID)', *Derivates Use, Trading Regulation* 11 (2004): 67-74. Still relevant, core literature on the ISD, such as, among many others: D. Bliesener, *Aufsichtsrechtliche Verhaltenspflichten beim Wertpapierhandel* (Berlin: de Gruyter, 1998); G. Ferrarini (ed.), *European Securities Markets – The Investment Services Directive and Beyond* (London et al.: Kluwer, 1998); P. Lastenouse, 'Les règles de conduite et la reconnaissance mutuelle dans la directive sur les services d'investissement', *Revue du Marché Unique Européen* 4 (1995): 79-120.
32. This will be the title and the topic of the annual Conference of the Society of European Contract Law in June 2009 in Florence.
33. R. Buxbaum, 'Is "Network" a Legal Concept?', *Journal of Institutional and Theoretical Economics* 149 (1993): 698-706; F. Caffaggi, 'Contractual Networks and the Small Business Act: Towards European Principles?', *European Review of Contract Law* 4 (2008): 493-539 (with ample further reference); S. Grundmann, 'Die Dogmatik des Vertragsnetzes', *Archiv für die civilistische Praxis* 207 (2007): 708-767; C. Ott, 'Contract Network in Distribution Systems', *Journal of Institutional and Theoretical Economics* 151 (1995): 212-217; G. Teubner, *Netzwerk als Vertragsverbund – Virtuelle Unternehmen, Franchising, Just-in-time aus sozialwissenschaftlicher und juristischer Sicht* (Baden-Baden: Nomos, 2004).

(credit transfer chains); nor in financing the business (syndicated loans or issues of bonds and shares). In the DCFR, one may find a rule here and there; this is not astonishing given that EC Contract Law is particularly rich in little bits and pieces already. The problem of network – and its relationship to the old principle of privity – is, however, in no way approached systematically, i.e., as a core piece of today's contract law system.

The same is true for regulation. At first sight, the DCFR would seem to be rather 'modern' in that it integrates the last major piece of contract law regulation – perhaps even very heavy regulation – which is the anti-discrimination law (Article II.-2:201 et seq.).[34] This, however, is again not much more than the transcript of very explicit EC secondary Law. Also, anti-discrimination law is a part of the 'market order'.[35] The market order is, however, not only established by anti-discrimination law. Again, those parts which the Community legislature has not yet structured and translated into contract law remain almost completely untouched. This is all the more astonishing as namely competition law is perceived not only as

34. The European standard has been set by four directives: Directive 2000/43/EC of the Council of 29.6.2000 implementing the principle of equal treatment between persons regardless of racial or ethnic origin, *EC OJ* L 180/22 (2000); Directive 2000/78/EC of the Council of 27.11.2000 establishing a general framework for equal treatment in employment and occupation, *EC OJ* L 303/16 (2000); Directive 2002/73/EC of the European Parliament and of the Council of 23.9.2002 amending Council Directive 76/207/EC on the implementation of the principle of equal treatment for men and women regarding access to employment, vocational training and promotion, and working conditions, *EC OJ* L 269/15 (2002); Directive 2004/113/EC of the Council of 13.12.2004 implementing the principle of equal treatment between men and women in the access to and supply of goods and services, *EC OJ* L 373/37 (2004). The directives prohibit discrimination on the ground of race, ethnic origin, and sex. Some national legislatures such as the German one even added other grounds, such as religion, age, disability, sexual orientation, and philosophy of life – the last criterion only regarding employment contracts. The typical sanctions are injunctions and damages.

35. *See* on the theory and the developments described: C. McCrudden & H. Kountouros, 'Human Rights and European Equality Law', *Oxford Law Working Paper*, no. 8 (10.4.2006); S. Fredman, 'Equality: A New Generation', *Industrial Law Journal* 30 (2001): 145-168; E. Howard, 'Anti Race Discrimination Measures in Europe: An Attack on Two Fronts', *European Law Journal* 11 (2005): 468-486; D. Mabbett, 'The Development of Rights-Based Social Policy in the European Union: The Example of Disability Rights', *Journal of Common Market Studies* 43 (2005): 97-120; A. Masselot, 'The State of Gender Equality Law in the European Union', *European Law Journal* 13 (2007): 152-168. German literature is particularly rich and highly critical for instance: E. Picker, 'Antidiskriminierungsgesetz – Der Anfang vom Ende der Privatautonomie?', *Juristenzeitung* 57 (2002): 880-882; J. Braun, 'Übrigens – Deutschland wird wieder totalitär', *Juristische Schulung* 5 (2002): 424-425. One of the core controversies is whether injunction also implies the obligation to contract: cf., for instance, C. Armbrüster, 'Bedeutung des Allgemeinen Gleichbehandlungsgesetzes für private Versicherungsverträge', *Versicherungsrecht* 28 (2006): 1297-1306; M. Worzalla, *Das neue Allgemeine Gleichbehandlungsgesetz* (Freiburg: Hauffe, 2006), 212; G. Maier-Reimer, 'Das Allgemeine Gleichbehandlungsgesetz im Zivilrechtsverkehr', *Neue Juristische Wochenschrift* 36 (2006): 2577-2583; W. Rühl, M. Schmid & H. P. Viethen, *AGG* (München: Beck, 2007), 150; D. Schiek (ed.), *AGG-Kommentar*, (München: Sellier, 2007), 21, para. 8 et seq. For the role of non-discrimination in market order *see also*: S. Grundmann, 'The Concept of the Private Law Society after 50 Years of European and European Business Law', *European Review of Private Law* 16 (2008): 553-581.

a protection of the other side of the market, but it is also perceived as a regime which should guarantee material freedom within the contract relationship. In short: no modern contract law can be written which does not take the regulatory dimension seriously; contract law nowadays is a mixture of party autonomy and policy regulation.

5. IT IS TIME FOR SYSTEM COMPETITION

This contribution, I am afraid, is critical. The question is whether this is 'constructive criticism'. I am afraid not, at least not with respect to the DCFR. The reason is that in my opinion it is not appropriate to remedy here and there and have the whole European legal Community help in this process where the overall structure is problematic – and, in my view, it is highly problematic for the reasons given. It would be as if one aimed to produce an Apple computer or at a Ferrari engine but tried to do so by adding to an International Business Machines Corporation (IBM) computer or adding to a normal street car's engine. This is just impossible. If one is convinced that modern contract law should be aimed at a re-formulation of the problems of contract law today (in a codified form of rules), taking into account the huge developments of the last thirty years and, quite prominently, also the *acquis*, all this based on a sound theory of social sciences and, of course, also traditional dogmatic thinking, amending here and there in the DCFR will just not suffice. One cannot infuse this into a structure which is mainly a comparative law synthesis of traditional Codes, with a certain Germanic bias, supplemented by the rules taken from the *acquis* (and generalized). The only way is to open the process to true competition again – competition which has been restricted quite consciously by the EC Commission's responsibles with the active consent of the groups involved by choosing to put all stakes into only one network at a stage where a truly European discussion (a 'market') had not yet developed. Competition would mean that there is time and there are funds for developing some competing designs, probably best with a clear definition of what fields of law should be included and with the courage to define the scope of the whole endeavour. Market order is order, and markets function much better when there is a transparent and reliable structure. Competition would mean as well that the decision about the designs is taken when the products are in the market and not on the basis of a monopoly. Whether a European Law Institute is helpful – as is suggested by quite a few writers, often from Germany – is less clear to me. Maybe, in any case, however: competition is of much higher and indeed primordial importance, competition actively fostered by the political bodies. If others have said that 'the moment is far from being reached for a politically legitimized text', this paper would answer: if the DCFR prompts a truly open competition which then produces own products – *not on the basis* of the DCFR – there are much better chances that, within a reasonable period of time, 'the moment will come for a convincing text which deserves political legitimization'.

Chapter 3

The DCFR: A Technical or Political Toolbox?

Ruth Sefton-Green

1. INTRODUCTION

The Council recently endorsed a CFR for European Contract Law, the purpose of which is stated to be 'a tool for better lawmaking targeted at Community lawmakers'.[1] The idea of a tool, or toolbox, can be traced back to the European Commission's Communication of 2004, in which the CFR is described as containing a set of model rules as a 'legislator's guide' or 'toolbox'.[2] The CFR itself was conceived in the Commission's 'Action Plan on a More Coherent European Contract Law' of 2003.[3] The DCFR, the fruit of research and collaboration undertaken by the Study Group on a European Civil Code and the Research Group on Existing EC Private Law (the Acquis Group) published in 2008,[4] and funded in part by the

1. Press Release of 18.4.2008, 8397/08 (presse 96), 18. My thanks to Jacobien Rutgers for her helpful and critical comments on a previous draft of this paper.
2. European Contract Law and the Revision of the Acquis: The Way Forward, COM (2004) 651 final, 11.10.2004 (the 'Way Forward'), s. 2.1.1, 3.
3. A More Coherent European Contract Law: An Action Plan. COM (2003) 68 final, 12.2.2003 (the 'Action Plan'), s. 4.1.1, 16-18.
4. *See* C. von Bar, E. Clive & H. Schulte-Nölke (eds), *Principles, Definitions and Model Rules of European Private Law: Draft Common Frame of Reference*, Interim Outline Edition (Munich: Sellier, 2008), prepared by the Study Group on European Civil Code and the Research Group on EC Private Law (Acquis Group).

Alessandro Somma, *The Politics of the Draft Common Frame of Reference*, pp. 39-50.

Sixth Framework Research Programme, purports to contain a set of principles, definitions, and model rules. Although it is emphasized that the DCFR is an academic draft, distinct from the political CFR,[5] it is clearly intended to serve as a basis for an ultimate Community instrument, whatever that will be.[6]

Despite the apparent dichotomy of a political CFR and academic DCFR, relating to their respective mode of elaboration, the two projects are presented as essentially technical, or even technocratic,[7] in nature. The CFR was proposed as an answer to the perceived problems of incoherence of legislation and market failures, caused, inter alia, by diversity. The obvious solution to these problems is therefore harmonization: the CFR is a means of achieving this goal. The primary objectives of the CFR are, therefore, greater transparency, coherence, and simplification of European contract law.[8] Following resistance to this approach, on the basis that the CFR was a disguised code,[9] the Commission has changed track and adopted a softer, even more technical, approach by presenting the CFR as a toolbox.

The DCFR, in turn, is thus partly presented as a set of model rules, a potential toolbox of a technical nature, which could be useful to achieve a future CFR. The Council has indicated that the legal effect of the CFR is intended to be 'a set of non-binding guidelines to be used by the lawmakers at Community level on a voluntary basis as a common source of inspiration or reference in the lawmaking process'.[10] Is the suggestion political rhetoric, i.e., a means of disguising the true aim of the instrument?[11] More to the point, how will such a toolbox help achieve the primary objectives of the CFR? The soft law, non-binding nature of the CFR clashes

5. Id., para. 4, 5 refers to 'an academic, not a politically authorised text'. *See also* C. von Bar, 'The Coverage and Structure of the Academic CFR', *European Review of Contract Law* (2007): 350-361.
6. Id., para. 6, 6 'a possible model for a political CFR' and paras 7-8 'a possible source of inspiration'.
7. The question of whether the CFR is going to be technical or in fact a political code has already been the subject of academic debate: *see*, M.W. Hesselink (ed.), *The Politics of a European Civil Code* (The Hague: Kluwer Law International, 2006), especially 3-8.
8. Confirmed in the Press Release (n. 1 above), 19.
9. *See*, e.g., H. Collins, 'The "Common Frame of Reference" For EC Contract Law: A Common Lawyer's Perspective', in *L'armonizzazione del diritto privato europeo*, eds M. Meli & M.R. Maugeri, (Milano: Giuffré, 2004), 107-124. 'The *common frame of reference* may, like a Trojan horse, smuggle into Europe a Code of Contract Law (. . .). Let's just call it a Code'; European Union Committee of the House of Lords, 'European Contract Law – The Way Forward?', HL Paper 95, 12th Report of Session 2004-2005 (5.4.2005), 23 'We doubt whether it is correct to describe the CFR as envisaged in the Communication as a thesaurus. It would be more than a book of synonyms or a book of specialized vocabulary. We hope the Government has not underestimated what the CFR might contain or involve. As we explain below, the CFR would be likely to have the potential to become an "optional instrument" and/or part of a European civil code'.
10. Press Release (n. 1 above), 18. The idea of a 'non-binding guideline' evokes the Open Method of Co-ordination, used in the area of social policy, for instance, as a means of circumventing problems of competence.
11. For an enlightening critique of the optional nature of the CFR, *see* B. Lurger, 'The Common Frame of Reference/Optional Code and the Various Understandings of Social Justice in

head-on with its primary aims to improve the quality, coherence, transparency and accessibility of the *acquis communautaire* through harmonization. Is it not self-defeating to suggest that soft law can achieve these goals?

This paper critically assesses the idea of the DCFR as a purely technical (academic) toolbox. The DCFR is an academic project but it does not follow that it is exclusively technical as a result; certain policy choices have been made.[12] The proposed hiatus between a technical and political toolbox will be examined in order to evaluate its accuracy. The argument proceeds in two stages: first, the proposition that the DCFR is purely technical is put to the test. This involves examining its content, methods, and aims, alongside those of the CFR. The purpose of the argument is to show that since the aims of the CFR are political/democratic in nature, then either the DCFR is political or (if merely technical), it cannot be a source of inspiration for the CFR, since its manufacture is of the wrong design. Secondly, the implications of the DCFR as a political toolbox are briefly considered.

2. THE DCFR AS A TECHNICAL TOOLBOX: TRUE OR FALSE?

According to the European Commission in its communications,[13] the project could be a useful source of inspiration for a future – politically authorized – CFR. Presenting the DCFR as a merely technical guide calls for interrelated paths of enquiry as to its method, content, and aims. Four main reasons why it might be a misnomer to call the DCFR a technical, i.e., apolitical, toolbox will be examined in turn. The first concerns the link between private law rules and the market order. The second relates to the DCFR's own goals, to set out the best solutions of European private law. The third relates to the capacity of the DCFR to achieve the CFR's goals of transparency, simplification, and coherence. Finally, the DCFR as a toolbox containing model rules and its capacity to achieve harmonization, or uniformity, will be examined.

2.1. Private Law Rules and the Link to the Market Order

The DCFR is an academic project, and academia is often accused of being stuck in an ivory tower, removed from political and social reality. In this vein, the drafters present the DCFR's content and aims as technical. However, an examination of its

---

Europe', in *Private Law and the Many Cultures of Europe*, eds T. Wilhelmsson, E. Paunio & A. Pohjolainen (The Hague: Kluwer Law International, 2007), 177-199.

12. The technical/political opposition is not a new criticism, *see*, e.g., D. Kennedy, 'The Political Stakes in "Merely Technical" Issues of Contract Law', *European Review of Private Law* (2001): 7-28.
13. *See* the Action Plan (n. 3 above), para. 60, 16 et seq.; The Way Forward (n. 2 above), Section 2, 2.1, 5.

aims or underlying principles, outlined in the introduction,[14] show that this is deceptive. There is always a political tendency or orientation involved in rules of private law.[15] The model of society and its economic system are tied to political issues. The DCFR, while recognizing this,[16] indicates that it 'mediates' between the differences between the underlying principles of Member States' law and EC law and adopts a 'balanced position'.[17] The latter is not a totally neutral stance, however, it involves making choices and arriving at a (political) compromise. This becomes perfectly clear when the Acquis Principles (ACQP)[18] are examined in conjunction with the DCFR. There is an indication that the ACQP and the DCFR have different functions.[19] Certain texts have been incorporated; others indicate that common accord could not be reached, explained by the use of square brackets, in Article II.-9:404, for example, on unfair terms. This epiphenomenon illustrates that the DCFR has 'deep moral-political implications'[20] that must not be occulted, for reasons of democracy and legitimacy. It is particularly difficult, in the interim, and while awaiting the publication of the final version of the DCFR, to analyze the policy arguments behind the rules of the DCFR, because they are not yet visible.[21]

Correcting market failures and eliminating obstacles to trade by means of harmonization are often used by the Commission as an explanation for the *raison d'être* of greater integration of the common market.[22] However, there are of course many ways of achieving an effective, efficient, and attractive single market. For instance, it has been suggested that differentiation might be good for consumers and thus indeed for businesses.[23] This would imply that the goal of achieving a single market could be obtained without necessarily using harmonization or uniformity and the elimination of consumer/business cultural particularities. The wide scope of private law rules which regulate relations between citizens makes it clear that we make political choices about the content of these rules: i.e., where to draw the line between protecting consumers and the principle of *caveat emptor.*[24] The DCFR's stance that it must position itself between 'free market and fair

---

14. DCFR (n. 4 above), para. 15, 22-36.
15. As the drafters of the DCFR recognize (n. 4 above), para. 22, 13.
16. DCFR (n. 4 above), para. 16, 11.
17. Id., para. 21, 12.
18. Research Group on the Existing EC Private Law (Acquis Group) (ed.), *Contract I – Pre-contractual Obligations, Conclusion of Contract, Unfair Terms* (Munich: Sellier, 2007). For a critical examination of the method of the ACQP; *see* N. Jansen & R. Zimmermann, 'Restatement of the *Acquis Communautaire*? A Critical Examination of the Principles of the Existing EC Contract Law', *Modern Law Review* 71 (2008), 505-534.
19. DCFR (n. 4 above), para. 58, 28.
20. R. Schulze & T. Wilhelmsson, 'From the Draft Common Frame of Reference towards European Contract Law Rules', *European Review of Contract Law* 2 (2008): 154-168.
21. *See* 2.2 and 2.3. below.
22. *See*, e.g., the Action Plan (n. 3 above), para. 57, 15.
23. G. Wagner, 'The Virtues of Diversity in European Private Law', in *The Need for a European Contract Law, Empirical and Legal Perspectives*, ed. J. Smits (Groningen-Amsterdam: Europa Law Publishing, 2005), 3-24.
24. *See*, e.g., M.W. Hesselink, 'The Politics of the European Civil Code', *European Law Journal* 10 (2004): 675-697.

competition theories and more invasive approaches in favour of consumers'[25] is far from neutral. The phrasing suggests that the starting point is a laissez faire economy; this viewpoint represents only one of the many ways of distributing welfare. The DCFR seems to have adopted implicitly the Commission's market-functionalist approach, leaving aside questions of social justice.[26] However, as the Manifesto on Social Justice and the debate it has engendered point out,[27] private law rules steer the direction of our welfare, both material and non-material,[28] and such crucial issues cannot be left for later discussion.

The information duties contained in Book II, Chapter 3 will be used to illustrate the proposition that the DCFR rules also contain an implicit political dimension, as suggested above. Articles II.-3:101 and 103 respectively contain a set of duties to disclose information about goods and services, in a business to business contract, in a business to consumer contract, and in a business to consumer contract when the consumer is at a particular disadvantage. These rules are drafted in a rather abstract manner; yet contain specific references to different kinds of contractual situations. Moreover, very precise rules follow concerning remedies in the event of a breach of such duties.

The very existence of a duty to disclose information (whatever the precise content and nature of the duty is) can be compared and contrasted with the other end of the spectrum where no such duty exists. To illustrate with a concrete example relating to contracts for the sale of goods or services, French law imposes a more general duty on the seller to explain clearly the subject matter of his obligation.[29] In addition, the Consumer Code contains a specific duty on the part of the seller to inform the buyer of the essential characteristics of the goods or services in B2C contracts.[30] Furthermore, French case law has inferred, or not, a pre-contractual duty to inform, on the basis of fraudulent concealment,[31] according to the circumstances of the case, the expertise of the contracting parties, the nature

25. DCFR (n. 4 above), para. 20, 12.
26. *See* O. Lando, 'The Structure and the Legal Values of the Common Frame of Reference (CFR)', *European Review of Contract Law* (2007): 245-256 who criticizes the lack of social orientation of the DCFR. It is generally admitted that the DCFR is a step backwards from PECL in this respect. *See also* Schulze & Wilhelmsson (n. 20 above), 167-168.
27. Study Group on Social Justice in European Private Law, 'Social Justice in European Law: A Manifesto', *European Law Journal* 10 (2004): 653-674. *See* for a collection of articles presented at the Social Justice Group meeting in September 2005, *European Review of Contract Law* 2 (2006): 131-286.
28. H. Collins, 'Does Social Justice Require the Preservation of Diversity in the Private Laws of Member States of Europe', in *Private Law and the Many Culture of Europe*, ed. Wilhelmsson et al. (n. 11 above), 153-176.
29. Article 1602, line 1 CC: 'Le vendeur est tenu d'expliquer clairement ce à quoi il s'oblige'.
30. Article L.111-1 C. consom (Law no. 93-949 of 26.7. 1993): 'Tout professionnel vendeur de biens ou prestataire de services, doit, avant la conclusion du contrat, mettre le consommateur en mesure de connaître les caractéristiques essentielles du bien ou du service'.
31. Article 1116, line 1 CC: 'Le dol est une cause de nullité de la convention lorsque les manœuvres pratiquées par l'une des parties sont telles, qu'il est évident que, sans ces manœuvres, l'autre partie n'aurait pas contracté'.

of the subject matter, etc.[32] In English law, no such duty to inform or disclose exists, as such, although it has been suggested that, with respect to B2B contracts of sale, Section 14 (3) Sale of Goods Act 1979, imposing a duty on the seller to ensure that goods are fit for the purpose, on the double condition that the seller knows or should have known of the buyer's purpose and that it was reasonable for the buyer to rely on the seller, is, in substance similar to a duty to disclose.[33] In Book II of the DCFR, the chapter on information duties follows on from those containing general provisions and non-discrimination and thus relates to 'contracts and other juridical acts' i.e., all types of contracts. A choice has been made to impose such a duty as a general rule in all types of contract even if the intensity of the duty varies according to the type of contracting parties. Presumably, these rules have been drawn up because it was considered necessary to harmonize the existing diverging rules in this domain. Arguments could be made in favour of introducing these rules in the name of promoting consumer confidence or enhancing transparency on the market. However it has already been pointed out that establishing the level of pre-contractual duties is a legal policy decision, which goes beyond the existing patchy *acquis*.[34]

Moreover, it is questionable whether such rules are capable of achieving harmonization, or even uniformity, for two reasons. First, it should be emphasized that the content or the norm in the DCFR is abstract and open-ended. For example, in B2B contracts, liability of the party providing information is measured against whether a failure to so provide constitutes a deviation from 'good commercial practice',[35] whereas in B2C contracts, the criterion is different but is equally open-ended, i.e., the provider of the information is liable to 'provide such material information as the average consumer needs in the given context to take an informed decision on whether to conclude the contract'.[36] It is submitted that such open-textured rules may give rise to diverging solutions in national jurisdictions. Secondly, a fuller explanation of what the various choices involve and the political implications of such choices are necessary in order to clarify what is actually at stake. If no such explanation is proffered and the rules are wrapped up in technical language, then the political dimension of these rules remains hidden. The crucial question for the legislator is where to place European contract law on the spectrum between protecting the party receiving information, be it consumer, small and

32. *See* M. Fabre Magnan, *Droit des obligations, Contrat et engagement unilatéral*, vol. I (Paris: PUF, 2008), 135, 318 et seq. Notice that the duty to inform lies with the seller and not the buyer; in other words it is not bilateral. *See* Civ 3, 17.1.2007, *Bull. civ.* III, no. 5, 3 where it was held that in a contract of sale between a seller, not acting in the course of business, and a buyer, acting in the course of business, the buyer is not obliged to inform the seller of the value of the goods ('l'acquéreur, même professionnel, n'est pas tenu d'une obligation d'information au profit du vendeur sur la valeur du bien acquis').

33. *See* S.A. Smith, *Atiyah's Introduction to the Law of Contract*, 6th edn (Oxford: Clarendon Press, 2005), 246-247.

34. *See* T. Wilhelmsson & C. Twigg-Flessner 'Pre-contractual Information Duties in the *Acquis Communautaire*', *European Review of Contract Law* 2 (2006): 441-470.

35. II-3:101 (2) DCFR.

36. II-3:102 (1) DCFR.

medium enterprises (SMEs), or another business and providing no protection at all. Surely if the DCFR is to serve as a guide, it needs to explain these various choices to the legislator more fully? For instance, a choice has been made to vary the content and intensity of the duty according to a categorical distinction between consumers and businesses. Other choices are possible, such as the question as to whether this categorization corresponds to the needs and difficulties of SMEs on the internal market, for example.[37] Furthermore, more information on the consequences of such a duty on the market should be adduced in evidence, so that the policy implications are more transparent. How or even can such a rule help enhance consumer protection, for example, and what are its effects on the free movement of goods? These considerations require empirical enquiries to be carried out to assess the impact of the rule.[38] The danger of the approach taken by the DCFR is that it obfuscates a sensitive policy issue. Would it not be preferable for academics to share their expertise, to make it more transparent and accessible, so that the decision-makers can arrive at a conclusion upon an informed basis?

2.2. The 'Best Solution': A Non-neutral Stance

Although the drafters of the DCFR tend to leave these questions for later discussion, in a rather airy-fairy way, as if it is of no concern to academics, a closer look at their statement of objectives shows how thin this veneer is. In order to comply with the instructions laid down by the Commission in 2004,[39] the drafters admit that they have carried out research to identify the 'best solutions', even though it is emphasized that the DCFR rules themselves are suggested as a source of inspiration for the legislator.[40] This appears to be a contradiction in terms. If the best solution is identified, then since it is the best, it will prevail. Here then is the contradiction: if the optimal solution is absolute, the DCFR cannot merely propose, it will impose. However, if the solutions found are only relatively optimal, a discussion will need to be organized. Only in this situation will the DCFR be able to provide a source of inspiration, a soft law proposal, among others, for subsequent debate.

Identifying the paradoxical nature of the best solution requires in turn that its nature – absolute or relative – be assessed. A simpler way of examining the question may be to consider the meaning of the 'best solution'. It is tempting to ask: best for whom? Does this mean best for Businesses or Consumers; or best for Businesses and Consumers? Once again, where do SMEs fit in? Does 'best' mean optimal or paramount in terms of expediency or morality? The dual distinction

37. For example, legal costs are identified as dissuasive for SMEs in the internal market, Action Plan (n. 3 above), para. 30, 10.
38. *See* Wilhelmsson & Twigg-Flessner (n. 34 above), 452-455: who discuss whether information requirements are an adequate and effective tool for consumer protection.
39. The Way Forward, Section 3.1.3, 11.
40. DCFR (n. 4 above), para. 63, 31.

between a perfectionist and conventionalist moral viewpoint may be of help. If a perfectionist (paternalistic) approach is adopted, then only the legislator has legitimacy to choose. If a conventionalist approach is used, then it becomes even more pertinent to emphasize that scholars have no legitimacy to identify what is best for society. In order to decide what rules of conduct we want to govern our society and market, democratic procedures should be put into motion. So scholars may propose, but then there should be competing models from which to choose and a full democratic deliberation process must be carried out.

This then confirms that if the DCFR is proposing soft law rules, there should be a choice of rules from which to elaborate a fuller political discussion. But the DCFR presents one set of elaborate and comprehensive rules. These rules do not look like suggestions, but rather they look like one-sided, carefully chosen, and ordered rules, ready for use. If this is the case, the DCFR is not a technical box of tools but a box full of politically sensitive ideas, that require detailed discussion to arrive at a common consensus. In other words, this is a misnomer, despite the irony that some jurists consider legal classification to be a pre-eminent exercise.

2.3. The Goals of Transparency, Simplification, and Coherency

We should not lose sight of the fact that an aim of the DCFR, and indeed one of the reasons why the Action Plan was launched in the first place, is to improve the *acquis communautaire.* This involves greater coherency, transparency, and simplification. The drafters of the DCFR explicitly recognize the latter two objectives when justifying the use of language and choice of terms.[41] The attempt to express legal rules in an accessible and intelligible way is highly praiseworthy. Rendering the language of the law less technical is not a purely academic exercise; its end-goal is surely to render the law accessible to everyone, not just jurists. Of course, a project that is accessible to a greater number and not a selected élite, is far from being objectionable and is entirely fitting for democratic ideals. However, it becomes clear that the DCFR is not a technical box of tools but rather a code of rules with a political content.

Moreover, despite the attempt to formulate legal (perceived as technical) rules to be accessible and intelligible, the result is not always conclusive. For instance, a 'juridical act' sounds much more like a term of art than anything else.[42] Although great efforts have been undertaken to avoid terms with 'unwanted baggage',[43] this has not always been successful. For example, the term 'fraudulent misrepresentation' (II-7:205) connotes the English law of misrepresentation. This is rather

---

41. Id., para. 49, 23.
42. *See* Schulze & Wilhelmsson (n. 20 above), 157: who call this 'abstract terminology'; H. Collins, 'Review on the DCFR', *Modern Law Review* 71 (2008): 840-844. *See* for an analysis of the meaning of the 'juridical act', R. Sefton-Green, 'Sense and Sensibilities: The DCFR and the Preservation of Cultural and Linguistic Plurality', *European Review of Contract Law* 3 (2008): 283-305.
43. DCFR (n. 4 above), para. 49, 23.

unfortunate and we must await the translations of the text to see how this connotation is neutralized. In addition, as has already been pointed out, certain terms, which call out for definition, are absent from the list of definitions, such 'good commercial practice' or 'comfort letters'.[44] The drafters are of the opinion that the DCFR contains language and definitions which could be useful for closely targeted legislation,[45] though this looks somewhat doubtful to the outsider. In short, the DCFR looks too abstract[46] and at times obscure. The criticism that the DCFR fails to address underlying policy arguments is, in my view, highly convincing.[47]

Furthermore, if the DCFR fails to achieve the goals of transparency and simplification, it may also be difficult for it to achieve greater coherence of European contract law. At first glance, coherence looks like a preoccupation for (academic) jurists. However, the suggestion that the coherence of European contract law has a concrete meaning must not be neglected. The European Commission is interested in the coherence of European contract law, not for academic reasons, but because of its perception of contract law as an ideal instrument to accomplish free movement and to guarantee consumer protection in the internal market.[48]

2.4. A Toolbox Containing Model Rules

As discussed above, the DCFR is presented as a set of model rules for the future CFR. In order to understand the kind of model rules contained in the DCFR and how they may be used as soft law, first, the effectiveness of soft law in general, then the question of whether the kind of model rules contained in the DCFR may fulfil their ambition, will be examined.

2.4.1. The Effectiveness of Soft Law

A threefold distinction can be made between soft law instruments as to their nature and function.[49] First, such instruments can be qualified as interpretative and decisional, with a post-law function. Examples include guidelines, communications, notices, codes of practice, etc. Secondly, there is the category of steering instruments,

---

44. Collins (n. 42 above), 842.
45. DCFR (n. 4 above), para. 71, 35.
46. It goes without saying that legal norms must be formulated at a certain level of abstraction, the question is rather to arrive at the optimal level. *See* T. Wilhelmsson, 'The Design of an Optional (Re)statement of European Contract Law – Real Life Instead of Dead Concepts', in *An Academic Green Paper on European Contract Law*, eds S. Grundmann & J. Stuyck (The Hague: Kluwer Law International, 2002), 353-372.
47. Schulze & Wilhelmsson (n. 20 above).
48. Id., 163. *See* the Action Plan (n. 3 above), para. 4.1.2, 18 et seq.; which contextualizes the need for 'high quality and consistency' of the *acquis* in European contract law as part of a drive to improve the regulatory environment. For a further discussion, *see* below.
49. *See* L. Senden & S. Prechal, 'Differentiation in and through Community Soft Law', in *The Many Faces of Differentiation*, eds B. de Witte, D. Hanf & E. Vos (Antwerp, etc.: Intersentia, 2001), 181-199.

with a para-law function. Thirdly, preparatory and informative instruments, with a pre-law function, such as Green and White Papers can also be identified.[50] To which category does the DCFR belong? This question highlights the fact that the categories are not necessarily watertight, since in a sense the DCFR may be used for more than one function. At first sight, the DCFR belongs to the third category; indeed it is to become the object of a forthcoming White Paper,[51] but it may also have an interpretative function for two reasons. First, it contains definitions, designed to help compile a coherent terminology for the future CFR, the purpose of which is to improve the *acquis.*[52] Secondly, the DCFR will ultimately contain essential background information, comparative law notes, and so forth.[53] It has been shown that interpretative instruments in general do not lay down new rules but are adopted to interpret an existing body of rules, case law, and so forth.[54] Moreover, although the aim of such instruments is to make the law more transparent, to contribute to compliance and a more uniform application, differentiation, which is even greater than that arising under Directives, may also result.[55] In fact, according to this analysis, the effectiveness of soft law instruments in achieving greater uniformity, consistency, and legal certainty will depend on their use and application.

Furthermore, the question of whether or not soft law instruments produce disintegrative consequences is controversial. It has also been suggested that as soft law allows its actors to pick and choose, paradoxically, this can lead to great uniformity and certainty.[56] However, there is no guarantee that this will be the outcome; indeed it is equally plausible that the opposite effect will occur. Moreover, in view of the multiple actors involved and the multi-levels of governance in the EU, there is no certainty that all the actors involved will produce the same results on all levels. So in my view, the risk of achieving greater disintegration, or differentiation, is tantamount, if not superior, to the end-purpose of achieving more consistency and uniformity of European private law rules. If we consider that national judges will also be encouraged, though not obliged, to make use of the DCFR, this argument becomes even more compelling. From this perspective, the possibilities for varying interpretations will simply increase, and there will be no mechanism for stopping the flow, except for the fact that the national judges will be bound by an interpretation coming from the ECJ. However, in the event that interpretation is left in the hands of national judges, such as has already occurred under the Unfair Terms Directive of 1993 regarding the concept of good faith,[57] it is very difficult to see why the DCFR, or even an eventual CFR will alter the status quo, thus constituting an improvement.

50. *Ibid.*, 188.
51. Resolution of the European Parliament of 3.9.2008, T6-TA-PROV (2008) 0397.
52. DCFR (n. 4 above), para. 64, 31-32.
53. Id., para. 72, 35.
54. Sendel & Prechel (n. 49 above), 190.
55. *Ibid.*, 197.
56. *Ibid.*, 198.
57. *See*, e.g., Case C-237/02 *Freiburger Kommunalbauten GmbH Baugesellschaft & Co. KG v. Ludger Hofstetter und Ulrike Hofstetter* [2004] ECR I-3404.

2.4.2. Open-Ended Rules and Uniformity

To pursue the argument it is necessary to look more closely at the content of the DCFR. The DCFR contains model rules with a high level of abstraction, combined with more specific rules. However, certain rules are subject to general or broad standards of conduct, such as good faith and fair dealing, good commercial practice, or inversely and cumulatively, a 'gross deviation from good commercial practice, contrary to good faith and fair dealing' (Article II.-9:406). Yet, as has already pointed out, such phrases 'tend to frustrate the Commission's ambition to harmonize or approximate the law of contract'.[58] In addition, Hugh Collins suggests that a distinction can be made between these two sets of open standards. Open-textured phrases like 'good commercial practice' (noticeably absent from the definitions contained in the DCFR) can never lead to a uniform application as they evoke customs, or normal of standards behaviour, which inevitably vary from one country, or even region, to another. Despite globalization of markets, there is evidence to suggest that both business and consumer cultures are inherently local, or even parochial.[59] According to this analysis, the lack of unity will be exacerbated by the use of terms referring to 'good commercial practice'. In contrast, broad concepts, such as good faith and fair dealing, are meant to refer to objective and morally founded principles. This would mean that the application of such principles have a greater chance of harmonizing, since there is a 'possibility that morally based concepts could develop a shared meaning'.[60] However, this possibility strikes me as being remote, if not utopian. Evidence that 'good faith' has a shared meaning at present seems pretty scarce, otherwise the ECJ would not have found it necessary to delegate the interpretation to the national courts' jurisdiction. Morally based concepts can only share a meaning if there is a European civil society in which such a meaning can be shared. This remains a mute point or a vicious circle: will the DCFR provide the building bricks to build the agora? How can this attractive sounding possibility (of shared meanings and understandings of moral concepts) be rendered more concrete? If the fear is justified that the language and the nature of the norms contained in the DCFR are too abstract,[61] then the likelihood that these model rules can achieve uniformity looks remote.

3. THE IMPLICATIONS OF THE DCFR AS A POLITICAL TOOLBOX

It follows from the above that the policy guidelines of the DCFR need to be brought into the open. It may become important to put the DCFR in the limelight so that

58. Collins (n. 42 above), 842.
59. T. Wilhelmsson, 'The Average European Consumer: A Legal Fiction', in *Private Law and the Many Culture of Europe*, eds Wilhelmsson et al. (n. 11 above), 243-268, especially 250-254.
60. Collins (n. 42 above), 842.
61. Schulze & Wilhelmsson (n. 20 above), especially 157-160.

politicians become more actively involved in the elaboration of the CFR, thus fulfilling the democratic requirements of transparency and legitimacy. It is equally possible that the DCFR be relegated to a bureaucratic shelf once its political nature is revealed since it is always difficult to predict the destiny of academic projects for law reform.[62] It has already been demonstrated that the DCFR is not a neutral, technical – purely academic – exercise. Indeed, the fact that the authors of the DCFR deny that it is political may simply contribute to suspicion.

It has already been pointed out that the DCFR largely exceeds its mandate and fails to correspond to the objectives of increasing the transparency and coherence of European contract law.[63] Indeed the ambit of the DCFR is much wider and more ambitious and seems to clash with its purpose of harmonizing European contract law and promoting the smooth functioning of the internal market. What then, or which parts of the DCFR will pave the way towards an optional instrument? A fuller discussion on the merits of adopting an optional instrument is necessary before its potential contents are drawn up by academics, as recently recognized by the European Parliament.[64] The DCFR, as a paving stone for an optional instrument, implicitly steers in a (political) direction, which cannot be covered up on the basis that it is just an academic project or a toolbox for technicians.

In conclusion, if the DCFR is truly technical, it cannot help achieve its declared aims of transparency, simplification, and coherence of European contract law, as these are democratic/political, not academic, ideals. It has been suggested that the DCFR is inherently political, even if its political overtones are not explicit. The opposition between a technical or political toolbox does not, therefore, stand up to the test.

It follows that if the DCFR contains rules with a moral-political dimension, and this comes as no particular surprise, it is all the more important that European decision-makers are aware of the DCFR's non-neutral stance. Furthermore, it is suggested that the DCFR be a building block to create an optional instrument for European contract law. The critical debate as to whether such an optional instrument could help improve the *acquis communautaire*, rendering it more transparent and coherent with the purpose of achieving greater harmonization of European contract law, is not our immediate concern. Suffice to say that it is difficult to fill a toolbox if it is not clear to what use the tools will be put. Is the DCFR a box containing a lot of tools or a tool without a box? It looks as if the DCFR cannot serve the aims it aspires toward, but it will certainly be helpful in the learning process.[65] The DCFR may, paradoxically, help crystallize the EU lawmaker's true aims by putting the political cards on the table.

---

62. *See* R. Sefton-Green, 'Les codes manqués', *Revue trimestrielle de droit civil* (2005): 539-552; id., 'The DCFR, the *Avant-projet Catala* and French Legal Scholars: A Story of Cat and Mouse?', *Edinburgh Law Review* 12 (2008): 351-373.
63. Schulze & Wilhelmsson (n. 20 above), 158 et seq.
64. Resolution of 3.9.2008 (n. 51 above).
65. T. Wilhelmsson, 'Private Law in the EU: Harmonised or Fragmented Europeanisation?', *European Review of Private Law* (2002): 77-97; Collins (n. 42 above), 844.

Chapter 4

Some Like It Soft: Soft Law and Hard Law in the Shaping of European Contract Law

Alessandro Somma

1. THE ALLURE OF SOFTNESS

'Soft law' is an expression which reflects many typical elements of postmodernist language. It goes well with expressions which combine terms that were traditionally considered antithetical so as to convey the sense of deep-running changes, while referring to the instability and contingency of human constructs.[1]

1.1. Overcoming Legal Positivism

Those who speak about soft law have no intention of creating an oxymoron or a paradox. Rather, they want to celebrate the overcoming of the traditional Western model of State-originated law-making according to the principles of legal positivism.

From many points of view, there can be no doubt that this model belongs to the past. In fact, everyone can see how the behavior of most of society's members is

1. Such as 'liquid modernity': *See* Z. Bauman, *Liquid Modernity* (Oxford: Oxford University Press, 2000).

Alessandro Somma, *The Politics of the Draft Common Frame of Reference*, pp. 51-68.

not only governed by formal legal sources, indirectly or directly related to State action.

Indeed, it could not be otherwise. The type of State legal positivism refers to does not encounter any external limits. If it does, it negotiates them on a level of formal equality with other States. Moreover, it is the kind of State which tends to recognize a system of law-making which is modelled on the formal scheme of the separation of powers, to contrast all sorts of intermediate bodies. It is ultimately the type of State which concentrates power in the hands of the sovereign and in exchange provides property rights to the individual.

A different model of the State is envisaged by the current reflections on soft law, regardless of whether soft law is used or invoked as an alternative to hard law or in combination with it. It is, first of all, a Welfare State which fosters forms of solidarity with and amongst citizens. Thus it is a State which aims to guarantee forms of wealth redistribution through alternative mechanisms to the market but also to model the market according to solidarity principles. It is also a State whose boundaries have become permeable to internal and external forms of sovereignty and which thus finds itself within a complex structure of territorial and non-territorial powers. Such powers in turn either aim at spreading solidarity or they belong to the opposite spectrum, i.e., they aim at shaping the market with measures tending to defend competition based mechanisms instead of preventing and fighting social weakness.

1.2. The Development of an Order with Graduated Normativity

Clearly, overcoming the traditional model of law-making in this sense implies at the same time a diversification of the instruments with which these laws are supposed to be enforced. These cannot all be referred to State coercion. A distinctive characteristic of soft law can indeed be identified. It is a non-binding legal source according to traditional standards. Nonetheless, it is legally relevant, part of a complex and differentiated flexible system of rules which are each endowed with a different prescriptive intensity and a graduated, relative normativity.[2] One could describe this system in terms of a network and no longer in terms of a pyramid. Obviously, it also has its hard spots, but it is continuously enriched by soft elements, functionally allowing the invasion typical of current motions of the economy and of technology.

Therefore, the absence of enforceability in the traditional sense is a typical trait of soft law. However, the same is not true for its being produced in ways which cannot be traced back to legal positivism, whose overhaul does not represent an exclusive characteristic of the current existing law.[3]

---

2. *See* P. Weil, 'Towards Relative Normativity in International Law?', *American Journal of International Law* 77 (1983): 440 et seq.
3. J. Klabbers, 'The Redundancy of Soft Law', *Nordic Journal of International Law* 65 (1996): 167 et seq.

If this is the case, it should not come as a surprise that the first reflections on soft law developed in public international law, an area of law which has long wished to emancipate itself from State powers without being able, at the same time, to envisage an order with real enforcement powers. Moreover, soft law has come to play a major role in other areas of the legal system. Here it has often been inserted into a discourse tending to legitimize forms of traditional power and thus establishing connections, at time invented, with past phenomena.[4]

1.3. The Genealogy of Soft Law

Such phenomena can be described by looking at the genealogy of soft law. One can identify two main paths. Both ultimately rotate around yet another characteristic element of soft law which we shall focus on in particular: its creation involving the participation of its addressees and thus the recourse to methods which can be defined as neo-corporatist.

As to the first path, soft law stems from legal pluralism, typical of the Middle Ages. At that time, a lex mercatoria developed from such pluralism. Similarly, today it can lead to a regulation of the market as intended by the business community, including consumers. As to the second path, soft law derives from the nineteenth century organicist approach. From this perspective, soft law may well contribute to rules capable of combining business efficiency and social solidarity.[5]

The medieval origins of soft law have been known for quite some time. They combine the construction of a Europe of markets with the other important claim to a position of pre-eminence of legal science in law-making. This genealogy starts from the proclamation of a historic lex mercatoria and from the observation that it re-emerges in current market tensions by developing a law which is as universal as mercantile law used to be in the past.[6] Today, these origins are repeating themselves in the construction of a European contract law as undertaken at EC-level and, in particular, with the creation of the CFR.

The recourse to sociological genealogy, used in particular in the process of building a Europe of rights, is less diffused or explicit. In that context, soft law is hailed as a discipline which originates from experience and from the various dimensions of social life. Soft law can be used to integrate hard law as part of a larger solution in which formal rules are combined with other non-binding instruments.[7] Similar statements are made in connection with the recent developments in European governance and, in particular, with the use of the so-called open method

4. The obvious reference here is to: E. J. Hobsbawm & T. Ranger (eds), *The Invention of Tradition* (Cambridge: Cambridge University Press, 1983).
5. A. di Robilant, 'Genealogies of Soft Law', *American Journal of Comparative Law* 54 (2006): 499 et seq.
6. *See* e.g., F. Galgano, *La globalizzazione nello specchio del diritto* (Bologna: Il Mulino, 2005), 56 et seq.
7. *See* e.g., P. Olivelli, 'Diritti sociali e metodo di coordinamento aperto in Europa', *Argomenti di diritto del lavoro* (2002): 314, 323.

of coordination. We will briefly refer to this issue below in order to highlight some points which will help to reflect upon a European contract law: the purposes for which social justice is achieved outside of the market are always connected to the ways in which that market is regulated.

By enhancing the genealogy of soft law, we may be able to draw some conclusions from the aims envisaged by referring back to it. In fact, one of the characteristics of postmodern language is that it hints at the values which it intends to overcome. In our case, it is the vision of State-originated legal sources. However, the values which are supposed to be promoted in their place are not as clear. Quite to the contrary, they are made unclear by the use of suggestive, albeit void, expressions, as they can lead to the most disparate constructs.

2. SOFT LAW AND A EUROPE OF RIGHTS

The development of social policies in the European Community is tied to the diffusion of soft law. According to many, this is due to the circumstance that the recourse to traditional instruments of harmonization of national legislation prevents the creation of a Europe of rights, besides a Europe of markets. Such instruments of harmonization do not respect national diversities and therefore cannot create a consensus about the solutions adopted from time to time.

2.1. Open Method of Coordination versus Harmonization

For this reason, it is no coincidence that the alternatives to harmonization are viewed favourably, especially by the Community institution closest to national governments: the Council of Ministers. Amongst those alternatives the open method of coordination, aiming at a coordination of national economic, labour, and welfare policies, occupies a central position.[8] The method is appreciated, since it allows the interested parties to intervene in the definition of the objectives to be achieved. However, it is criticized because it leaves the parties free to determine the means by which to reach those aims and because it goes hand in hand with practically ineffective control measures.[9]

One can also agree with the promoters of soft law in that it allows one to deal with subject matters which would otherwise not fall within Community competence. However, a similar position does not heed the development of a system of fundamental European rights, which could easily become crucial for the definition of hard social policies.

8. *See* Art. 5 EU Treaty.
9. How the open method of coordination works can be gleaned from the European Council of Luxemburg on 20-21.11.1997, *Presidency Conclusions*, n. 3 et seq. and 13 et seq. and from the European Council of Lisbon on 23-24.3.2000, *Presidency Conclusions*, n. 1 et seq. and 37 et seq.

Hence, one has to look elsewhere for reasons justifying an expansion of the area reserved for soft law. For example, one could mention the intent to increase the recourse to forms of neo-corporatist democracy, which necessarily anticipates the expansion in discourse, an aspect which we will look at shortly. The intent to water down social values by combining them with business values seems equally relevant: it is not a coincidence that one looks to soft law in order to combine flexibility and security of and in employment,[10] or solidarity and competitiveness of the productive system, or economic growth and environmental sustainability.[11]

From this point of view, the observation that the open method of coordination has many things in common with various forms of competitive federalism, such as competition amongst legal orders, also seems to be correct. These forms are formally introduced to protect national identity but are equally able to produce incisive forms of harmonization. In referring to criteria of economic efficiency, a race to the bottom, at least from a point of view of social policies, has started.[12]

2.2. EC-Fundamental Rights versus National Fundamental Rights

According to some, this situation could change significantly if the systems of soft law functioned within a space defined by a system of hard fundamental rights. This system would obviously not be a mere attachment to a Europe of markets, where State intervention is only conceived and developed in case of market failures.

Yet, it does not seem possible to envisage such a change with reference to the fundamental Community rights as codified in the Nice Charter of Fundamental Rights of the EU.[13] The social rights included in the system have been listed starting with the declaration of the principle of formal equality, meaning that they are not accompanied by a State obligation to remove any obstacles to the achievement of substantive equality. In fact, social rights simply fall under the domain of the principle of non-discrimination. To give two typical examples, the right to health care is only the right of everyone to 'access to preventive health care and the right to benefit from medical treatment under the conditions established by national laws and practices' (Article 35), whilst the right to social inclusion is only the right to 'social and housing assistance' of 'all those who lack sufficient resources,

10. Combined in the term 'flexicurity'. On this point *see* the critical position of di Robilant (n. 5 above), 506.
11. This leads to the famous notion of 'sustainable development': On this point *see* A. Somma, 'Exporting Economic Democracy', in *Private Law and the Many Cultures of Europe*, ed. T. Wilhelmsson (The Hague: Kluwer Law International, 2007), 201 et seq.
12. *See* T. Treu, 'Diritti sociali europei', *Lavoro e diritto* (2000): 444 et seq.; A. Lo Faro & A. Andronico, 'Metodo aperto di coordinamento e diritti fondamentali. Strumenti complementari o grammatiche differenti?', *Giornale di diritto del lavoro e di relazioni industriali* 4 (2005): 518 et seq.
13. Article 6 of the EU Treaty now attributes 'the same legal value as the Treaties' to this Charter, as adapted at Strasbourg, on 12.12.2007.

in accordance with the riles laid down by Community law and national laws and practices' (Article 34).[14] Moreover, 'in order to promote the social cohesion of the Union', the Charter 'recognizes and respects access to services of general economic interest' (Article 36), in accordance with a scheme which does not create any new right.[15] Thus drafted, the provisions establishing social rights are a 'considerable step back', and not only for the reasons just mentioned.

One also needs to criticize the fact that EC-fundamental rights, formulated in the way they are, will not be deemed a benchmark for ordinary legislation.[16] This results from the provision stating that the addressees of the Charter – the 'institutions', the 'bodies of the Union with due regard for the principle of subsidiarity' and 'the Member States only when they are implementing Union law' – shall 'respect' the rights and only 'observe' the principles recognized (Article 51). All this, whilst, according to an official statement, 'principles are different from subjective rights in that they may call for implementation through legislative or executive acts'.[17]

This scenario may call into question an assumption that is widespread in many civil law countries; namely, the assumption that the distinction between constitutional provisions having merely a programmatic or prescriptive character does not influence their normative character. Eventually, it also leads to subordinating the implementation of fundamental rights to economic and budgetary compatibility. This corresponds precisely to the mechanism theorized about with reference to the Open method of coordination[18] and not surprisingly invoked as a useful instrument for the implementation of the Charter of Nice.[19]

3. A EUROPE OF MARKETS

As we have seen, the discourse on sociological genealogy is not the only existing one around the use of soft law. It intertwines with the medieval genealogy, which has expanded at equal pace with the expansion of the Europe of markets across the boundaries traditionally imposed by the State. Just as in the case of the construction of a Europe of rights, here too, the references to soft law lead to the proposal of making rules which are developed with the contribution of their addressees and which are not enforceable by means of State intervention.

---

14. The *Text of the explanations relating to the complete text of the Charter as set out in* CHARTE 4473/00 CONVENT 49, establishes that 'the reference to social services relates to cases in which such services have been introduced' and 'does not imply that such services must be created where they do not exist' (31 et seq.).
15. See n. 14 above, 33.
16. D. Grimm, 'Il significato della stesura di un catalogo europeo dei diritti fondamentali', in *Diritti e Costituzione nell'Unione Europea*, ed. G. Zagrebelsky (Rome and Bari: Laterza, 2003), 10 et seq.
17. The European Convention – WG II – Working doc. 23, 4 et seq.
18. European Council of Luxemburg on 20-21.11.1997, *Presidency Conclusions*, n. 3 and 7.
19. EU Network of Independent Experts in Fundamental Rights, *Report on the Situation of Fundamental Rights in the European Union and the Member States in 2002*, 25 et seq.

3.1. The Contribution of Neo-Pandectistic

Nevertheless, it is not only the medieval method to be hailed, i.e. its being a model for reconstructing the ancient European academic unity.[20] Often the so-called Neo-Pandectists also make direct references to the Roman law foundations of this unity;[21] as if Roman law were really a kind of legal supermarket in which lawyers belonging to various time periods have regularly found what they needed;[22] and the history of law in the Western world were a chain of legal transplants starting from Roman law.[23]

It is widely known that there are no traces whatsoever at the Community level that such a path has indeed been taken.[24] The distance separating our present time from the past is less known. Legal science is often the ally of a political power weakened by recourse to neo-corporatist mechanisms that are encouraged by recourse to soft law. The political power in turn is the ally of an economic power committed to building an ordoliberal Private law society.[25] Hence, if one likes the point that European private law is based on the principles of 'Roman law clad in modern clothes', it is only because the rules necessary to build and consolidate this type of society are to be found in these principles. For example, the implicit principle contained in the statement that 'contracts based on nothing else but informal consent are usually binding',[26] is advanced by those who want to keep private law insulated from instances of solidarity or redistribution.[27]

3.2. The Role of Legal Science in Drafting the DCFR

We can find confirmation of these phenomena in the stark contrast existing between the scenarios developed by the Neo-Pandectists and what is happening, on the contrary, with reference to the current initiatives aiming at developing the CFR.

20. On this point *see* recently C. Prieto, 'Une culture contractuelle commune en Europe', in *Regards croisés sur les Principes du droit européen du contrat et sur le droit français*, ed. C. Prieto (Aix-en-Provence: Presses Universitaires d'Aix-Marseille, 2003), 37 et seq.
21. E.g., P. Caroni, 'Der Schiffbruch der Geschichtlichkeit', *Zeitschrift für neuere Rechtsgeschichte* 16 (1994): 85 et seq.
22. As advanced by P. Stein, *Roman Law in European History* (Cambridge: Cambridge University Press, 1999), 2.
23. *See* A. Watson, *Legal Transplant Legal Transplants and European Private Law*, 2nd edn (Athens, Georgia: University of Georgia Press, 1993), 107 et seq.
24. *See* A. Somma, *Introduzione critica al diritto europeo dei contratti* (Milano: Giuffré, 2007), 18 et seq.
25. *See* Section 4.1. below.
26. R. Zimmermann, 'Roman Law and European Legal Unity', in *Towards a European Civil Code*, eds A. Hartkamp et al. (Nijmegen: Ars Aequi libri, 1994), 72.
27. H. Eidenmüller et al., 'Der Gemeinsame Referenzrahmen für das Europäische Privatrecht', *Juristenzeitung* (2008): 535.

Its drafting has been entrusted to an international network of academics, which has been charged with the preparation of a draft (DCFR)[28] that was recently published in its interim outline edition.[29] Yet, as can easily be guessed, the above-mentioned network is neither the only nor the main actor in this phase of creation of a European private law. A primary role is and has been played by the so-called 'stakeholders',[30] who have been grouped in a commission representing on the one hand businesses and the legal profession, and on the other hand consumers (CFR-net). This commission has had the task of directing the drafting efforts of the DCFR, to contribute to the initial 'identification of the main problems which need to be addressed'[31] and to then provide comments on the drafts made by the academic network. The latter must then revise the drafts accordingly or, in case of disagreement, explain the reasons for not doing so.[32]

For their part, the academics needed to justify any political decisions they may have taken. Any decisions which are not in line with the fundamental principle of contractual freedom are deemed to fall into that category.[33]

From this point of view, as highlighted by its authors, the DCFR can be viewed as an academic and not a political text.[34] However, this is only the case in as far as it has been materially drafted by these academics and not as an autonomous product of legal science. This is a situation that is clearly different from that imagined or hoped for by the Neo-Pandectists.

3.3. The DCFR as an Academic Codification

But there are further considerations concerning the role soft law plays in the elaboration of a contract law in line with the above-mentioned premises. The use of soft law is important on two different levels: on the one hand, the choice of the normative instrument, packaged according to the neo-corporatist scheme and, on the other hand, the selection of the rules which are supposed to become mandatory.

The normative instrument, which combines softness with scholarly power, is the 'academic codification'. This is what the Community documents hint at when they mention an 'optional instrument',[35] which the parties are free to choose

28. Contract 513351 within the Sixth Framework Programme (FP6 – *Priority 7 – Research topic 5.1.3. Towards a European Contract Law*).
29. C. von Bar et al. (eds), *Principles, Definition and Model Rules of European Private Law: Draft Common Frame of Reference (DCFR)*, Interim Outline Edition (München: Sellier, 2008).
30. Section 5.2. below.
31. This is being requested in the Call for expression of interest with a view to setting up a network of stakeholder experts on the CFR in the area of European contract law (CFR-net), in OJ S 148, 31.7.2004.
32. COM/2005/456 final (para. 2.2.2.).
33. Id. (para. 2.6.3.).
34. *See* R. Schulze, 'The Academic Draft of the CFR and the EC Contract Law', in *The Common Frame of Reference and Existing EC Contract Law*, ed. R. Schulze (München: Sellier, 2008), 3.
35. Many have held that the expression intended to make reference to a proper codification but this has been excluded in absolute terms: COM/2004/651 final (para. 2.3.).

as applicable law to their relationship and whose success therefore relies on its persuasive authority.[36] This is the case of the DCFR, the starting point for the possible future optional instrument, which aspires at becoming yet another authoritative text such as the earlier International Institute for the Unification of Private Law (UNIDROIT) Principles of International Commercial Contracts or the PECL, drafted by the so-called Lando Commission and widely re-used in the DCFR.[37]

The attempt at comparing these academic codifications to one of their most well known predecessors, the Restatements prepared by the American Law Institute starting from the 1920s, has probably followed the aim to increase their authoritativeness. With reference to the DCFR, this comparison is made directly at the Community level, to show and stress, for example, the invitation to make it a coordinated document made up of open formulas.[38]

Nonetheless, many believe that the possibilities of comparing such formulas to the work of the famous American institute stop there. In other words, according to them, there are no other instances of convergence, in particular with reference to the principles derived from national laws. In fact, these cannot be compared to the formulas contained in the Restatements, since they are taken from legal orders which are often not comparable and which are the result of a creative process.[39]

The connection to the Restatement by the American Law Institute seems more appropriate when referring to the reconstructive efforts of the *acquis communautaire*, a normative order which developed along autonomous interpretative lines.[40] However, even this connection is contested, given that the entire process of drafting the DCFR is different from the one followed by the famous US-American institution.[41]

Moreover, the *acquis communautaire* includes both the 'principle of an open market economy with free competition' (Article 4 EC Treaty) and the 'fundamental rights' as found in the 'constitutional traditions common to the Member States' (Article 6 EU Treaty). It is a principle and rights which are both referred to in the DCFR, where it identifies the objectives in interpreting its provisions: on the one hand 'human rights and fundamental freedoms' and on the other hand 'any applicable constitutional laws' (Article I.-1:102). A principle and rights which, nevertheless, are often in conflict with each other, so that the reconstruction of the *acquis communautaire* becomes an activity for which it is

---

36. B. Fauvarque-Cosson, 'Droit européen et international des contrats', *Dalloz* (2007): 96 et seq.
37. Von Bar et al., 'Introduction', in C. von Bar et al. (n. 29 above), 24 et seq.
38. COM/2001/398 final (n. 7) and COM/2003/68 final (Annex).
39. This is what is being said about the Lando Principles: *see* Commissione per il diritto europeo dei contratti, *Principi di diritto europeo dei contratti – Parte I e II* (Milano: Giuffré, 2001), 17.
40. G. Ajani & H. Schulte-Nölke, 'The principles of the existing EC Contract Law: A Preliminary Output of the Acquis Group', in *Principles of the existing EC Contract Law* (Acquis Principles) (Munich: Sellier, 2007), xi.
41. *See* P.G. Monateri, 'Contratto rugiadoso e contratto rude nel diritto europeo e comunitario', in *Buona fede e giustizia contrattuale*, eds A. D'Angelo, P.G. Monateri & A. Somma (Torino: Giappichelli, 2005), 65.

necessary to confront contradictions and lacunae which are not very different from those found when trying to determine the essence of national laws.[42]

3.4. The Prestige of the DCFR

The truth is that by referring to the US-American Restatements, the academic codifications are trying to establish themselves as technical normative products and to acquire authoritativeness by distancing themselves from the arena in which the basic political choices are being made. At this point, it is important to remember that the circulation of legal models is not merely determined by their prestige: neglecting that law, whether soft or hard, is an expression of power and leads to hiding the values on which these models are based.[43]

Hence, the critique of the idea of packaging a European contract law in an academic codification,[44] whose application would depend on a choice by those parties who might be, for some reason or another, interested in referring to what could be considered a twenty-eighth Community legal order.[45] In fact, if it were a reference to a text which is on the whole favourable to the weak party, it would stand little chance of giving birth to a consolidated practice. However, if the text favoured the strong party, such reference would result in damage for the weak one.[46] Thus, we would find ourselves, yet again, in a case of soft law used to suppress a Europe of rights in favour of a Europe of markets.

4. MANDATORY AND NON-MANDATORY RULES IN EUROPEAN CONTRACT LAW

Before considering the second level at which the recourse to soft law becomes relevant in the construction of a European contract law, namely the level of selection of those rules which will become mandatory, one has to provide some comments on the ordoliberal Private law society and the bigger legal policy picture in which it is placed.

4.1. The Private Law Society

Ordoliberalism was developed during the Nazi period by a group of scholars who had the idea of according the State the power to implement the natural economic

42. Citations in A. Somma, 'Social Justice and the Market in European Contract Law', *European Review of Contract Law* 2 (2006): 191 et seq.
43. Citations from A. Somma, 'Tanto per cambiare. Mutazione del diritto e mondializzazione nella riflessione comparatistica', *Politica del diritto* (2005): 105 et seq.
44. E.g., O. Lando, 'Culture and Contract Laws', *European Review of Contract Law* (2007): 19.
45. *See* H. Schulte-Nölke, 'EC Law on the Formation of Contract', *European Review of Contract Law* (2007): 332 et seq.
46. *See* B. Lurger, 'Il futuro del diritto europeo dei contratti', in *Giustizia sociale e mercato nel diritto europeo dei contratti*, ed. A. Somma (Torino: Giappichelli, 2007), 144.

order and thus to unite general and special interests.[47] With the end of Nazism, ordoliberalism was completed with the development of a formula of the Private law society, even though it is indifferent, if not hostile, to the coordination with the functioning of a democracy. In such a society the State is given the only powers necessary to defend the functionality of the Private law mechanisms, in particular the freedom to act of the economic actors.[48]

In the Private law society, the tax contribution paid in proportion to one's earning capacities and destined to finance the structures of the Welfare State is the privileged form of solidarity. These structures may reduce the territory of the market in as far as they mark the boundaries of an area outside of its logic. However, the market as such is not undermined by measures destined to promote solidarity: in the Private law society, social interventionism only represents a historical condition of its existence.[49]

4.2. The Social Market Economy

In EC-language, this scheme is summarized in the expression 'social market economy':[50] the situation in which economic freedoms are encouraged if they promote competition, and fought if they hinder it.[51] Thus, in the Private law society, the role of the State is far from being scaled down. The State is the instrument through which the behaviors of economic actors are forced into the logic of a system. Therefore, professionals are transformed into efficient multipliers and consumers into rational selectors of goods and services offered.

Similar considerations are at the core of the debate dedicated to the construction of a European contract law. This debate starts from the assumption that those provisions which are supposed to prevent market failures must have a mandatory character. Since they cannot be derogated by economic actors, they must be harmonized in order to avoid distortions of competition.[52] This explains why at the Community level the opportunity of proceeding with a harmonization of contract law is not under discussion. What is at stake, is the elaboration of criteria useful to identify the areas of mandatory character and those areas in which it is sufficient to establish non-mandatory rules.

---

47. A classic is F. Böhm, *Die Ordnung der Wirtschaft als geschichtliche Aufgabe und rechtsschöpferische Leistung* (Stuttgart: Kohlhammer, 1937).
48. K. Mayer & J. Scheinpflug, *Privatrechtsgesellschaft und die Europäische Union* (Tübingen: Mohr-Siebeck, 1996), 75.
49. M. Foucault, *Nascita della biopolitica: corso al College de France (1978-1979)* (Milano: Feltrinelli, 2005), 133 et seq.
50. Article 2 EU Treaty. Today *see* Art. 3 in the version modified by the Lisbon Treaty of 13.12.2007.
51. W. Eucken, 'Die Wettbewerbsordnung und ihre Verwirklichung', *Ordo* 2 (1949): 52 et seq.
52. COM/2003/68 final (25 et seq.).

4.3. Mandatory Contract Law

First we will analyze hard contract law before looking at the functions of non-mandatory law. Our starting point is the provision contained in the DCFR, according to which the parties are free to enter into a contract and to determine its content 'in observance of the rules on good faith and fair dealing and of any other applicable mandatory rule', integrated by the additional provision that the parties may exclude the application of all rules in contract matters 'unless it is not otherwise established' (Article II.-1:102).

Therefore, the main provision deemed to be immediately mandatory by the DCFR concerns the obligation of good faith and fair dealing.[53] When analyzing the context in which this obligation appears, it becomes clear that it represents a kind of rule of ordoliberal extraction referring to a mercantile morality, and in particular an invitation to cooperate so as to maintain and develop competition.[54]

This is equally true in those cases in which the references to good faith and fairness concern aspects of contract regulation, which can be used to conform the market according to solidarity schemes and which are therefore mindful of wealth redistribution. However, such a use characterizes the core of national contract law but not Community law.[55] A typical example is the provision allowing courts to re-establish the balance between contractual obligations (Article II.-7:207). In fact, this is a balance which is part of commutative justice rather than distributive justice: of contractual justice rather than social justice – a balance, the re-establishment of which is only permitted in as far as it allows the extension of the market mechanism to the weaker participants.[56]

The observations concerning other provisions of the DCFR, whose mandatory character derives from the explicit specification that their application cannot be excluded by the parties, are not much different. This is the case, for instance, for those provisions that prohibit forms of discrimination capable of preventing consumer categories from exercising their function as selectors of goods offered on the market (Article II.-2:101 ff.). It is equally the case for the definition of the information duties (Article II.-3:107) or for the regulation concerning the right to withdraw (Articles II.-3:107 and II.-5:101), both aimed at placing the consumer in a position from which he or she can rationally evaluate the terms of the deal and correctly exercise the above-mentioned function.[57]

---

53. The Outline Edition of the DCFR makes no explicit reference to good faith in art. II.1:102, but still refers to it as an aspect of contractual security, which is listed amoung the underlying principle in European contract law.
54. On this point, *see* G. Alpa, 'I Principi Unidroit 2004 e i Principi di diritto europeo dei contratti', in Lurger (n. 46 above), 38.
55. *See* D. Blanc, 'Droit européen des contrats', *Dalloz* (2008): 566.
56. In this sense M. Storme, 'Freedom of Contract', *European Review of Private Law* (2007): 242.
57. For additional details on this normative political reading, *see* the scholarly writings cited in Somma (n. 24 above), 59 et seq.

4.4. DCFR and National Laws

Once the hard contractual provisions have been identified, Community law naturally, asks itself how to neutralize the mechanisms of private international law which might thwart the policy choices. This issue touches upon the core of the reflections surrounding soft law, since they ultimately concern the limits of State prerogatives in defining the normative policies decided at a supra-national level. Indeed, it is not the State which the Community level intends to shelve, but rather the national parameters which are incompatible with the ordoliberal way of thinking.[58]

Here, the most important provision of the DCFR is that which declares contracts void whenever they infringe 'a principle recognized as fundamental in the laws of the Member States of the European Union' (Article II.-7:301). This provision only refers to the fundamental principles shared by national laws as a whole as well as at the Community level and not those which are typical only of some legal orders. Also of note is that this nullity is only required to give effect to that principle (Article II.-7:301).

Thus, mandatory law ensures that the individual contract is regulated according to its connection with the general economic system. This leads to an explicit adaptation of economic freedoms in an ordoliberal sense and with it also to the identification of the legal order's reaction, which is most appropriate to keep the system in balance. However, it does not lead to allowing adaptive interventions typical of contract law based on solidarity values, which have characterized national law.[59]

4.5. Non-mandatory Contract Law

That said, we can formulate a couple of observations on soft contract law, i.e. on the non-mandatory provisions by the DCFR.

Obviously, these describe the course of the contractual relationship in harmony with the whole ordoliberal framework governing this area. However, such a course is subject to market controls, given that the proposed solutions can be replaced with those freely chosen by the parties or adopted from national law or from another legal text of different origins.

Thus, the use of soft law generates competition amongst legal orders also in contract law. This is not a coincidence, since it is being advocated to include the

58. Citations from A. Somma, 'La cittadinanza nella società del diritto privato', *Politica del diritto* (2008) *forthcoming*.
59. Clearly, national legal orders have also used and still are using mandatory rules for ordoliberal purposes. *See*, e.g., H. Kötz & A. Flessner, *Europäisches Vertragsrecht*, 1st edn (Tübingen: Mohr-Siebeck, 1996), 235 et seq. However, *see* the important use of them for other purposes: e.g., M.R. Marella, 'The Old and New Limits to Freedom of Contract in Europe', *European Review of Contract Law* (2006): 265 et seq.

circulation of rules in competition amongst themselves as a fifth freedom protected and promoted by the Community order.[60]

However, in this way, contrary to the assumptions of the promoters of competition amongst legal orders, one does not preserve his own identity, which is actually threatened by the penetrating logic of harmonization. Such a competition leads to a harmonization that inevitably harms the weak parties and, in the long term, undermines national social policies.[61]

5. SOFT LAW VERSUS DEMOCRACY

For some years, and especially since the popular rejection of the so-called European constitution, there has been an ongoing discussion concerning participation in decision-making processes as an effective answer to the citizens' mistrust, not only of State institutions, but also of supra-national ones.[62] This determines a shift from participatory democracy to deliberative democracy. Hence, the growing favour towards soft law which represents a central aspect of this shift.

5.1. Towards a Neo-corporatist Democracy

Nevertheless, the intention is not to analyze the above-mentioned method in depth nor, more generally, the different forms of deliberative democracy, which have been put in place to remedy the problems attributed to participatory democracy. The intention is rather to show how these forms are not the sign of a stronger democracy which requires the real possibility of everyone of influencing political results, but of a strong liberal society in which only formally free possibilities of influencing those results are envisaged.[63]

This highlights the implications of an approach which has led to exasperating the process of proceduralization in European governance, transforming it increasingly into an end in itself and decreasingly into a means to an end.[64] Thus, we are on the slippery slope towards a neo-corporatist conception of decision-making processes which is fed by an invitation to cooperate, typical of soft rhetoric. This determines the

60. R. Van den Bergh, 'Subsidiarity as an Economic Demarcation Principle and the Emergence of European Private Law', *Maastricht Journal of European and Comparative Law* 5 (1998): 152.
61. On this point *see* N. Reich, 'Competition between Legal Orders: A New Paradigm of EC Law?', *Common Market Law Review* 29 (1992): 861.
62. COM/2001/428 final (n. 3). *See also* COM/2002/278 final and COM/2003/71 final and the observations of L. Senden, 'Soft Law, Self Regulation and Co-regulation in European Law', *European Journal of Contract Law* 9 (2005): 1 et seq.
63. Crouch states that, 'maximal democracy certainly cannot flourish without strong liberalism. But the two are different things, and at points even conflict'. See C. Crouch, *Post-democracy* (Malden, MA: Polity, 2004): 17.
64. Lo Faro & Andronico (n. 12 above), 540 et seq. *See also* H. Frykman & U. Mörth, 'Soft Law and Three Notions of Democracy', in *Soft Law in Governance and Regulation: An Interdisciplinary Analysis*, ed. U. Mörth (Cheltenham: Edward Elgar, 2004), 155 et seq.

inevitable dominance of the strong interest over the weak one, which in turn is a typical effect of the transition from a strong democracy to a strong liberal society.[65] This goes to show how the attention to procedures does not imply a disinterest in the result of their application. Procedural rules are not neutral and the control over them ensures the Community level maybe a hidden power, but certainly not a weakened one.[66]

The corporatist and neo-corporatist views of social dynamics coordinate well with the reference to both the sociological and medieval genealogy of soft law which is hailed as an instrument able to adapt to social dynamics. These views stand at the basis of the idea of building an organic society, as an alternative to the classical liberal model, which supports an atomistic society centred on democratic representation.[67]

5.2. The Role of Catholic Ethics

These are the typical characteristics of catholic corporatism, as it resulted from the attempt to finding a third way between classical liberalism and socialism; a third way which was elaborated at the same time as Fascism elaborated the outlines of the ordoliberal school of thought with the same purpose;[68] a third way very similar to the one debated at the Community level, which trying to overcome the alternative between classical liberalism and social democracy.[69]

Catholic ethics lies, in particular, at the origins of the theory of stakeholders. Many developments around the participation in decision-making processes at Community level, such as the reference to the open method of coordination or the method used to create a European contract law, are based on this theory.

According to its tenets, the decision-making processes attributed to any given organization must ensure the participation of anyone who might be affected by such an organization or who may potentially affect it.[70] Thus, consumers and producers are viewed as holders of interests which are in competition with each

65. U. Mattei, 'Hard Code Now!', *Global Jurist Frontiers* 2 (2002): 14. *See also* G. Falkner et al., *Complying with Europe: EU Harmonization of Soft Law in the Member States* (Cambridge: Cambridge University Press, 2005), 348 et seq.
66. M. Barbera, 'A che punto è l'integrazione delle politiche dell'occupazione nell'Unione Europea?', *Diritto delle relazioni industriali* (2000): 165.
67. G. Tarello, *Corporativismo*, in *Enciclopedia Feltrinelli-Fischer*, vol. 27, 2nd edn (Milano: Feltrinelli, 1980), 71 et seq.
68. *See* Encyclical *Rerum novarum*, dated 1891, n. 2 and 37 and the Encyclical *Quadragesimo anno*, dated 1931, n. 79 et seq.
69. S. Fredman, 'Transformation or Dilution: Fundamental Rights in the EU Social Space', *European Law Journal* 12 (2006): 43 et seq.
70. According to the scholar who has been generally held to be the founder of the theory of stakeholders: R.E. Freeman, *Strategic Management: A Stakeholder Approach* (Boston: Pitman, 1984), 5.

other and whose coordination is useful in order to obtain more success in terms of performance.[71]

5.3. Echoes of the Fascist Corporatism

The Community level has not drawn its inspirations only from the catholic corporatism. The preference for public decision-making less distant from citizens and for private over public decision-making stems from this tradition.[72] The result of such preference instead, namely the enhancement of society's members limited to their role as economic actors and the constraint of their behaviour into totalitarian cooperative schemes destined primarily to promote the balance of the system, is due to fascist corporatism.

Fascism claimed to be the reaction to the liberal principle of the separation of politics and economics. However, eventually it aimed at generalizing the latter[73] and subjecting the former to the ultimate goal of achieving an economic system already vexed by the separation of society and the State.[74] This explains the idea of the citizen as a producer[75] or as a consumer[76] and the attempt at abolishing the dialectic between classes and at re-characterizing workers as a category of producers.

From a similar point of view, the gap between fascist corporatism and the models of participatory democracy developed at the Community level does not seem to be unbridgeable. As we have seen, once again the interest groups called upon to take part in the decision-making process are mostly those identified according to their position in the market system, or at least special attention is dedicated to them. There is equally an attempt at excluding the working world from this process. More than that, precisely the mechanisms used to enhance labour, in particular the social dialogue, are accused of being corporatist and undemocratic. The social dialogue supposedly grants the Community bureaucracy an exceedingly important role, allegedly leading to a drafting of hard legal instruments, not suitable for reforming national social policies, and it represents the expression of an authoritarian and centralizing approach in regulating common social life.[77]

---

71. T. Donaldson & L. E. Preston, 'La teoria degli stakeholder dell'impresa (1995)', in *Teoria degli stakeholder*, ed. E. Freeman et al. (Milano: F. Angeli, 2007), 50 et seq.
72. M. Luciani, 'Diritti sociali e integrazione europea', *Politica del diritto* (2000): 380 et seq.
73. U. Spirito, *Liberalismo*, in *Enciclopedia italiana*, vol. 6 (Rome: Istituto G. Treccani, 1934), 40.
74. E.g., W. Steinmetz, 'Introduction', in *Private Law and Social Inequality in the Industrial Age: Comparing Legal Cultures in Britain, France, Germany, and the United States*, ed. W. Steinmetz (Oxford: Oxford University Press, 2000), 13.
75. 'Relazione al Re n. 13', in G. Scarpello, M. Stella Richter & G. Dallari, *Codice civile – Libro della proprietà* (Milano: Giuffré, 1941), 43.
76. G. Stammati, 'L'impresa nell'ordinamento corporativo', *Diritto e pratica commerciale* 1 (1940): 117, 121.
77. *See* J. Scott & D. M. Trubek, 'Mind the Gap', *European Law Journal* 8 (2002): 1 et seq.

Such views tend to forget that it is thanks to the labour world that the Welfare State's mechanisms of solidarity between and with citizens were introduced.[78] For that matter, trade unions are possibly the only interest group which has any chance of confronting the production world, which is certainly not the case for consumer associations.

6. PRAISE OF DEMOCRATIC CONFLICT

The truth is that in order to draw a clear line between the fascist experience and the current situation, one has to abandon the cooperative background of Community law, be it soft or hard. Whatever is being reproached of this phase in terms of absent transparency and participation in the decision-making process[79] cannot be avoided by amplifying the circle of interest groups called upon to cooperate. In fact, one finds conflict again, as a generator of this process, by taking it back to those places destined to critically assess it according to the rules of democratic representation: national parliaments and, above all, the European Parliament.

Parliaments should give indications concerning the content of employment or social inclusion policies and not only provide observations on the ways in which other instances are bound to identify them; as if it were possible to separate the method from the merits of political decision making.[80] Parliaments must outline the base values from which the preparation of a European contract law must draw its inspiration. Instead, today this task is performed by an artificial environment, called upon to reproduce a would-be European civil society.[81]

It is no coincidence if the promoters of ordoliberalism, which is an ideology directed at keeping the balance of the existing economic system, recognize themselves in a cooperative vision of civil society. In fact, it leads to a rejection of conflict, viewed as a symptom and at the same time as a source of a system's malfunctioning.

Obviously, the conflict whose enhancement is advocated here is not that typical of the classical liberal tradition in which the result is simply acknowledged and controlled by the State. Constitutionalism in the Welfare State promotes solidarity with and amongst citizens. In addition, it requires forms of intervention aiming both at creating a system of resource allocation removed from the market and at developing market conformations which achieve substantive equality in economic relationships.

78. U. Romagnoli, 'I diritti sociali nella Costituzione', *Diritto del mercato del lavoro* (2005): 524 et seq.
79. R. Schulze & T. Wilhelmsson, 'From the Draft Common Frame of Reference towards European Contract Law Rules', *European Review of Contract Law* (2008): 168.
80. Barbera (n. 66 above), 350 et seq.
81. H. Micklitz, 'Review of Academic Approaches to the European Contract Law Codification Project', in *Liber Amicorum Guido Alpa: Private Law beyond the National Systems*, eds M. Andenas et al. (London: British Institute of International and Comparative Law, 2007), 728.

This demands normative policies, which are aware of the distributive effects of legal rules. This is the exact opposite of what the future system of fundamental rights at EC-level, aided by recourse to soft law, will look like.

Thus, one can infer the main, if not the only, function clearly exercised and exercisable by using soft law: namely, to substitute participatory democracy with a kind of democracy defined in procedural terms and not in substantive ones and based on the mediation of particular interests. Thus, the substantive contents become a dependent variable of procedures and thereby transform the Community construction into a neo-corporatist one. In any case, this construction protects a clearly defined, and in this sense hard, outcome.

The past century has experienced a period characterized by a similar scheme now in fashion and has come to know the motivations and outcomes of such an adventure: the reform of economic liberalism and the contemporaneous ruin of political liberalism.[82] Even if today the motivations are not shared, we shall not believe that the same outcome may not occur: the construction of a Europe of markets and the destruction of a Europe of rights.

82. A. Somma, *I giuristi e l'Asse culturale Roma-Berlino* (Frankfurt am Main: Klostermann, 2005), 81 et seq.

Part Two

Freedom of Contract and Social Justice

Chapter 5

Party Autonomy and Freedom of Contract Today

Guido Alpa

1. THE CONTRACT IN ITS OVERALL CONTEXT

The opportunity for reflection on the fate of freedom of contract in modern times was offered firstly by the advent of the new millennium, which seemed to open up a new season, inspired by fundamental values of Western society, but also by the new needs of the now completely globalized economy.[1] Next, this reflection was prompted by initiatives, originally merely academic, but which then were subsequently received favourably by the European Community bodies. These initiatives were intended to promote the achievement of a common terminology and the identification of common principles in the legal experience of Member States of

1. In Italian law, F. Galgano, 'Diritto ed economia alle soglie del nuovo millennio', *Contratto e impresa* (2000): 189 et seq.; id., *Il contratto* (Padova: Cedam, 2008); V. Roppo, *Il contratto del duemila* (Torino: Giappichelli, 2000); N. Irti, 'Scambi senza accordo', *Rivista trimestrale di diritto e procedura civile* (1998): 347 et seq.; G. Oppo, 'Disumanizzazione del contratto?', *Rivista di diritto civile* (1998): 525 et seq.; and the discussion promoted by S. Rodotà on the new development of contract law, 'Il contratto: nuovi itinerari di ricerca', *Rivista critica del diritto privato* (2001): 161 et seq.; in French Law, 'La réforme du droit de contrats', *Revue de contrats* 1 (2006); English common law and French law are included in J. Harris & D. Tallon (eds), *Contract Law Today* (Oxford: Clarendon Press, 1989); E. Mc Kendrick, *Conract Law*, 2nd edn (Oxford: Oxford University Press, 2008).

Alessandro Somma, *The Politics of the Draft Common Frame of Reference*, pp. 71-93.

the EU in the subject of contracts and all other sources of obligations.[2] Finally a new perspective opened, connected with the application of the fundamental rights, recognized in the constitutional charters and in the constitutional experiences of Member States, by the European Charter of fundamental rights and more recently by the Treaty of Lisbon. On the historical level, research has been promoted to compare common roots within the individual systems and the parallel evolution of principles, rules and models, sometimes with commendable in-depth analysis, at other times indulging in excessive simplification.

Meanwhile, the economic and social conditions of European citizens have changed, partly as a reflection of the world economic crisis, which has struck consumers, savers and also small businesses. The information revolution and the new techniques of distribution of products and services have left their mark in this sector too, putting the traditional conception of the contract as a consensual encounter, the 'meeting of the minds' of nineteenth century tradition, into crisis. Taking into account the reality of transactions, namely those performed through new technologies, it has been underlined that the 'meeting of the minds' is a pure intellectual abstraction: the will of one of the parties is aimed at the purchase of the goods or service and the will of the other party is aimed at achieving the price, and each will is directed to reach the thing/price without any meeting. So the exchanges occur 'without accord'.

The principle of freedom of contract is charged with two roles which are in conflict with each other. On the one side, there is the desire to construct with the contract a single system (free and supranational) of regulation of the relationships between private parties, tending to consider the contract as a plain 'business between individuals' precluding any supplement, evaluation, or control coming from outside. In this sense, freedom of contract, that is, the freedom for contracting policies to make any choice that they desire, so long as it is shared, coincides perfectly with autonomy, that is, with the private laws of the parties. On the other hand, there is the desire to entrust the contract with tasks of corrective and distributive justice, of protection of the person, of efficient allocation of resources, which once was the exclusive reserve of the legislature; thus the freedom of contract, in this sense, understood as freedom 'from' the contract as a binding instrument of the weaker party, strays away from autonomy, in that the contract is supplemented, assessed, and controlled from the outside.[3]

The older dialectic relationship between freedom and authority is represented in various guises, e.g., between the pole of a contract subject to the rules of common law and the other pole of a contract governed by special legislation; or between the 'guarantee' model and the 'paternalistic' model: in the first paternalistic model,

2. G. Alpa & M. Andenas, *Fondamenti del diritto privato europeo* (Milano: Giuffré, 2005); G. Alpa & G. Conte, 'Riflessioni sul progetto di Common frame of reference e sulla revisione dell'Acquis communautaire', *Rivista di diritto civile* 54 (2008): 141; *see also* M. Paradiso (ed.), *I mobili confini dell'autonomia privata* (Milano: Giuffré, 2005).
3. *See* A. Smith, 'Future Freedom and Freedom of Contract', *Modern Law Review* 59 (1996): 167 et seq.; C. Bridgeman, 'Liberalism and Freedom from the Promise Theory of Contract', *Modern Law Review* 67 (2004): 683 et seq.

the legal order (that is the State) is at the service of individuals in order to render their pacts binding and enforceable, without however interfering with free choice and self-governance; in the second (opposite) paternalistic model, the State interferes in the choices, but above all offers, for reasons of public interest, a safeguard to those categories in a weaker position, and governs, so to speak, a public dimension of the relationship created between the parties. A third way to represent this matter has been found in the model of a 'regulated' agreement – rather than governed completely from the outside – in which autonomy does not conflict but rather harmonizes with the re-balancing intervention; this model takes account precisely of the interests protected by the public sphere, above all when the weaker parties are employees, consumers, savers, tenants and so forth.

Further, in multiplying the sources of rules, the parliamentary legislature is now supplemented by bodies delegated for the formation of *soft law*, such as independent administrative authorities and the enunciation of codes of conduct, protocols of understanding, and negotiated procedures.

Various actors alternate or divide the parties on the stage: not only the legislators and the judges, not just the independent administrative authorities, nor only the academics and researchers, but also the professionals and more generally the stakeholders, who have a claim to intervene and contribute to the construction of the new physiognomy of contract. This is because stakeholders propose, through their activity of representation, solutions to the judges and arbitrators, or else, by participating in the legislative commissions, solutions to those who have kept the power of regulation, and also because through their representation they express the needs of civil society.

The debate on the fate of freedom of contract, and thus of the contract in modern times, reflects then the complexity of the economic and social situation which has come to be outlined in the last few years and the complexity of sources, which depend on the application of rules of private international law, of the European Community regulations on the choice of forum and the applicable law, on the expansion of Community legislation, on the legal relevance of the European Charter of fundamental rights and the common constitutional principles of the Member States, on the 'normative production' of the case law of the ECJ, as well as the evolution of the national systems.[4]

The complexity of the situation is due also to the emergence of contractual models and practices which from the international market tends to expand into the European Community market and thus into national experience. It is also due to the spread of models of decision-making, or extra-judicial determination, of the disputes in the competence of ordinary judges or arbitrators, and to procedures of mediation and conciliation. Then there is the multiplication of remedies – sometimes restricted to categories of persons characterized by their particular social and economic role – as well as the defense (at least in theory) of fundamental

4. O. Lando & H. Beale (eds), *Principles of European Contract Law, Parts I and II* (The Hague: Kluwer Law International, 2000).

rights and values of the individual; this aspect is mentioned last since it is the most problematic and at this stage is almost experimental.[5]

It is not possible, however, to abandon the conceptual framework which has come about by construction and refinement in the course of time. Every word has a relationship with its past; concepts of contractual dogma continue to play their part. So still today one talks of freedom of contract understood in the sense of the manifestation of free will, in which one reconnects with the importance of the trust and expectations of the parties and the techniques of internal equilibrium of the contract.[6]

The 'political' debate on the freedom of contract has revived, as a consequence of the European Community initiatives, on the harmonization of the rules concerning relations with consumers (*acquis communautaire*) and on the harmonization/ standardization/unification/ codification of the rules of a common law of contracts. The concept of contractual freedom has been discussed as an expression of an authentic 'liberal' vision of the action of the parties (confused often on purpose with a more brutal liberalism and the responsibility of the legislature Community or national) in pursuing social interests which could be neglected, or worse, denied by agreement between the parties.[7]

Then we are asked, faced with the endeavours to systemize entire sections of the business law, or of law relating to special contracts, and even the law of obligations, whether this uniformity is advantageous for the economy,

---

5. G. De Nova, *Il contratto alieno* (Torino: Giappichelli, 2008); Renzo Maria Morresi, *La redazione dei contratti internazionali*, trans. Marcel Fontaine & F. de Ly (Milano: Giuffré, 2008); V. Lasbordes, *Les contrats déséquilibrés* (Aix-Marseille: Presses universitaires, 2000); J. Ghestin, *Traité de droit civil. La formation du contrat* (Paris: L.G.D.J, 1993), 45 et seq.; M. J. Bonell, *Un 'Codice' Internazionale del Diritto dei Contratti. I Principi Unidroit dei Contratti Commerciali Internazionali*, 2nd edn (Milano: Giuffré, 2006); M. Trebilcock & J. Leng, 'The Role of Formal Contract and Enforcement in Economic Development', *Virginia Law Review* 92 (2006): 1517 et seq.; A. Stone Sweet, 'The New Lex Mercatoria and Transnational Governance', *Journal of European Public Policy* 13 (2006): 627 et seq.; J. M. Smits, 'Law Making in the European Union: On Globalization and Contract Law in Divergent Legal Cultures', *Louisiana Law Review* 67 (2007): 1181 et seq.
6. *See* D. Kimel, 'Neutrality, Autonomy, and Freedom of Contract', *Oxford Journal Legal Studies* 21 (2001): 473 et seq.; the discussion was originated by G. Gilmore. *See* Andrea Fusaro, *La morte del contratto*, trans. Grant Gilmore (Milano: Giuffré, 1988); P. S. Atiyah, *The Rise and Fall of Freedom of Contract* (1979) (reviewed by B. Mensch, 'Freedom of Contract as Ideaology', *Stanford Law Review* (1980): 753 et seq.); M. Trebilcock, *The Limits of Freedom of Contract* (Cambridge: Harvard University Press, 1993); H. Collins, *Regulating Contracts* (Oxford: Oxford University Press, 1999); H. N. Scheiber (ed.), *The State and Freedom of Contract* (Stanford: Stanford University Press, 1998); A. Schwartz & R. E. Scott, 'Contract Theory and the Limits of Contract Law', paper no. 275 given at Yale Law School (2003); M. Andenas & G. Sanders (eds), *Enforcing Contracts in Transition Economies* (London: European Bank for Reconstruction and Development. British Institute of International and Comparative Law, 2005).
7. But *see* A. Somma, *Introduzione critica al diritto europeo dei contratti* (Milano: Giuffré, 2007); id., *Autonomia privata e struttura del consenso contrattuale. Aspetti storico – comparativi di una vicenda concettuale* (Milano: Giuffré, 2000); M. R. Marella, 'The Old and New Limits of Freedom', *European Review of Contract Law* 2 (2006): 257 et seq.

advantageous for the parties, or just advantageous for the professionals who assist them.[8]

If one makes an exception for the Lex mercatoria of medieval origin, or for the principles of Roman law collected in the '*Regulae Iuris*', accidents of history which have their own logic and their own cultural and practical environment, the first attempts at uniformity go back to the 1930s. It is a pleasure for me in this respect to recall, as well as the works of Rabel, the attempt to draft a code of contracts and obligations promoted by a bilateral Italian-French commission (*Projet franco-italien de code des obligations*, 1927).[9]

The formulation of shared constitutional principles has cemented the European juridical culture, even if the debate is still open on the constitutionalization of contractual freedom, while the inclusion of constitutional principles of full protection of the person is now accepted, and in particular (but not exhaustively) the principles against discrimination between the rules which the parties may not contravene.[10]

To summarize the expressions 'contractual freedom' and 'party autonomy' must be put in their context in order to be able to adequately understand their significance. This is inevitably a *relative* significance.[11]

It is a meaning which must be reconstructed also in the light of the traditions which legal culture has ploughed in the course of time, such that in the perspective of the harmonization of European private law, the task appears very difficult for those who have proposed to draft texts which gather together an unambiguous

---

8. S. Vogenauer & S. Weatherill, *The Harmonization of European Contract Law. Implications for European Private Laws, Business and Legal Practice* (Oxford: Hart, 2006).
9. G. Alpa & G. Chiodi, *Progetto di codice italo-francese delle obbligazioni (1927). Un modello di armonizzazione nell'epoca della ricodificazione* (Milano: Giuffré, 2007).
10. There is a very wide literature in this field, since M. Giorgianni, 'La pianificazione economica e i diritti della persona umana', *Giurisprudenza costituzionale* (1962): 93 et seq.; S. Rodotà, *Le fonti di integrazione del contratto* (Milano: Giuffré, 1967); R. Sacco & G. De Nova, *Il contratto* (Torino: UTET, 1993); G. Iudica & G. Alpa (eds), *Costituzione europea e interpretazione della costituzione italiana* (Napoli: Edizioni Scientifiche Italiane, 2006); English law of contract has been influenced by the enactement of the Human Rights Act 1998: *see* R. Brownsword, *Contract Law. Themes for the Twenty-First Century*, 2nd edn (Oxford: Oxford University Press, 2006), Ch. 10; B. Markesinis, H. Unberath & A. Johnston, *The German Law of Contract. A Comparative Treatise* (Oxford: Hart, 2006); R. Youngs, 'Constitutional Limitations on Freedom of Contract: What Can the Germans Teach Us?', *Anglo-American Law Review* 29 (2000): 498 et seq. In French Law *see* C. Lajoye, 'De la valeur constitutionnelle de la liberté contractuelle', *Cahiers de la recherche sur les droits fondamentaux* (2002): 118; P. Terneyre, 'Le législateur peut-il abroger les articles 6 et 1123 du Code civil? Sur la valeur constitutionelle de la liberté contractuelle', in *Mélanges en l'honneur du Professeur Gustave Peiser* (Grenoble: Presses Universitaires de Grenoble, 1995): 473-486; M. L. Izorche, 'La liberté contractuelle', in *Libertés et droits fondamentaux* (Paris: Dalloz, 2002); in the economic analysis perspective *see* A. S. Venderberghe, 'The Economics of the Non-discrimination Principle in General Contract Law', *European Review of Contract Law* 3 (2007): 410 et seq.
11. In particular *see* B. Lurger, 'The Future of European Contract Law Between Freedom of Contract, Social Justice and Market Rationality', *European Review of Contract Law* 1 (2005): 442 et seq.

terminology, a conceptual armour, usable in all situations, general principles and abstracts formulated for the purpose of the rules for a 'code'.[12]

Thus the course which has led to the writing a DCFR has been inevitably long, tortuous, and haphazard.

The Draft, as is well known, does not come from one pen alone, but results from the confluence of many researches, texts, initiatives, and the work of many protagonists with different aims amongst themselves.

The genealogical tree of the body of rules which the stakeholders are called to evaluate goes back on the one hand to the principles of the *acquis communautaire* (ACQP)[13] and, on the other hand, to the Principles of European Law (PEL); in turn, both of these projects come from the PECL; the PECL is inspired by the Principles of International Commercial contracts (PICC) and both are inspired by the principles of the Convention for the International Sale of Goods (CISG).

Up to now – also considering the restricted times allowed from its publication to the request by the European Commission for comments and the open views of the European Parliament, expressed recently (Resolution of 3 September 2008 on the CFR for European contract Law) – the examination of the Draft has been effected with regard to the textual and systematic choices made by the draftsmen. In particular for the ACQP, one wanted to verify whether these were the products of improvement of the regulatory texture reserved for consumers or whether they also encompassed new principles, affecting the generally applicable law, and whether these thus had claims to be abstract and general principles. For the PEL, was it a matter of a simple *restatement* or did it contain innovations dictated by the requirements of a modern economy? To this trend there is to be added that which takes account the purposes – which are divergent – of the two bodies of rules, one dedicated (at least in its original intentions) to the coordination of the Community directives on the subject of the protection of the consumer and the other to the preparation of a single unified normative model of contract law concerning all categories of persons and all relations of obligation instituted within the national systems or trans-national relations. These analyses are completed by the critical examination of basic values, sometimes express, sometimes implied, used by both bodies of rules.

Are these the *desired* objects of the European Community Legislature, or of national legislatures, or of the governors and the government? The reply awaits the future, but what matters today is the attitude with which the jurists approach this

12. Many are the contributions of professor Christian von Bar in this field: the most recent is the introduction to the DCFR: C. Von Bar et al., 'Introduction', in C. von Bar et al. (eds), *Principles, Definition and Model Rules of European Private Law: Draft Common Frame of Reference (DCFR)*, Interim Outline Edition (München: Sellier, 2008); for a critical view *see* A. Somma, 'Verso il diritto privato europeo? Il quadro comune di riferimento nel conflitto tra diritto comunitario e diritti nazionali', *Rivista trimestrale di diritto e procedura civile* 62 (2008): 1097 et seq.
13. The text prepared by G. Ajani e H. Schulte-Nölke on the Acquis principles has been criticized by N. Jansen & R. Zimmermann, 'Restating the Acquis Communautaire? A Critical Examination of the Principles of the Existing EC Contract Law', *Modern Law Review* 71 (2008): 505 et seq.

text. In order to examine it, taking account the requirements of learning and practice as well as those subjected to these rules, it is necessary to approach with an open mind and develop if possible an understanding attitude. A solely destructive criticism would not render justice to the immense efforts which over the last thirty years have sustained researchers, draftsmen, and coordinators, nor would it respond to the expectations of those who believed in the appropriateness (if not the necessity) of promoting the development of European private law.

2. 'PARTY AUTONOMY' AND THE DEFINITION OF CONTRACT IN THE DRAFT

In the opening of Book 2 of the Draft dedicated to contracts and other 'juridical acts', there are gathered together some provisions which have a general character, a wider version then, of the rules contained in the body of the text, which themselves are already considered general, in the light of principles, rather than detailed and precise rules. In Article II-1:101, a definition of contract is offered, which would merit an analytical examination, taking account of both the nature and the scope of the Draft, as well as the conceptions of contract which have matured in the different experiences of Continental Europe and the systems of common law in Europe. In the definition, the contract is given a binding value. Rather it is stipulated that the contract, in that it is an 'agreement' is intended to constitute a *binding* legal relationship or have some other juridical effect.[14]

Following that there is envisaged a provision entitled 'party autonomy' (Article II-1:102) on the basis of which 'the parties are free to make a contract... and to determine its contents, subject to the rules on good faith and fair dealing and any other applicable mandatory rules'.

One can then talk of how the provision is expressed in the other paragraphs and whether it is possible to derogate from the rules contained in the Draft. However, one should pause initially on the necessity or otherwise of an opening rule such as that noted above.

The rule is placed immediately after the definition of contract. It could have been absorbed in the same definition, if only it had been said that 'the contract is the agreement *freely* made by the parties . . . etc.'. Contrarily, the emphasis on the 'autonomy' is linked with: (i) the decision to make a contract; (ii) the respect of good faith and fair dealing; and (iii) the other applicable mandatory rules.

As so formulated, neither the first nor the second rule may be included in a contractual text: thus not all the articles of the Draft may satisfy that requirement which is enunciated in the equivalent rules placed at the opening of the PECL, on which is conferred also the role of contractual clauses, if referred to or directly inserted by the parties in their contract. It is evident that in the contractual text there would not be a definition of contract, nor would one enunciate the principle of party

14. On the nature of the binding element refer to Art. II-1:103, which laconically but firmly enunciates the principle according to which 'a valid contract is binding on the parties'.

autonomy. At most one would explain that the contract has been freely negotiated between the parties, subject to the problem raised as to the value and effect of such a course.

In this sense, both the definition of contract and the position of the principle of party autonomy must be understood as allocated in the context of a text assuming the role of a model code or possible outline for a 'Community instrument' (in the species of Directive or Regulation). In such a case, though the text would remain still as a mere draft of academic import, given that only its inclusion in a binding framework, which a Community source could be, or only its recognition by a provision of positive law – Community or national – of the CFR, once having overcome the status of a mere draft, could have a binding legal value between the parties. A mere text not related to a norm of positive law would not by itself be capable of acquiring that value.

Scholars of private international law and international commercial law are well aware of this premise. They turn to the *lex fori* and the Community Regulation on contractual obligations to stress that it is not possible to acknowledge binding legal effect on any writing whatsoever made between the parties as such.

Yet there is more on this subject. The notion of contract which emerges from the two rules, or at least that which appears to be understood, is the *written* contract. However, one knows that a contract may be concluded by means of *conduct*, or other *signs* of expression of the will, by means of direct performance of the service, without a need for acceptance, by means of all the methods which can be listed to give rise to the contractual obligation which may be created between the parties, knowingly or otherwise. Thus the Draft does correct its aim with other provisions which concern the performance of the promise (Article II-1:103, c. 2) or the formative conduct (Article II-1:105), but it must always be intentional. The problem area of the *declaration* and of *reliance* is seen then as extraneous to the text and to the 'legislative' will of the draftsman of the Draft, notwithstanding the discussion over a good century which it has marked.

Thus, a choice of this type implicates: (i) a limited notion of autonomy of the parties; (ii) a limited application of the Draft – provided that the interpreters do not wish to extend its application by taking advantage of the *objective* definition of a contract; (iii) a cryptic election for the theory of will, even though 'the will of the parties' earns a brief mention in the definition of contract, in the guise of *intention* and then, in the provision which encompasses in the contract also the consciousness of the conduct maintained (Article II-1:105) always *intentionally* or with some other mental state.

The choice appears curious, since it is justified neither by the scope of the Draft nor by the nature of the rules proposed, which would be directed to disciplining all contractual relations (C2C, B2C, B2B) and concluded by parties which are not qualified in any particular manner.

Yet the words of the text are one story, whereas the commentary is another, and yet another is the description of the purposes of the text and the values sustained by it as appear from the introductory essay of the printed edition.

The importance of the principle examined is underlined several times in the introduction, in the warning to the reader and the potential legal operator that the rule which codifies contractual freedom – indeed one talks of *freedom* in this context – normally refers to 'justice', but this condition is fulfilled only where the parties are completely well-informed, have equal negotiating power, when they meet to make the agreement, and choose its content, which implies – normally – a choice made in their respective interests and thus responding to justice. Therefore, there would be no reason to interfere with the choice of the parties except when one of these is weaker and the other takes advantage of it, abuses it, or violates fundamental rights. The limitations to contractual freedom are thus intended as techniques which impose observance of mandatory rules or which strike out onerous clauses.

Contractual freedom is understood also in the sense of freedom from any external intervention, which is justified only 'in relation to certain situations or to certain types of contract'. Contractual freedom is not ensured where it would result in discrimination founded on 'gender, race or religion'. The freedom to choose the content of the contract, in its turn, is limited in the case of unfair conduct in the process of formation of the contract, in the abuse of contractual power, in the acquisition of excessive advantages which work to the benefit of the stronger party. The external intervention – due thus to reasons of public order, safeguard of the weaker party and a re-balancing of the contract – is considered as an exceptional circumstance, 'minimal', and as such as somehow to assist the party which is subjected to the limitation so that it is possible to allow it to carry on its activity in an economically efficient way. From this we see the drafting of simple rulings, instead of the imposition of standards, and the employment of flexible formulae, such as *fairness*, in the control of contractual tools, in imposing mandatory rulings, in foreseeing *default rules*, where the parties have not otherwise provided.

Still in the introduction, it is stated that the contractual rules, as well as encouraging efficiency, must promote fundamental rights, solidarity (understood as a duty of cooperation) and social responsibility (understood as an incentive to the performance of altruistic activities). Good faith also plays an important role. But contrary to the PECL, in which good faith is considered a general principle (Article 1:201), in the Draft, good faith appears scattered through the various sections, while being considered by some as a general rule of conduct and by others as a legal instrument in order to obtain improved fair dealing and efficiency.

3. A TEXTUAL COMPARISON BETWEEN THE FORMULAE OF THE DRAFT, OF THE PECL, AND THE PICC: 'PARTY AUTONOMY' AND 'FREEDOM OF CONTRACT'

In relation to the PECL, which partly inspired the rules of the Draft, and whose development the Draft followed for a certain period of time on a parallel track, one notes firstly the systematic concern to give a definition to the contract, which could have better been included in a list of definitions of terms or principles, as elaborated by the French participants. There is, besides, a sudden deformation of vocabulary, which, however, does not preclude the Draft from repeating the contents of the equivalent rules of the PECL (Article 1:102): freedom to make a contract, its subjection to principles of good faith and fair dealing, as well as norms declared to be mandatory by the PECL itself. In the case of the PECL, it would be difficult to call them 'imperative', as though emerges from the Italian translation of the text, given that the PECL are an academic creation, and even if they were to assume, in place of the CFR, a role of 'model rule', they would never be able to express the imperium, or power, which is typical of all norms of positive law.[15]

There is, however, a novelty which apparently seems to be only etymological. In the English version, the provision on party autonomy is expressed in terms of 'freedom of contract', instead of contractual autonomy, as recited in the Draft. Autonomy is given priority in the Italian translation of the PECL, perhaps by allusion to the title of Article 1322 of the Italian Civil Code, entitled precisely 'contractual autonomy', although bearing a much richer and more significant content.

It returns to *freedom of contract*, moreover with the same contents in relation to the freedom to contract and to choose the contents of the contract from the text of the PICC.

Is this just a choice of vocabulary or does the terminology used have a greater significance?

The French text refers to contractual freedom. The French research group on the terminology and principles of European contractual law has indeed proposed a reformulation of the entire introductory part to Book II, regrouping the provisions in three subsections respectively dedicated to: (i) contractual freedom; (ii) certainty in contract; and (iii) fair dealing in contract.

In Section I on contractual freedom, a wide meaning is given, in that the expression is understood in the sense of: (i) freedom to contract and to choose one's contracting party; (ii) freedom to determine the content of the contract; (iii) some rules of form applicable to it; and (iv) freedom to either modify the contract by common agreement or to terminate the contract.

Still in the context of the introductory discipline, one finds the possibility of concluding the contract only for the benefit of the parties themselves, unless otherwise provided; the production of effects which do not involve injury or alteration of the rights of third parties; the effectiveness of unilateral withdrawal from contracts for an indefinite term.

4. CONTRACTUAL AUTONOMY IN THE SYSTEMATIC CONTEXT OF THE GENERAL PART OF THE DRAFT

After examining the rules of the Draft, it appears appropriate to make use of the terms as they have been used in the text. As the Draft speaks of 'party autonomy'

15. M. E. Storme, 'Freedom of Contract: Mandatory and Non-Mandatory Rules in European Contract Law', *European Review of Private Law* 15 (2007): 233 et seq.

rather than 'freedom of contract', I shall make reference to the first phrase, even if from a merely preliminary reading of the text one can infer that the draftsmen made no distinction between the two formulae.

The Draft cannot be considered as a typical civil code of the European continental tradition. Not only have the Community organs involved in this question and related initiatives insisted very strongly on this – the European Parliament, the European Commission, and the Council itself – but also the draftsmen of the text and the coordinators of the workgroups dedicated to the different programmes converging on it. All the same, the criteria for reading, for coordinating its provisions, the internal references, the techniques of broad interpretation, analogy, and the other techniques which would need to be observed for its application in a *European context* are really those of the codified culture expressed by the national experiences.[16] Faced with a text of rules (proposals, and recommendations, optionals, and so forth), the reactions of the reader are exactly those of the culture in which the reader was brought up and carries through life.

I must say though that, for the *civilian* lawyer, the temptation to treat – that is to read, interpret, coordinate, scan – the chapters, the sections, and the individual rules as if in the presence of an 'old-style' code is strong, almost natural, if not to say invincible. Besides, if the Draft, in its definitive version, should become a 'model code', the attitude of the *civilian* lawyer could not be very different. Just as inevitable is the comparison with the text of the codes currently in force or in preparation, like those of the French preliminary project.

Thus – at least from the perspective which comes to me naturally, but also in the views of the draftsmen of the text – one can speak of a *systematic interpretation* of the introductory rules and the rules which relate to the special parts.

It is also true that the Draft dictates the rules on its own interpretation. But beyond those rules which are expressly indicated and which should be understood as self-contained, autonomous, and self-sufficient, it is quite difficult not to consider that, placed in a European context, rather than a Community context, the text, even if it were to be understood in its narrowest meaning, that is as a model of rules to which the parties may refer to discipline their relations, this would not diminish the interpretative rules, which are precisely Community instruments.

In any case, Article I-1:102 does not leave the interpreter deprived of self-contained rules: indeed, there is:

(a) a call to teleological interpretation;
(b) the provision that the rules of the Draft should be understood 'in the light of any applicable instruments guaranteeing human rights' and any applicable 'constitutional laws' (an obscure expression which is intended to make reference to common constitutional principles, shared by the Member States, as they had been nurtured and defined by the ECJ in its opinion

16. *See* Alpa & Conte (n. 2 above), 141-142.

relating to the signature of the European Convention of Human Rights by the European Community);

(c) a recall to the values of uniformity of application, of good faith and fair dealing and certainty of the law;
(d) a recall in a rather curious manner to the application of analogy;
(e) a reference to the principle of the supremacy of the *lex specialis* over the *lex generalis*, in other words, the priority of the rules contained in the books containing 'special rules' over those envisaged as 'general'.

The limits set to autonomy of the parties as recalled by Article II-1:102 are thus systematically and already integrated in the rules of interpretation recorded above. In other words, any agreement whatsoever which may be created by the parties shall be interpreted in a manner that does not contradict 'human rights' and 'fundamental freedoms'. The second Chapter of Book II envisages specific limits relating to the implementation of the principle of non-discrimination (by sex, ethnic group or race). However, the remedy is not invalidity of the contract – as one could suppose if the rules against discrimination were to be considered as mandatory – but in compensation for damages, either pre-contractual or contractual. Yet, there is a provision for inversion of the burden of proof, since it is for the other party to the person who considers him or herself discriminated to prove that there has not been any discrimination (Article II-2:101 et seq.). There are no limits set to the form, other than specific provisions (Article II-1:107).

One can ignore, for the moment, the rules on the pre-contractual phase, which showed the wide openness of the Draft, compared to the preclusions coming from the experience of English common law, and the rules on the formation of contract.

According to some authors and according to those writing the Draft,[17] amongst the limits set to party autonomy (the cited text prefers to speak of 'freedom of contract') can be listed the rules on mistake, fraud, duress, omission of due information, and abuse of economic dependence. One is dealing though with hypotheses which are very different one from the other: error, fraud, and duress (Articles II-7:201 et seq.) are defects of consent and have nothing to do with freedom of contract. It is a different case for reliance on incorrect information supplied in the course of negotiations, which implies the transfer of effects from the prior negotiating phase and formation of a contract to the phase of execution of a contract, with related remedies (Article II-7:204).

The case of abuse of economic dependency, though, does affect freedom of contract; this effectively refers to the contractual power used by one side in relation to the other and it is appropriate that the provision applies also to contracts from business to business (B2B) (Article II-7.207); again there is the power by one party to confirm a voidable contract (Article II-7:211).

Clauses of agreement relating to the exclusion or limitation of remedies deserve special consideration by themselves (Article II-7:215). In contrast with that provided by Article 1462 of the Italian Civil Code, which provides full ineffectiveness

17. C. Von Bar et al. (n. 12 above), 15.

in case of nullity, voidability, and rescission of the contract, the provision in the Draft allows the efficacy (or validity?) of the clause which excludes or limits remedies arising out of error, subject to its compliance with good faith and fair dealing. However, this condition appears incomprehensible from the consideration that such a clause cannot be other than contrary to good faith.

The limits to party autonomy return in evidence in Chapter VII, in which amongst the causes of invalidity is contemplated the violation of *fundamental principles* or mandatory rules. The first expression is ambiguous, as well as laconically formulated and as appears from the words of the draftsmen, entrusted to the Introduction itself,[18] and as is well known by those who have studied in depth the subject considering the history, the elaboration of dogma, philosophy, and practice of principles of private law of individual legal systems and then of the European private law. A wide discretion then is left to the interpreter, which certainly does not square with the need for certainty of the law, which again is assumed as a basic value for the purposes of the Draft. But the fundamental principles do not make up a coherent framework; they are in conflict with each other, and they must be first identified and then balanced. The Draft, in the pages of the Introduction, and in the rules of the general part, is the expression to indicate some of these, in the form of 'scope' or 'values' to be reached and safeguarded, but the universe of principles is a laboratory in constant activity, glowing and with unclear frontiers.

A question naturally springs to mind when one reads in the text of 'human rights' and 'fundamental freedoms', 'fundamental principles', 'non-discrimination' and so forth: why is there no reference to the Charter of fundamental rights, which now has a recognized legal value, and to its direct application to contractual relations? We must return to this point later, since it is a subject of capital importance.

Particularly significant is the provision which considers as contractual clauses certain declarations exchanged between the parties in the course of negotiation. These are significant not just for their novelty, but also for the importance assigned to conduct – and to declarations – of the parties at the stage when, being prior to the making of the contract, they relate to a preliminary situation, not yet defined, which could be completely modified at the time of conclusion of the contract. This is strange, since there are traditions, such as English law, in which the conduct prior to conclusion is considered completely irrelevant, even for purposes of interpretation of a contract. Here the principal of reliance applies, which is not resolved by a remedy of compensation but which is resolved in the form of integration of the contract determined not by external sources to the will of the parties, as occurs in dealing with circumstances codified by the Italian Civil Code at Article 1374, where there is mention precisely of the law or uses and equity, but rather from the context in which the negotiations took place. The provision must be put into relationship with the 'merger clause' which we shall deal with below (Article II-4:104).

Just as significant for its novelty is the rule which allows clauses dictated by one party and not known by the other prior to or during the phase of formation of the contract to be rendered ineffective (or null?) (Article II-9:102).

18. *Ibid.*, 12.

Freedom of contract is limited by the 'non-binding' nature of the clauses imposed by one party on the other, thus not negotiated, to those which have been drafted and communicated in a 'clear and intelligible language'. The expression has been drawn from Directive 13/1993 on unfair terms in consumer contracts (Article 4.2) and is repeated in the 1999 Regulations by which the United Kingdom implemented Directive 13/1993 (Article 6).

A significant fact is that the Draft distinguishes the evaluation of unfairness of the clauses according to whether the contract was concluded: (i) between a professional and a consumer (Article II-9:404); (ii) between parties not qualifiable as professionals (Article II-9:405); (iii) and just between professionals (Article II-9:406). In this latter case, as well as being contrary to good faith and fair dealing, it is necessary that the clause 'grossly deviates from good commercial practice'.

Particular limitations have been provided for unfair clauses in consumer contracts (Article II-9:410 on the appropriate forum, Article II-9:411 on other clauses already considered in the said Directive).

There are two further considerations. Within the scope of the discipline of remedies for breach (or non-performance), governed by a separate book from that concerning the rules for contract and centred on obligations (Book III), one comes back to a provision which concerns exclusion or limitation clauses of liability, limited however to damages arising from personal injuries caused intentionally or through gross negligence (Article III-3:105). To these one should add the clauses which exclude or limit a remedy for breach, which are considered valid, provided that they are not in conflict with the rules for oppressive clauses governed by Book II, Chapter 9, and which do not appear contrary to good faith and fair dealing in their exercise (Article III-2:105).

Finally, as for clauses relating to compensation for damage,[19] there are no such restrictions, other than the discipline for the penalty clause, which is valued without any examination of the damage suffered (Article III-9:710), and that may be reduced to a 'reasonable' amount if 'grossly excessive'.

There is no specific discipline envisaged for the hypothesis relating to the institute of rescission, which however could be encompassed within the scope of the rules relating to 'unfair exploitation'. Nothing is envisaged in relation to 'presupposition', which in different systems comes from time to time to be ascribed to *imprévision, Geschäftsgrundlage, frustration*, and thus in relation to hardship clauses, express termination clauses, and many other clauses which the individual civil codes or international commercial contracts normally foresee.

5. CODIFICATION OF THE MERGER CLAUSE

In the face of formation, the Draft provides that the parties may include a clause for the entirety of the contract (the so-called merger clause) in the written text.

19. Which includes also moral damage, consisting in 'pain and suffering and impairment of the quality of life' (Art. III-3:701).

It may appear strange that in a model Civil Code intended to govern the three categories of contracts which one can classify, according to the position of the persons, of the contracting parties (C2C, B2B, B2C) to which should be added a fourth category of contracts between strong professionals and weak professionals (B2b), reference should be made to the merger clause. This is a typical clause contained in international commercial contracts and in that economic context has its perspicuous purpose. It wants to reassure the parties in relation to the autonomy and sufficiency of a contract that they have negotiated and concluded, to avoid there remaining doubts both on the documents exchanged between them (or the conduct maintained by them) in the course of the formation of the agreement. It is also intended to exclude any authority whatsoever (judicial or arbitral) which may be vested with the power of adjudicating upon the economic operation as agreed between them from altering its meaning or the equilibrium by modifying the contents. The merger clause implies in short that the 'desire' of the parties corresponds, by that agreement, to that which the contract reflects, and only to that may one refer to evaluate its performance. It is as if the contract were a 'closed box' which the judge or the arbitrator may open, without any power to alter its content (Article II-4:104). It is strange also that this can be allowed in a model code such as this, referring to a merger clause which has not been negotiated, even with the qualification of mere presumption of its effect. It is all the same true that the text provides other qualifications: for example, that the declarations of the parties effected prior to conclusion of the contract may be used in order to interpret the contract, a rule which must be coordinated with the provisions concerning the content of the contract and the declarations made in the course of negotiations (Article II-9:102). It is also true that there is a presumption of priority of the declarations made over the merger clause, if there has been reliance by the party subjected to it on the importancc of these declarations (Article II-4:104).

The fact remains that the Draft desires to give importance to this technique of making the contract, and thus to this strong expression of the will of the parties.

6. DEFAULT AND MANDATORY RULES

Italian scholars have discussed with notable authority the distinction between non-excludable rules, imperative rules, excludable rules, and default rules.

There are no doubts on the appropriateness that in a code – however it may be conceived – default rules should be contemplated: these compose in a systematic manner a framework of complete directives to confront the majority of circumstances which may arise in the course of execution of the contract, and may also be included in the contract text, if the parties assume a common determination in this direction.

Not all non-excludable rules may be described as mandatory rules. There are rules which the parties cannot exclude which do not give rise to the penalty of nullity, which is the ordinary consequence of a violation of a mandatory rule. Also from this point of view, however, Italian legal opinion is not uniform. Not all imperative rules provoke per se the nullity of the contract; not those placed for the protection of just one of the parties, as occurs for the essential rules which protect the consumer; it is not the case for those that the legislature proclaims without specifically connecting them with the penalty, since in such case there is the availability of other remedies, such as compensation for damages, rather than invalidating the contract; nor for those cases in which – by a broad interpretation – there may arise the so-called virtual nullity rule.

It is thus appropriate that the mandatory rules should be explained, so as not to give rise to uncertainty in interpretation. This understanding has not been followed in the Draft effect.

The Convention of Rome, now the Regulation on the law applicable to contractual obligations, distinguishes between three categories of mandatory norms: ordinary mandatory norms, mandatory rules of immediate application, and rules of public policy. The last two categories cannot be waived.

Learned authors have listed the categories of imperative rules contained in the international conventions, in the PICC, in the national systems, in the PECL, and in the PEL, which more or less correspond to those contained in the Draft. It is still true that of all these categories of rules in the Draft, there is only reference to *illegality* and the consequences of their *infringement*, but as many commentators have observed, the PECL, from this point of view, are better expressed, more complete, and more precise.

It is clear that – these rules being the hub of the discipline of the contract and, in a certain sense, the expression of the characters of the European model of contract – the situation cannot appear satisfying to those who think of contract not only as a formal clothing of a 'private' economic operation, and not even as a *transaction* which must be justified, but also as the collocation of private interests, promoted by the State or by other public authorities, which may not take a position in conflict with fundamental principles, with the values of the person, and the values expressed by public policy and solidarity.

It is then the limit of *solidarity* – between the parties on one side and the parties within the community on the other side – which does not emerge with that evidence which was already expressed (albeit weakly) in the PECL, and which the tenor of the European Charter of fundamental rights and the new text of the Treaty of Union approved in Lisbon would claim.

The same Union has made it clear that the Treaty of Lisbon has repeated the model of a 'Europe of rights and values, of freedom, solidarity and safety, which provides new mechanisms of solidarity and guarantees a better protection for European citizens', a model which 'sets forth and reinforces the values and objectives on which the Union is based' since they serve 'as a point of reference for European citizens and demonstrate that which Europe may offer to its partners in the rest of the world'. The Treaty of Lisbon maintains existing rights and introduced new ones. In particular, it guarantees the freedoms and principles approved by the Charter of fundamental rights, rendering them legally binding.

The Treaty contemplates civil, political, economic, and social rights. Since the Draft makes reference to these rights, the contract can only be supplemented in its content with these values, and any clause whatsoever provided in it which is in conflict with the same must be considered null.

7. RETHINKING CONTRACTUAL FREEDOM?

In the context of the Draft, the 'freedom of contract' and 'party autonomy' no longer have the old meaning which is centred around the boundaries between which the parties had desired and that which the authority could impose upon them (from the contract to a contractual relationship, through the course of supplementation and control by the authorities) or else between internal will, manifested will and representation (from the contract understood in its subjective sense to the contract understood in an objective sense). 'Freedom of contract' and 'party autonomy' have acquired a new meaning, that the Draft, the PECL and the 'code' prepared by the Study Group attempt to put in evidence with words and concepts other than those used traditionally, and which rely upon the interpreter to express with all the potentiality offered by the interpretation and the coordination of the sources outside the contract: good-faith (also as a supplement), cooperation, solidarity and the safeguard of fundamental rights.

A common factor emerges, however: the contract is understood as the expression of party autonomy, which may be decided from outside. It is thus free but with limits set by fundamental principles, by general clauses, and by mandatory norms. In contrast with the Continental experiences and, in particular those in Germany and Italy, autonomy is recognized in so far as it abides by the system and is, so to say, born with shackles.

The model contract constructed by the Draft diverges from the model expressed by the principles drafted by UNIDROIT, since these are oriented towards the international market, nor is it similar to those outlined in the new Lex Mercatoria, for similar reasons, and it does not represent even the instrument which is substituted for law, as now many authors who have identified in the contract the hub of the discipline of private relations in the phase of market globalization maintain. Nor is it even the fall-out of the *acquis communautaire*, nor the reflection of a restatement of principles expressed by the ECJ or by the national experiences understood as a whole. However, instead of being considered as a sort of 'deviation' from the received mandate, this choice is a result imposed by the path which has been rationally straighter than the researchers have been able to do previously.

There has been a different argument, an argument which, as one has been able to observe in progress, concerns the individual choices made by the draftsmen.

One has the impression, besides the important innovations already noted, that for certain national models, the Draft may be more innovative and may respond better to the 'social' situations, while for others it may be, so to say, more backwards in relation to the results reached by the internal order, consisting of (in codified countries) the written rules of the legislature, the constitutional principles, the rules set by courts, and interpretative and professional practices. And again it is possible that the Draft may be more sensitive to freedom of contract understood in a formal manner than that understood in a substantive sense.

In this sense, the model of the Draft appears, to the eyes of an Italian jurist, more articulated compared to the French and English development, but less so compared to the German and Italian models.

7.1. The Formulae

In the English experience, the two formulae, at least understood in their ordinary meaning, are not the same: 'freedom of contract' is wider, and 'private autonomy' refers only to the freedom of the parties to conclude the contract and to choose their contracting party (the so-called 'parties' autonomy).

On the contrary, French thinking considers freedom of contract as a sub-species of party autonomy, but scholars and courts prefer to refer to the first rather than to the second. In the Italian experience, the two terms have been used interchangeably, even though autonomy is an originally ethical and juridical category, while freedom of contract has more of a political and social flavour. In German thinking, party autonomy is the general category which covers the acts of private persons, while freedom of contract, which derives its origin from that, is divided into all its sub-species.

7.2. The Environments

English thinking is still marked by the irrelevance of the conduct of the parties in the course of negotiation, by the obsessive fear of 'good faith' (while a similar sentiment is not found in relation to 'fairness' or 'fair dealing'), by the literal nature of interpretation of a contract and by the substantial declining of judicial control other than in exceptional cases. Instead, the Italian and German experience are similar in considering the contract as an expression of the will (or the declaration) but also of the strong internal control exercised by the judge. In the German experience, the courts tend to consider freedom of contract as guaranteed by the Constitution, but only within the limits in which it does not violate the values of the person. Contractual freedom in France is particularly valued by scholars and courts in public law, and the applications of the rules of the Civil Code indicate that its categorization is similar to that found in Italian experience, also as far as negotiations are concerned.

7.3. Contractual Justice

If exception may be made for undue influence, it is rare to find mechanisms in English and French law for the control of the equivalence of respective performance, except for the application of *consideration/cause, frustration/imprévision*, while in Italy and Germany *good faith, equity, and presupposition* help to restore a balance to the economic paradigm of the operation of contract; certainly, one is dealing with a 'commutative' justice, which becomes 'corrective', but is not yet 'distributive'. Distributive justice cannot be found in the rules of contract in general, but in the legislation in favour of consumers, savers, and so forth, where the legislature has wanted to retain a power of discretion over the content of the contract or to otherwise fix rules on the determination of the price, or to introduce mechanisms for withdrawal, or automatic renewal, or minimum duration off a contract, and so forth.

There are also authors who are worried in particular about the social aspects of the rules of the contract. They are concerned about the legitimization of the disadvantages which one party may impose upon the other, about the persistent notion of contractual freedom as a reflection of the market, or about the role which general clauses could have in order to introduce a contractual justice which is more coherent and effective.

The debate is in course and certainly will not be stopped by the preparation of the Draft, which, on the contrary, stimulates a further refining of terminology, of principles, and of models as a result of all the groups involved in this daunting adventure.

8. FREEDOM OF CONTRACT IN A FORMAL SENSE AND IN A SUBSTANTIVE SENSE: AN INDIVIDUALISTIC CONCEPTION AND A COLLECTIVE CONCEPTION OF CONTRACT – AN AMBIGUOUS OR COMPROMISING POSITION OF THE DRAFT?

Freedom of contract, born under the star of formalism, could not be neglected by the Draft, still less for reasons of textual consistency, even if the research effected precisely to collaborate with the Community programmes on the codification of European law have demonstrated that not all Continental codes have expressed this principle. Its express recognition then, in the text under examination, has more a symbolic and systematic nature than a real, substantive, and efficient one: it is a value implicitly understood in all codifications, and also where codes do not exist, one may find it from case law and practice; what instead emerges are its *limitations.*

It is interesting to note, reading the more recent contributions on the subject, that there is now a general widespread conception of a contract as a 'clean slate', on which the parties inscribe the rules established by agreement; it is like an island. From the outside, the legislature (whichever that may be) rushes in to outline the borders. This conception is incorrect: already by entering a binding obligation, the parties are subjecting themselves to all provisions which are connected to the contractual circumstances created.

Standardization of contracts has been considered, in the different experiences, as one of the more massive and profound manifestations of the limits to the freedom of the parties. In reality, if this can be true for contracts in which there is asymmetry (of information, decision-making or operative) between the contracting parties – a situation which one may find both in B2C-contracts and in B2b-contracts – it is not necessarily the case that the clauses and standard models may not be well received in international commerce, and in relations between professionals. This is because they simplify individual relations, they allow anticipated management of any results of disputes, and they may be re-used over and over again with all the parties, allowing them to reach a rapid comparative evaluation of the advantages and disadvantages both in a horizontal and vertical sense.

The fact that the investigations conducted on the subject have demonstrated how professionals appreciate not only the standard models and clauses, but also uniformity of terms, principles, and rules of European contractual law goes to signify that the road undertaken by the Community bodies, which aims at a simplification of rules, is really not just proclaimed, but it is heralded as efficient.

It is freedom in the substantive sense, which poses problems of an ideological, dogmatic, systematic, and operational nature. But this is the challenge of European contractual law, of the model which the EU must design in order to distinguish itself from alternative models, while, however, maintaining the connotation of competitiveness as vital. From this point of view, the idea of a contract, which is not only an expression of commutative justice (so to speak natural in any exchange) and corrective justice (so to speak natural to a developed economy) but also of distributive justice, may be the vehicle to attain the definition of the model and its approval.

The Draft has appeared to many as rather less sensitive to social justice than that which was already the case with the other projects which had preceded it.[20] Does it suffice to insist on the fundamental principles (which however reflect a traditional concept of contract), on good faith and fair dealing (which however are also understood broadly in somewhat different manners in the national cultures) and on the fundamental rights of the person? The compromising choice of the Draft is not reassuring, if one has to rely on the interpreter alone to exalt the innovative contents of the 'European' conception of a contract.

It is for this reason that the works must be considered to be still in course.

9. DRAFTING OF THE INDIVIDUAL CONTRACT IN THE INTEREST OF A CLIENT AND THE CHOICES OF THE DRAFT IN RELATION TO FREEDOM OF CONTRACT

Up to now, the debate has concerned in a general perspective the merits and defects of the Draft from the point of view of a lawyer.

Some arguments which have been the subject of sections or chapters of the Draft and which constitute the results of research of various centres which have

20. *See* Study Group on Social Justice in European Private Law, 'Social Justice in European Contract Law: A Manifesto', *European Law Journal* 10 (2004): 653 et seq.

participated in drafting, have been submitted, in the course of various seminars, to the stakeholders, amongst whom lawyers are obviously included.

The impact with the texts presented, particularly amongst those who do not have familiarity with European private law, who had not been aware of the research in course, who did not have any scientific curiosity generally and comparative in particular, has been very disconcerting; these first reactions have been such as to congeal opinions with which the students of the subject are familiar, since they correspond to the first phase of the edification of European law. First they asked themselves why they should approve or in any way participate in such a programme, then they asked whether the EU should have a responsibility in the matter or not, and lastly they queried whether uniformity as thus proposed would not end up sacrificing the traditions, values, and cultural and conceptual context expressed by the national legal systems precisely in the subjects which constitute the pillars of private law (and more generally for the entire legal system): that is, obligations, contract, liability, and in reflection property.

All these objections, which stem also from ancient fears towards that which is new or that which is unknown, have been overcome by the intense, deep, and refined scientific debates, by research done in practice, such as the investigation carried out at Oxford on the reactions of entrepreneurial groups to uniformity of European contractual law. It is not appropriate to indulge for too long these interrogations which risk impeding the progress of the Draft.

More serious and important, however, is another question which professionals, in particular lawyers, have asked. Would the use of the Draft as a rule of contract – given that one day the Regulation on the applicable choice for contractual obligations (Rome 1) may allow the parties to choose the Draft (or its definitive version) – or its use already, if some national system were to allow such an option, be convenient for the lawyers?

The evaluation of the advantages (or disadvantages) may be made from three different viewpoints: the interest of the category itself, the interest of the client, and the interest of the lawyer.

The application of a framework of rules created *ex novo* (but derived from different experiences and drafted taking account the need for a modern society), rather than from the domestic law or the law chosen by the parties, may engender problems for the lawyers who are not familiar with any system other than their own. The choice of a law different from the domestic law and unknown to the lawyer is similar to the choice of the rules of the Draft; it presents, however, one other advantage which should not be underestimated: the fact that a national law is not presented so to speak 'laid bare' like the Draft, in that a national law is accompanied by commentaries, of experimentation of contractual practices and thus may engender greater trust, even if it is foreign to the lawyer familiar only with his or her own law, since it allows that lawyer to become better informed and equipped. Conversely, a 'naked' text offers the advantage of not having precedents and thus being able to be read afresh which could be profitable for the lawyer. Regarding Italian lawyers, having to compete with foreign lawyers on the basis of a new text for everybody constitutes an undoubted advantage, it being very rare, as is well known, that the parties of a different nationality opt for Italian law, for reasons primarily of ignorance of the language, of the law, and of its application by Italian courts. At other times, the choice is discouraged by the negative image which is given by the system of administration of justice in Italy, but this is a quite different argument which has some foundation even if abroad it is peppered with prejudices.

The interest of the client must in any case – also for ethical reasons – overcome the choice of the applicable law by the lawyer. In this perspective, the argument becomes more complex because it implies that the lawyer is placing himself in the shoes of the client, who, as a contracting party, may be in good or bad faith, to make the contract because he has not found a better opportunity but to be ready to escape from the obligation if it should be convenient, and may be fortunate or unfortunate in the course of performance of the contract, and so forth. I pause for a moment on the execution and performance of the contract, even if most of the problems relating to the choice of law arise primarily in the phase of negotiations.

The execution of a contract negotiated individually may occur between parties who have equal contracting power or between parties who find themselves in an asymmetric position, one stronger, the other weaker.

Also in this case, the argument must be restricted, because the lawyer who defends the weaker party belonging to the category of consumers is already favoured by the rules which the Draft provides for the benefit of consumers. Following the policy proposed by the Community bodies, indeed, the law for consumers, wherever this is possible, is integrated into civil and commercial law, and thus the Draft does not envisage a chapter expressly for the rules intended to discipline relations between professionals and consumers. Rather, in the Draft there is a place for the revision of the *acquis communautaire*, which brings up to date, coordinates, and makes the multiple rules which have crowded into this sector systematic. Almost two pages of the index of the Draft are dedicated to the list of rules which mention consumers with the intent of protecting their rights and interests.

The consumer's lawyer should not then be contrary to the choice of the Draft, unless the domestic or another national law which the consumer manages to impose on the counterpart does not give greater guarantees. This implies obviously that the lawyer knows the rules of implementation of the Directives in the various Member States, the case law of the ECJ and the interpretation of those rules by national judges. This is an encyclopaedic task, which nevertheless may become less onerous if the lawyer is specialized in a particular sector and thus has succeeded in becoming notably competent at the level of Community and comparative law.

The 'weakness' of the party, then, or at least in this context, does not depend on status, but rather it depends on other factors, including the financial.

Concerning the professional in a weaker position, more particularly, the business which finds itself in a situation of economic weakness in relation to the other party, the Draft offers chances which not all national legal systems offer: I refer above all to the onerous clauses (Article II-9:406) and to the 'undue exploitation' (Article II-7:207) and to the information duties (Article II-3:101 et seq.), either in the pre-contractual phase, or in the phase of execution of a contract, which relate, at least to a large extent, to both the parties, whatever status they may have.

Yet a party may be weak also for other reasons: for example, because assisted by an incompetent lawyer, or else because it finds itself in a situation in which, for the purpose of starting further relationships or preserving existing ones with the other side, the party does not intend to hold out much against the requests of the other or to impose necessarily its own reasons. With or without the Draft, it appears to me that the situation does not change much in these cases.

And does the lawyer who represents a 'strong' party have advantages in the choice of the Draft? The obligation to respect fair dealing and good faith, as well as the rules which are qualified as mandatory, would, in any case, be imposed on that party by the national laws. If at all, there could be another argument: to give effect to and impose a non Community law, where the Community regulations and national rules of the parties may impose limits to freedom of contract not envisaged elsewhere. But in this case, the problem of the applicability of the Rome I Regulation remains open, as well as the enforceability in the countries to which the parties belong of the provisions of foreign judges or international arbitrators.

The provision on a merger clause could provide some opportunities which are not envisaged by the national law. The same can be said for the lack of provision of mechanisms which allow escape from the binding obligation in the case of the occurrence of certain circumstances stipulated by the parties (hardship clause); and this always supposing that, examined in the light of the intervening circumstances, they could have placed that party in a position of advantage.

The frequent reference to the fundamental principles could increase the area of uncertainty which any interpretation of contract carries with it, an uncertainty which grows and which increases the basic uncertainty, that is, the normal risk which is typical for any transaction. Many other hypotheses could be made and taken into consideration, and this again could be enriched by a discussion of individual cases in order to verify how they would be resolved by application of the rules of the Draft.

As an Italian lawyer, of course I would be favourable to the application of the Italian Civil Code in any situation in which I should find myself in defense of the parties represented by me, but, as noted elsewhere, one needs a more elastic mentality. One's own law is not always the best law; the evaluation depends on so many circumstances which professional practice brings to our attention.

Chapter 6

The CFR and Social Justice

Martijn Hesselink

1. INTRODUCTION

This paper aims to evaluate the DCFR in terms of social justice.[1] It is a normative paper written by someone who was actively involved in the drafting of the DCFR as a member of the Study Group on a European Civil Code, and who was also part of a group of scholars who expressed their social justice concerns with regard to the European Commission's Action Plan (the Social Justice Group).[2]

1.1. CFR in a Broad Sense

At this stage, it is unclear exactly what role the final CFR will play in European contract law.

Its original aim, as envisaged by the European Commission in its Action Plan on European contract law, was for it to be the main tool in making European

1. Von Bar et al. (eds), *Principles, Definitions and Model Rules of European Private Law*, Draft Common Frame of Reference (DCFR), Interim Outline Edition (Munich: Sellier, 2008).
2. I have been a member of the SGECC since it was founded and was responsible, in particular, for the drafting of the PEL on Commercial Agency, Franchise and Distribution Contracts on which Book IV E DCFR is based, and of the Study Group on Social Justice in European Private Law that published its manifesto in 2004: 'Social Justice in European Contract Law: A Manifesto', *European Law Journal* 16 (2004): 653-674 (*see* further below).

Alessandro Somma, *The Politics of the Draft Common Frame of Reference*, pp. 95-113.

contract law more coherent.[3] In particular, the CFR was meant to play a key role in the revision of the existing Community contract law and in enacting new EU legislation in the area of contract law. Moreover, it could provide the basis for an optional European code of contract law. The process of revising the *acquis* is already underway. It is limited, for now, to eight directives concerning consumer protection. A Green Paper was published two years ago and a framework directive was proposed last year.[4] What new *acquis* we can expect in the future is, of course, uncertain. For the moment, political attention in the area of consumer protection seems to have shifted from substantive rules to civil procedure (especially collective action). The idea of an optional code of contracts also seems to be lower on the political agenda.[5] However, it may well be that the project is simply on hold until the content of the final CFR, on which any optional code will have to be based, is known. This would make sense since it is impossible to discuss the idea properly in the abstract.[6] The same holds true for a possible inter-institutional agreement (IIA) concerning the CFR as is envisaged by the European Commission:[7] none of the institutions will be willing to commit to such an agreement, whatever its terms,[8] without knowing the content of the CFR.

---

3. *See* A more Coherent European Contract Law, an Action Plan, Brussels, 12.2.2003, COM (2003) 68. *See also* European Contract Law and the revision of the acquis: the way forward, 11.10.2004, COM (2004) 651.
4. *See* Green Paper on the Review of the Consumer Acquis, Brussels, 8.2.2007, COM (2007) 744; Proposal for a Directive of the European Parliament and of the Council on Consumer Rights, 28.11.2008, COM (2008) 614.
5. *See* First Annual Progress Report on The Common Frame of Reference, 23.9.2005, COM (2005) 456; Second Progress Report on The Common Frame of Reference, 25.7.2007, COM (2007) 447.
6. In itself, the idea is appealing, both in b2b and in b2c-contracts. As to the former, the CISG is quite a success especially as a default system for contracts between unsophisticated parties who cannot afford the expert advice that is needed for making an informed choice of law, but it contains several gaps and is anyhow limited to sales contracts. As to the latter, at least in theory the 'blue-button idea' (cf. H. Schulte-Nölke, 'EC Law on the Formation of Contract – From the Common Frame of Reference to the "Blue Button" ', *European Review of Contract Law* 3 (2007): 332-349), where consumers (e.g., on the Internet) would be given the choice between the law of the place of business of the seller and European law (by clicking on a button representing the European flag), could create a win-win situation where businesses could save so much in terms of transaction costs that they could accept a somewhat higher level of consumer protection than they would otherwise be prepared to accept, and still be better off. However, one should not be naive about the bargaining process. Cf. B. Lurger, 'The Common Frame of Reference/Optional Code and the various understandings of social justice in Europe', in *Private Law and the Many Cultures of Europe*, eds T. Wilhelmsson, E. Paunio & A. Pohjolainen (Alphen a/d Rijn: Kluwer Law International, 2007), 177-199.
7. The idea was launched by Commissioner Kyprianou in his opening address at the conference on 'European contract law: better lawmaking to the common frame of reference' (first European Discussion Forum), London, 26.9.2005. Cf. also Action Plan, 80 and The Way Forward, 6. On the constitutional dimensions of such a IIA, *see* M. W. Hesselink, J. W. Rutgers & T. Q. de Booys, *The Legal Basis for an Optional Instrument on European Contract Law*; Short study for the European Parliament on the different options for a future instrument on a CFR in EU contract law, in particular the legal form and the legal basis for any future optional instrument, PE 393.280, <http://ssrn.com/abstract=1091119>, February 2008.
8. The most likely content of such an IIA *see*ms to be that the Commission, the Parliament and the Council commit themselves to taking the CFR into account when preparing and enacting legislation within the scope of the CFR.

In addition to its formal purposes, the CFR is likely to play additional roles as well. Because of its task as an independent interpreter and developer of European Community law, it is unthinkable that the ECJ or, for that matter, any national court would take part in any IIA concerning the CFR. However, this does not mean that the ECJ and national courts will not be influenced by it. On the contrary, if the CFR is indeed going to inspire the revision of the *acquis* and the drafting of new *acquis* (both specifically as a resource for drafting consumer protection rules and more generally as a background of general private law rules against which the specific consumer law rules are drafted), then it will become virtually inevitable for a court that tries to find the proper interpretation of a certain part of the *acquis*, and to further develop it in a coherent way, to consider the CFR.[9] The same holds true for legal scholars and for legal education. In other words, it seems likely that the CFR will become a CFR, in a much broader sense, for all actors involved in the developing multi-level system of European private law. Indeed, the CFR is likely to become the cornerstone of a European legal method of private law.[10] Finally, the CFR is even likely to affect private parties (individual citizens and businesses) as well. After all, it will only be rational for them to anticipate the possible roles that the CFR will play in the legislation and adjudication that may affect them. Therefore, whatever the limits to its formal role will be, in substantive terms the CFR is likely to have a certain 'horizontal effect'.

Therefore, in this paper I will take the notion of a CFR in this very broad sense with a view to this very broad possible range of applications. In practical terms this is very similar to regarding the DCFR as a model European Civil Code.[11] Indeed, apart from the principles and definitions contained in the introduction and the annex, the Draft mainly contains 'model rules', which are organized in exactly the same systematic way as a civil code.[12]

---

9. On this binding effect, not formally but substantively, of the CFR *see* further M. W. Hesselink, 'The Ideal of Codification and the Dynamics of Europeanisation: The Dutch Experience', *European Law Journal* 12 (2006): 279-305.
10. *See* M. W. Hesselink, 'A European Legal Method? On European Private Law and Scientific Method', *European Law Journal (forthcoming)*.
11. In the same sense, after the publication of the Action Plan, E. H. Hondius, 'Towards a European Civil Code', in *Towards a European Civil Code*, eds A. S. Hartkamp et al. (The Hague, London, New York: Kluwer Law International, 2004), 13; H. Collins, 'The "Common Frame of Reference" for EC Contract Law: A Common Lawyer's Perspective', in *L'armonizzazione del diritto privato europeo*, eds M. Meli & M. R. Maugeri (Milan: Giuffrè, 2004), 107-124. Cf. House of Lords (European Union Committee), European Contract Law – the way forward? (HL Paper 95) (London: The Stationery Office Limited, 2005), 115, that expressed the concern that the CFR might turn out to be something of a Trojan Horse.
12. The difference, of course, is that the CFR will probably never be enacted in its totality and completely replace national private laws. Only in this more limited sense is the European Commission correct when it underlines that it is not preparing a European Civil Code (*see* The Way Forward, 8). *See also* the Dutch Minister of Justice (Tweede Kamer, vergaderjaar 2007-2008, 23 490, n. 482) answering questions in Parliament after a cover story entitled 'A European Civil Code through the backdoor' in the newspaper NRC Handelsblad (9.10.2007).

1.2. Social Justice and Contract Law

As said, this paper aims to evaluate the DCFR in terms of social justice. One could argue that this is unfair because social justice was not one of the aims or parameters that the Commission had in mind when it announced its plan to adopt a CFR and when it entrusted a joint network of legal academics with the task of providing the first draft. Indeed, the Action Plan focuses exclusively on the coherence of the *acquis communautaire* and on the functioning of the Internal Market; social justice is not even mentioned in the Plan. However, that argument is not convincing. In view of its intended use, and of the other uses that it is likely to have (*see* above), a CFR simply must be in accordance with the conceptions of social justice prevailing in Europe. A socially unjust CFR could not properly serve any of its intended specific purposes, let alone be a CFR for the conduct of European citizens and businesses. Ideally, the model rules in the DCFR should represent the European model for just conduct between private parties, a more detailed elaboration of the concept of a social market economy that is enshrined in the Lisbon Treaty. Indeed, in a resolution in 2005 the European Parliament 'highlights the importance of taking into account the European social model when harmonising contract law'.[13] Therefore, the CFR has to pass the social justice test. Fortunately, unlike the Commission, the drafters of the DCFR were aware of this: the introduction to the DCFR explicitly addresses the issue of social justice.[14]

The next question is whether such a test is actually feasible. How can one possibly measure the degree of social justice contained in the DCFR? Admittedly, there is no generally accepted procedure for objectively measuring the justice of a legal rule (the philosopher's stone). Not only are there many different well-established but mutually incompatible theories of social justice (utilitarian, deontological, libertarian, positivist, realist, and deconstructivist, to name but a few), but these general theories and the specific rules of private law also largely operate on different levels of generality. None of the leading theories of social justice yield any remotely complete answer to the questions concerning private law that are on the table in Europe today. In particular, they do not provide a yardstick for objectively measuring the amount of social justice contained in the DCFR. This also applies to the economic analysis of law which, as is well known, is based on controversial normative assumptions (the utilitarian idea that the law should mainly, or even only, aim at welfare maximization) and needs empirical data (the 'preferences' of individuals and their relative importance) that are simply not available (and therefore are very often substituted with the normatively biased empirical assumption that most of the time individuals are actually rationally pursuing the increase of their own wealth).

However, this does not mean that nothing meaningful can be said about the CFR from the perspective of social justice. On the contrary, articulated normative

13. European Parliament resolution on European contract law and the revision of the acquis: the way forward (2005/2022(INI)), no. 8.
14. 'Introduction', DCFR, 16.

evaluations of the DCFR are very much needed at this stage. And such normative analyses can certainly benefit from insights from social and political philosophy. The fact that social justice analysis of private law is not an exact science does not make it arbitrary or turn it into mere opinion in the strong sense that it differs categorically from scientific knowledge.[15]

1.3. Private Law and Democracy

Jan Smits recently advocated that European private law should become a spontaneous order. In response to the Manifesto on social justice in European contract law,[16] he wrote:[17] 'what constitutes the best rules for Europe cannot, in my view, be decided by an almighty legislator that has the power to change the existing distribution of power and riches – if this is what one wants to do at all. The present legal system is the result of a long process of trial and error through which a partly spontaneous order has come into being. . . . To me, law is not primarily the result of conscious choice, but of spontaneous development. In this respect, I am influenced by the work of Nobel Prize winner Friedrich Hayek.' Frankly, I find this Jungle Book version of European private law unappealing.[18] Hayek was an extreme libertarian who completely rejected the notion of social justice and who insistently warned that any interference with the free market (which he called the 'spontaneous order') based on any notion of social justice (including utilitarianism!) would inevitably lead to a totalitarian State where individual freedom would be completely abolished.[19] If this were true, we would certainly have to think twice whether in Europe we want to have a social market economy (*see* Article 3 Lisbon Treaty) and a social private law. However, Hayek never produced any evidence that could make this apocalyptic scenario even remotely plausible. Indeed, his essentially empirical claim is demonstrably false.

The Welfare States as they developed in Western Europe in the second half of the twentieth Century had many defects and, after abandoning their excessive faith in central planning in the 1970s, most governments have gradually revised the balance that they had struck between individual freedom and social solidarity. But no country can seriously be said to have come even close to the total abolition of

15. *See* Hesselink (n. 10 above).
16. *See* n. 2 above and *see* n. 28 below.
17. J. M. Smits, 'European Private Law: a Plea for a Spontaneous Legal Order', in *European Integration and Law*, eds D. M. Curtin, J. M. Smits, A. Klip & J. McCahery (Antwerp and Oxford: Intersentia, 2006), 85.
18. The metaphor is imprecise because in Kipling's and Walt Disney's Jungle Book it is not the fittest (Shere Khan) but the most vulnerable (Mowgli) that prevails (as a result of the conception of social justice shared by most of the animals, i.e., that weaker parties must be protected).
19. Hayek presents an elaborate theory of law in F.A. Hayek, *Law, Legislation and Liberty; A new statement of the liberal principles of justice and political economy* (London and New York: Routledge, 2003). However, all the basic ideas are already present in F.A. Hayek, *The Road to Serfdom* (London and New York: Routledge Classics, 2005).

individual freedom in a way similar to that of the totalitarian regimes of Nazism and communism. On the other hand, Hayek's analysis fails to take into account the reality that in functioning Welfare States individuals actually enjoy greater freedom (in the substantive sense of capabilities to live the lives they want to live) than in many crudely capitalist countries.[20] Indeed, there is no evidence of any positive link between unrestricted capitalism and personal freedom.[21] As Ole Lando puts it, 'Experience seems to show that societies, which build on a market economy combined with solidarity, fairness and loyalty, fare better than those where the law of the jungle governs.'[22] The all or nothing – in other words: totalitarian – character of Hayek's theory (he explicitly rejected any third way because it would lead straight to socialism and from there to totalitarianism)[23] and its Cold War rhetoric make it largely irrelevant to most contemporary debates, including the one on the future of European private law, for the simple reason that all existing systems are mixed economies. And the key question that we have to answer is: what is the right mix? For private law this means: how much freedom of contract? What to do with unbalanced contracts? How much strict liability in tort? What limits to property rights and to the rights of shareholders in companies? On these questions, and on the more general question of what role distributive and other social justice elements could play in contract law, Hayek has nothing to say. Richard Posner (hardly a socialist himself!) remarks:[24] 'a mixed system is what we and our peer nations have; what help Hayek's thought offers to someone trying to evaluate such a system is unclear.'

Although the idea of a spontaneous order in the sense of Hayek is out of touch with both reality and morality, the opposite idea where the legislator would start from scratch and design a private law that corresponds perfectly to its own idea of social justice, without having any regard to existing experience, is equally

---

20. *See* e.g., A. Sen, *Development as Freedom* (Oxford: Oxford University Press, 1999); M. C. Nussbaum, *Sex and Social Justice* (Oxford: Oxford University Press, 1999).
21. As Kymlycka puts it, referring to Hayek, 'this defence of market freedom must also be a contingent one, for history does not reveal any invariable link between capitalism and civil liberties. Countries with essentially unrestricted capitalism have sometimes had poor human rights records (e.g., military dictatorships in capitalist Chile or Argentina; McCarthyism in the United States), while countries with a extensive welfare state have sometimes had excellent records in defending civil and political rights (e.g., Sweden).' (W. Kymlicka, *Contemporary Political Philosophy: An Introduction* (Oxford: OUP, 2001), 102. *See also* N. Klein, *Shock Therapy; The Rise of Disaster Capitalism* (New York: Metropolitan Books, 2007), who argues that market fundamentalism of the Chicago School brand (Milton Friedman was inspired by Hayek) cannot be introduced except in an authoritarian and violent way. She reports (on 84) that Hayek travelled to Pinochet's Chile several times to admire the free market laboratory, and (on 131) that he wrote a letter to Margaret Thatcher to urge her to use Pinochet's model for transforming Britain's Keynesian economy.
22. O. Lando, 'The structure and the legal values of the Common Frame of Reference (CFR)', *European Review of Contract Law* 3 (2007): 245-256.
23. F. A. Hayek, *Law, Legislation and Liberty*, vol. III (London and Henley: Routledge & Kegan Paul), 151.
24. R. A. Posner, 'Hayek, law, and cognition', *New York University Journal of Law & Liberty* (2005): 147.

unrealistic: this would be so unwise that it is unthinkable that any legislator would even consider making such a fresh start on a clean slate. That makes the debate on whether the democratically elected legislator has a right to design private law as it pleases largely sterile.

Indeed, with regard to the CFR, the European Commission has essentially asked for a codification of best solutions (without, frankly, instructing the drafters what standard should be adopted when determining the quality of the solutions).[25] And the drafters have produced a DCFR that was inspired mainly by the national traditions of the different Members States, the developing international tradition in the area of contract law (CISG, Unidroit Principles, PECL) and the admittedly fairly recent Community tradition (*acquis communautaire*).[26] On the detailed level of specific rules, the CFR certainly contains a number of innovations. However, on the whole it is best characterized as an attempt to codify existing law rather than as an attempt to design an entirely new private law from scratch. If anything, what is so far missing is rather the democratic input. Although in this respect the CFR process is perfectly in line with the tradition and the current practice in many Member States, where private law legislation is usually prepared by academic experts, an attempt at involving the European and Member State parliaments in a much earlier stage of the drafting could and should have been made.[27] It is to be hoped that Members of the European Parliament (MEPs) and Members of Parliament (MPs) will not be intimidated by the erroneous impression of the CFR as a delicately balanced system that will collapse like a house of cards as soon as one dares to touch a single rule contained therein.

1.4. Neo-Liberal or Social-Democratic?

When it launched the CFR process, the European Commission used a lot of neo-liberal rhetoric. This worried a group of European legal scholars so much that they published a Manifesto on social justice in European contract law in which they underlined that private law in Europe, both on the Member State and the Community level, is a mix between autonomy and solidarity, between liberalism and socialism, and that it should continue to be so, also in the CFR.[28] The group pointed out that this question is all the more important since, as result of privatization, European citizens depend, for many essential things in their lives, on private contracts. Now that a first Draft has been published, a key question is whether the DCFR is a liberal or a socialist system or something in between.

25. Action Plan, 62.
26. 'Introduction', DCFR, 21.
27. This could have been done e.g., by submitting the politically most important issues, in the form of policy questions, to the European and national parliaments before the drafting started. For a tentative list of fifty such questions, *see* M. W. Hesselink, 'The Politics of a European Civil Code', *European Law Journal* 10 (2004): 675-697.
28. Study Group on Social Justice in European Private Law (n. 2 above), 653-674.

Private law rules can be analyzed in terms of private autonomy and social solidarity. For every question of private law, it is possible to imagine rule alternatives which can be placed on a scale from strong autonomy (or individualism) to strong solidarity (or altruism).[29] These results can be aggregated and in this sense a system of private law can be said to be more or less autonomy-oriented. Translated into ideological terms, a system such as the DCFR can thus be said to be more or less liberal, more or less socialist. By the same token, private law systems in different but sufficiently similar countries also can be compared in political terms.[30] Obviously, neither the political analysis nor the political comparison of private law is an exact science.[31]

When compared to the PECL, the DCFR is more liberal.[32] Where the corresponding parts of the DCFR deviate in substance from the PECL, it is almost always in the direction of more party autonomy. Some striking examples include the control of unfair terms and the role of good faith. Another crucial difference between the PECL and the DCFR, which gives it a distinctly liberal outlook (sometimes form is substance), is that the latter introduces the notion of a juridical act and gives it a prominent place in Book II. It is a well-known fact that not only is this abstract concept closely related to the Germanic professorial legal culture,[33] but it is also the flagship of nineteenth Century laissez-faire liberalism: it

---

29. *See* D. Kennedy, 'The Political Stakes in "Merely Technical" Issues of Contract Law', *European Review of Private Law* 10 (2002): 7-28. For European contract law *see* Hesselink (n. 27 above). For European sales law *see* B. van Zelst, *The Politics of European Sales Law* (Alphen a/d Rijn: Kluwer Law International, 2008). This method clearly has its limits. T. Wilhelmsson, 'Varieties of Welfarism in European Contract Law', *European Law Journal* 10 (2004): 712-733, has proposed a different framework for the political analysis of private law.
30. *See* C. Mak, *Fundamental Rights in European Contract Law; A comparison of the impact of fundamental rights on contractual relationships in Germany, the Netherlands, Italy and England* (Alphen a/d Rijn: Kluwer Law International, 2008), who undertakes a political comparison of contract law rules on subjects where fundamental rights play a role.
31. On a theoretical level, arguably, legal systems can be said to be incommensurable in the sense that there is no common denominator (e.g., a 'function' that a rule or doctrine or concept could objectively be said to fulfil) by which they can be compared. *See* G. Frankenberg, 'Critical Comparisons: Re-thinking Comparative Law', *Harvard International Law Journal* 26 (1985): 411 and P. Legrand, *Que sais-je? Le droit comparé* (Paris: PUF, 1999). As a consequence, it is not possible to develop abstract sets of rule alternatives (to be placed on a scale from autonomy to solidarity) because these alternatives are always answers to a functionally defined problem (nor can autonomy or solidarity themselves be said to provide such a standard because these concepts have no intrinsic abstract meaning independent of a continuum of rule alternatives). However, it is submitted that in the context of European contract law this theoretical difficulty has no practical significance because private law systems in the Member States play sufficiently similar roles to allow for broad and general (but still essentially functional) comparisons in terms of autonomy and solidarity.
32. In the same sense Lando (2007), who writes that 'As it now appears the CFR tends to pay more heed to the liberals than does PECL', 252, and speaks of 'the liberal philosophy behind the present CFR', 256 and argues in favour of preparing 'a more socially oriented CFR', 256. Unlike the structural and terminological changes the substantive deviations from PECL are not justified in the Introduction (*see* Introduction, 50-54).
33. Cf. Lando (n. 22 above), 250.

epitomizes the idea of party autonomy. This structural change should be reversed. It can easily be done by returning to the structure of the PECL and adding one article to the effect that the rules on contracts apply with appropriate modifications to unilateral acts. This would have the additional advantage – not without importance from the point of view of social justice – of being much more intelligible to the ordinary European citizen who has not been trained as a lawyer in the Germanic academic tradition.

That said, the mere fact that the DCFR, where it deviates in substance from the PECL almost always does so in the direction of autonomy, and that therefore the DCFR is more liberal than the PECL does not imply in itself that the DCFR is neoliberal per se, and not even that it is more liberal than the civil codes of the Member States. On the contrary, the DCFR is certainly less autonomy-oriented than most classical civil codes that are still in force today (such as the French civil code), which are outdated in this respect and had to be heavily supplemented by the courts, and indeed the more modern re-codifications, such as those of Italy, Portugal, and the Netherlands. With rules on pre-contractual information duties,[34] pre-contractual good faith and confidentiality,[35] unfair exploitation,[36] the obligation to cooperate,[37] and change of circumstances,[38] to give only a few examples from contract law, the DCFR is a modern code in this respect. It is even more modern than German law, since the reform of the law of obligations in 2002 (which did not affect the rather liberal law of juridical acts, relevant for the formation, validity and interpretation of contracts) and the law reform proposed in France in 2005 by the Catala Committee.[39]

2. UNDERLYING VALUES AND PRINCIPLES

2.1. Useful?

The Introduction to the DCFR contains a statement of underlying principles and values, which is meant to become a Preamble to the final CFR.[40] At first sight, one might think that such a statement is mere rhetoric and of no practical importance. However, that perception would be a mistake. Once adopted, this list of underlying principles and values is likely to play an important role in the interpretation and further development of the CFR, especially by the courts (national and the ECJ) and as a broader frame of reference for legislators, courts, and academics, at both the Community and the national level, when further developing the existing multi-level system of private law in European and its common European legal method. Indeed,

34. Articles II.-3:101-II.-3:107 DCFR.
35. Articles II.-3:301 and II.-3:302 DCFR.
36. Article II.-7:207 DCFR.
37. Article III.-1:104 DCFR.
38. Article III.-1:110 DCFR.
39. Avant-projet de réforme du droit des obligations (Arts 1101 à 1386 du Code civil) et du droit de la prescription (Arts 2234 à 2281 du Code civil) (22.09.2005).
40. *See* 'Introduction', DCFR, 15-36. Cf. The Way Forward, Annex I.

the DCFR explicitly states that issues within its scope which are not expressly settled by its rules must be settled in accordance with these underlying principles.[41]

Think, as an example, of the role that the introductory recitals play in the interpretation of directives by the ECJ. Admittedly, directives are explicitly meant to be instrumental and therefore the courts have to establish the purpose of each directive; that is not necessarily the case for the CFR. Nevertheless, a better idea of the aims of the CFR can obviously facilitate its interpretation. Think also of the aims of the EU as they are stated in the founding Treaties. The ECJ regularly invokes them, also in private law cases. A good example is the Mostaza Claro case, where the ECJ invoked Article 3(1)(t) EC in order to underline that the Directive on unfair terms was 'a measure which is essential to the accomplishment of the tasks entrusted to the Community and, in particular, to raising the standard of living and the quality of life in its territory', and thus to justify that a national court be required to assess the unfairness of a term of its own motion.[42]

The introduction to the DCFR explicitly invites comments on whether a statement of fundamental principles would be useful and therefore should be completed and included in the final version of the DCFR.[43] The answer is clearly yes: the final CFR should include a statement of fundamental principles.

2.2. Balanced?

Since the list may play an important role in solving hard cases within the scope of the CFR, it becomes crucial, of course, to know whether from the perspective of social justice the list is well balanced.

It is certainly much more balanced than the one presented by the Acquis Group. The Acquis Group attributes five possible fundamental principles on contract law to the *acquis communautaire* (while underlining at the same time that making a restatement means by definition 'to reflect the law as it stands and not to invent artificial rules which would be ideal in the view of the makers').[44] These principles are politically very one-sided (liberal-conservative). Freedom is the key word; solidarity and even dignity are absent. It is as if we were back in the nineteenth Century. It is therefore astonishing that according to the drafters, the core content of these five principles 'does not seem to be very controversial'.

The list of principles and values in the CFR is somewhat similar to those enshrined in the Nice Charter, but it is not identical. The Charter is not even mentioned. It is unclear why a more explicit link is not made. That would also affirm the constitutional dimension of private law. In some Member States, that

41. Article I. 1:102 DCFR.
42. Case C-168/05, *Elisa María Mostaza Claro v. Centro Móvil Milenium SL*, 26.10.2006.
43. 'Introduction', DCFR, 17.
44. *See* G. Ajani & H. Schulte-Nölke, 'The principles of the existing EC Contract Law: A Preliminary Output of the Acquis Group', in *Principles of the existing EC Contract Law* (ACQP) (Munich: Sellier, 2007), xi.

dimension is well established. However, the DCFR still seems rather detached. This may become problematic especially if one day it will be enacted (in part), e.g., as an optional Code. Pursuant to Article 2 Lisbon Treaty, which could not have been taken into account by the drafters of the DCFR, 'The Union is founded on the values of respect for human dignity, freedom, democracy, equality, the rule of law and respect for human rights, including the rights of persons belonging to minorities. These values are common to the Member States in a society in which pluralism, non-discrimination, tolerance, justice, solidarity and equality between women and men prevail.' It would be advisable to make explicit in the final list that these values (i.e., human dignity, freedom, equality, respect for human rights, pluralism, non-discrimination, tolerance, justice, solidarity, and equality) also underlie private law and that its interpretation and further development (in other words the resolution of hard cases) should also be inspired by these values. The present list in the introduction to the DCFR is therefore incomplete and should be supplemented.

Another problem with the list is that not all principles and values mentioned therein have equal status. Since the way in which principles operate is through balancing,[45] it is crucial that principle and counter principle have an equal formal status. However, the principle of party autonomy has made it to the black-letter rules (II.-1:102 DCFR) whereas solidarity, its counter principle, has not been given an equal formal status. This omission should be corrected in the final CFR: the principle of solidarity should be upgraded to the level of a black-letter rule.

2.3. Justice

This is not the place to go into all the values listed in the Introduction to the DCFR and into the way in which they are described, and whether the description corresponds to the way in which they are implemented into model rules. However, obviously here an exception has to be made for the value of justice.

According to the introduction, 'every model rule in the DCFR pursues the aim of reaching a just and fair solution for the situation to be regulated.' This raises the question of what theory or standard the drafters have adopted for testing the justice and fairness of solutions.

Today, there are many different theories of justice. Did the drafters follow Rawls's two principles of justice, Sen & Nussbaum's capabilities approach, Hayek's idea that social justice is a mirage, or Habermas's discursive approach? No, they resorted to the classical Aristotelian notion of corrective justice: 'the DCFR is particularly concerned to promote what Aristotle termed "corrective" justice. This notion is fundamental to contract, non-contractual liability for damage and unjustified enrichment.... The DCFR is less concerned with issues of "distributive justice", but sometimes distributive or "welfarist" concerns may be reflected in the DCFR, for instance when it is decided that a consumer should always have certain rights.'

45. *See* explicitly 'Introduction', DCFR, 23.

This notion of justice is unduly narrow and conservative. It is too reminiscent of the days when legal scholars, especially in Germany,[46] tried to set private law apart from the remainder of our legal system as being based on an entirely different notion of justice.

Moreover, it is doubtful whether the abstract notion of corrective justice alone can point the way to reaching a just and fair solution. What does commutative justice mean in contract law? It is well known that in the late Middle Ages the most important application of the notion of commutative justice in the Aristotelian tradition became the fair price (iustum pretium) doctrine. However, this doctrine has not been accepted in the DCFR. On the contrary, price is explicitly excluded from the policing of unfair terms,[47] just as in the directive on unfair terms.[48] But in spite of the fact that the issue was raised in the Green Paper on the revision of the *acquis*,[49] no explanation is given in the DCFR. An unfair price doctrine should at least have been considered. For example, a rule where a deviation of fifty percent from the market price (where there is one) is presumed to be unfair. Such a safety net facilitates access to the market of weaker parties who would otherwise fear a great loss, which is an important social benefit in itself (especially if it concerns markets for goods and services of primary importance), and could thus even increase social welfare.[50] Moreover, it is not clear that the notion of commutative justice, which aims at restoring the status quo ante, can explain expectation damage and specific performance as remedies for breach of contract. However, these are the main remedies in the DCFR (and in all Member States).[51]

3. THE PROTECTION OF WEAKER PARTIES

3.1. Consumer Protection

This subject is best analyzed in terms of more or less consumer friendliness. The most relevant yardsticks are the current level of protection in the *acquis* and the alternatives suggested by the European Commission in its Green Paper on the review of the consumer *acquis*.[52] Obviously, the level of protection in the DCFR never goes below the minimum required by the directives. But does it ever go beyond or does the minimum requirement in the directives become the

46. *See* for a recent attempt C.W. Canaris, *Die Bedeutung der iustitia distributiva im deutschen Vertragsrecht*, (Munich: Verlag der Bayerischen Akademie der Wissenschaften, 1997).
47. Article II.-9:407 (2) DCFR.
48. Article 4(2) unfair terms directive.
49. Question D3, Option 1.
50. *See* further M.W. Hesselink, 'Capacity and Capability in European Contract Law', *European Review of Private Law* 11 (2005): 491-507.
51. *See* Book III, Chapter 3 DCFR.
52. Green Paper on the review of the Consumer Acquis COM (2006) 744 final. *See* for a thorough analysis of the Green Paper, B.M. Loos, *Review of the European Consumer Acquis* (Munich: Sellier, 2008).

maximum in the DCFR? The Green Paper asks a number of detailed questions concerning the level of consumer protection. The main answers contained in the DCFR can be classified as follows.

Consumer friendly:

(a) The notion of consumer is extended to mixed contracts.[53]

(b) The list of terms in the Annex to the Unfair terms directive, which currently operates as an indicative list with low formal status,[54] is upgraded to a grey list (a rebuttable presumption of unfairness) and one type of clause is even blacklisted (deemed to be unfair).[55]

(c) The DCFR contains a clear set of remedies for the breach of pre-contractual duties which not only goes beyond the protection provided in several directives (which provide no remedies) but also beyond the most protective option suggested in the Green Paper.[56]

(d) The uniform cooling-off period is fourteen calendar days which is longer than in the existing directives, and corresponds to the most consumer-friendly alternative suggested in the Green Paper.[57]

(e) The exercise of the right of withdrawal is informal and returning the subject-matter of the contract constitutes a withdrawal. This settles, in a consumer-friendly way, a question that was left open in the *acquis*.[58]

(f) The DCFR does not exclude consumer protection in the case of second-hand goods sold at a public auction, something the Consumer sales directive allowed the Member States to do.[59]

(g) The protection provided by the Consumer sales directive is extended to digital content and software.[60]

(h) In consumer sales contracts the risk does not pass until the consumer takes over the goods.[61]

(i) The DCFR gives the consumer buyer a free choice of remedies (abolition of the hierarchy of remedies).[62]

---

53. *See* DCFR, 329: 'any natural person who is acting primarily for purposes which are not related to his or her trade, business or profession.' Cf. Green Paper, Question B1, Option 2.
54. In Case 478/99 *Commission v. Kingdom of Sweden* [2002] ECR I-4147 (ECJ) the Court decided that the Annex did not have to form an integral part of the provisions implementing the Directive for the reason that it 'docs not limit the discretion of the national authorities to determine the unfairness of a term'.
55. *See* Arts 9:411 and 9:410 DCFR respectively. Cf. Green Paper, Question D2.
56. *See* Art. II.-3:107 DCFR. Cf. Green Paper, Question E.
57. *See* Art. II.-5:103 DCFR. Cf. Green Paper, Question F1, Option 1.
58. *See* Art. II.-5:102 DCFR. Cf. Green Paper, Question F2, Option 3.
59. Cf. Green Paper, Question H2, Option 1.
60. *See* Art. IV.A-1:101(2) DCFR, and Book IV, Part B (Lease of Goods). Cf. Green Paper, Question H1, Option 4.
61. *See* Art. IV.A.-5:103 DCFR. Cf. Green Paper, Question 12.
62. *See* Art. IV.-4:201 DCFR. The only limitation is that the consumer buyer may not terminate the contact if the lack of conformity is minor. *See* IV.-4:201 DCFR. Cf. Green Paper, Question K1, Option 2.

(j) The consumer buyer is not under a duty to notify the seller within a reasonable time of the non-conformity (failing which he would lose certain or even all his remedies).[63]

(k) The DCFR makes the commercial guarantee ('consumer goods guarantee') binding in favour of the buyer and subsequent owners, regulates its minimum content and makes limitations of the guarantee to specific parts not binding on the consumer unless the limitation is clearly indicated.[64]

Not consumer friendly:

(a) The scope of the unfairness test has not been extended to the definition of the main subject-matter of the contract and the adequacy of the price.[65]

(b) The consumer who exercises his right of withdrawal may become liable to pay for the benefits he has received from the contract. This is a rather extreme application of the principle of unjustified enrichment. It unfavourably deviates from the *acquis* that left the matter to the Member States and, for consumers in some Member States, is worse than the least favourable option in the Green Paper.[66]

(c) The reversal of the burden of proof that the defects existed at the time of delivery has not been extended.[67]

Undecided:

(a) The question whether the policing of unfair terms should be limited to terms that have not been individually negotiated has remained undecided, the Acquis Group rejecting the more consumer-friendly solution proposed by the Study Group on a European Civil Code (SGECC).[68] Frankly, the notion of an 'individually negotiated term' is so problematic (when can a term be meaningfully said to have been negotiated in the case of unequal bargaining?)[69] that it would be wiser (quite apart from considerations of fairness) to drop this categorical limitation and to take this circumstance into account, if necessary, when applying the fairness test.

The balance is clearly positive, i.e., the cases where consumer protection is extended beyond the minimum required by the directives clearly outnumber the cases that maintain the status quo. In addition, the DCFR

63. *See* Art. III.-3:107 DCFR. Cf. Green Paper, Question K2, Option 3. Contrast Arts 4: 301-4:302 Principles of European Law Sales (PELS) which did impose such a duty on the consumer buyer.
64. *See* Arts IV.A.-6:102, IV.A.-6:102 and IV.A.-6:105 respectively. Cf. Green Paper, Question M1, Option 2, Question M2, Option 2 and Question M3, Option 2.
65. *See* Art. II.-9:407 DCFR. Cf. Green Paper, Question D3, Option 2.
66. This follows from Art. II.-5:105 (2). Cf. Green Paper, Question F3.
67. *See* Art. IV.A.-2:308 DCFR. Cf. Green Paper, Question J4, Option 1; Option 2 was to the effect that the burden of proof was reversed for the entire duration of the legal guarantee, as long as this would be compatible with the nature of the goods and the defects.
68. *See* Art. II-9:404 DCFR. Cf. Question D1 Cf. Green Paper, Question B1.
69. *See* the extremely lengthy and rather cumbersome definition in Art. II-9:403 DCFR.

introduces consumer protection for a number of subjects that are not so far covered by the consumer *acquis*. The question is, of course, whether this is enough. Frankly, this depends on the purpose. As a maximum beyond which Member States are not allowed to go it is still too restrictive, but as a twenty-eighth system that can be chosen by clicking on a blue button, it is certainly acceptable.

3.2. The Protection of SMEs

SMEs may be equally vulnerable as consumers when it comes to lack of information, inexperience and dependence. Nevertheless, within the DCFR there is a sharp contrast between the way consumers and small businesses are treated, even though they are often in a very similar position. SMEs are not only completely excluded from the definition of consumer, but here are also no other rules contained in the DCFR that categorically protect certain SMEs (e.g., the smallest ones) in certain situations (e.g., in very unbalanced contracts). Franchisees and commercial agents are among the few exceptions. This is an omission.

The DCFR is too harsh on small businesses. A striking example is Article II.-9:406 DCFR on unfair terms where artisans and small family business are treated in exactly the same manner as large multinationals. This article should be changed. Of course, there are practical difficulties (mainly relating to definition), but these are typical of any categorical protection and are not per se insuperable. It has been done in a number of Member States.[70] Again, the PECL were better in this respect. There, the same unfairness test that remains limited in the DCFR to consumer contracts (just like in the directive on unfair terms) is extended to b2b contracts.[71] The treatment of small businesses in the DCFR is not only unfair, it is also out of line with the EU policy to protect SMEs.

3.3. Non-discrimination

A major innovation in the DCFR compared to the civil codes of all the Member States (and the PECL) is that it contains a chapter on discrimination in contracts.[72] The codification of this subject in the DCFR underlines that discrimination is a concern for private law just as much as for public law. Moreover, the chapter is not a mere declaration of good intentions. It provides that discrimination amounts to a breach of contract which gives rise to all the remedies for breach of contract including damages for economic and non-economic loss.[73]

70. *See* M.W. Hesselink, 'SMEs in European Contract Law', in *The Future of European Contract Law*, eds K. Boele-Woelki & W. Grosheide (Alphen a/d Rijn: Kluwer Law International, 2007), 349-372.
71. Article 4:110 PECL. Cf. explicitly Comment A (266).
72. DCFR, Book II, Chapter 2: Non-discrimination.
73. *See* Art. II.-2:104 DCFR.

That said, it is not clear why the right not to be discriminated against is limited to the grounds of sex, ethnic, and racial origin. One should not discriminate between different grounds of discrimination. It is true that this is still an extension compared to the directive on unequal treatment,[74] which was limited to discrimination on the grounds of race and ethnic origin. However, Article 21 of the Charter of Fundamental Rights of the EU declares that 'Any discrimination based on any ground such as sex, race, colour, ethnic or social origin, genetic features, language, religion or belief, political or any other opinion, membership of a national minority, property, birth, disability, age or sexual orientation shall be prohibited.' There is no reason why the same protection, with the same remedies, should not also be given in cases of these types of discrimination in contractual relationships.[75]

3.4. Other Weaker Parties

As a model European Civil Code, the DCFR is certainly not complete. Not only are several important general subjects of private law still missing (most prominently: property law), but it also lacks much of 'special private law', (i.e., the private – especially contract – law rules that were developed everywhere in Europe to protect the weaker parties in certain contractual relations, such as employees and tenants). That makes the DCFR look more like a classical nineteenth Century pre-Welfare State Civil Code than is necessary. The more modern civil codes usually include all sorts of rules that are meant to protect these weaker parties against the consequences of unequal bargaining. With regard to the most immediate purposes of the CFR, this may not be so problematic. However, for its broader role as background rules and as a frame of reference, it is. In the words of Hondius, the inclusion of 'special private law' into the Dutch civil code was a paradigmatic change which made visible to what extent private law is a mix of freedom and protection. This is important if a civil code is regarded as the model for the conduct between private parties (civil constitution). Obviously, the CFR is not meant to be a Civil Code (let alone a constitution). However, the concept of a 'common frame of reference' very much suggests the idea of a model of conduct for European citizens and businesses. As such a model, the CFR certainly looks pale, without any rules on the protection of minors, the mentally ill, tenants, employees, small businesses, and other weaker parties. Strategic arguments such as that these subjects are too political, that the traditions in Member States differ, that there is no EU legal basis, and so forth are not convincing, because they also apply to many subjects that have been included in the CFR. Therefore, the DCFR should be completed with labour contracts, landlord and tenant contracts, and so forth in order for it to become a

74. Directive 2000/43/EC implementing the principle of equal treatment between persons regardless of racial and ethnic origin (OJ L 180/22).
75. Moreover, although for the DCFR the problem of legal basis does not exist, it is worthwhile pointing out that pursuant to Article 13 EC the Community is allowed to combat discrimination based on sex, racial or ethnic origin, religion or belief, disability, age or sexual orientation.

more balanced model (frame of reference) for today's private law and private conduct in Europe.

4. THE ROLE OF GOOD FAITH

General clauses can play an important role in promoting social justice in contract law, especially in adding to and in counterbalancing the binding force of contract. Although there may be no logical or necessary link between good faith and social justice, there certainly is a historical one.

The PECL contain a general good faith clause. In the words of Ole Lando, Article 1:201 PECL is 'an over-arching principle, which a court can apply to enforce community standards of decency, fairness and reasonableness even when there is no specific provision in PECL, which it can invoke'.[76] However, Hugh Beale replied:[77] 'first, Article 1:102 [PECL] needs to be revised to make clear that good faith and fair dealing is not an over-arching control mechanism. And secondly, it needs to be made clear that the principle merely excludes the unreasonable'. If indeed this were to happen, it would be wrong, because with one brush it would remove what has served as the basis for most of judge-made social private law. It would also be in vain, because, as the history of the application of the concept in virtually all Member States (i.e., all except the common law countries) shows, courts will not be limited by the wording of the good faith clause but will exercise what they regard as their task when applying abstract rules to concrete cases: they will interpret, supplement, and correct the abstract rules where, in their view, fairness requires this for the type of case at hand.[78]

Nevertheless, this is exactly what has happened in the DCFR. Article III.-1:103 (3) reads as follows: 'breach of the duty [to act in accordance with good faith and fair dealing in performing an obligation] does not give rise directly to the remedies for non-performance of an obligation but may preclude the person in breach from exercising or relying on a right, remedy or defense which that person would otherwise have.' This is a clear attempt to curtail the courts' possibility to develop new obligations (as they have done in the past in the case of duties to inform, to cooperate, of care) that without excessive fiction (as in the common law

76. *See* O. Lando, 'Is good faith an over-arching general clause in the Principles of European Contract Law', in *Liber amicorum Guido Alpa; Private law beyond the national systems*, eds M. Andenas et al. (London: British Institute of International and Comparative Law, 2007), 601-613.
77. H. Beale, 'General clauses and specific rules in the Principles of European Contract Law: the "Good Faith" clause', in *General Clauses and Standards in European Contract Law*, eds S. Grundmann & D. Mazeaud (The Hague: Kluwer Law International, 2006), 205-218.
78. *See* S. Whittaker & R. Zimmermann, 'Good faith in European contract law: surveying the legal landscape', in *Good Faith in European Contract Law*, eds R. Zimmermann & S. Whittaker (Cambridge: CUP, 2000), 7-62, at 32; M.W. Hesselink 'The Concept of Good Faith', in *Towards a European Civil Code*, eds A. Hartkamp et al. (The Hague/Boston/London: Kluwer Law International, 2004).

doctrine of implied terms) cannot be said to be based on the contract. Including this new rule in the final CFR would mean a severe blow to social justice in European private law. Therefore, in the words of Ole Lando, good faith should be given back its teeth.[79]

5. CONCLUSION

The DCFR has all the characteristics of a typical European compromise. Ideological and esthetical purists will certainly be disappointed. In this respect, it has much in common with the Constitutional Treaty. This is not necessarily something to worry about. A CFR is not made, in the first place (if at all), for esthetical or ideological reasons; it is meant to provide some normative guidance in the further development of European contract law.

European citizens are likely to have very different interests, preferences, and opinions in relation to almost all the subjects dealt with in the DCFR. A DCFR consistently based on only one such conception would inevitably disappoint all European citizens who have a different idea of social justice in European private law. Therefore, if we really want the further Europeanization of private law, we will have to accept that it will probably look different from both the particular Member State law that each of us has been accustomed to and our personal ideas of social justice. The publication of the interim outline edition of the Draft CFR, which is the result of collaboration between hundreds of legal scholars from all Member States, has brought that message home.

Overall, from the point of view of social justice, the DCFR is fairly balanced. There is certainly room for improvement. The concept of juridical acts should be removed. The list of underlying values, which may play an important role in the interpretation and further development of the CFR by the courts, must be made more balanced. The protection of consumers should be extended to SMEs at least in certain cases (notably unfair terms). The classical role of good faith as a basis for new judge-made obligations should be restored. However, the characterizations of the DCFR as 'a law for big business and competent consumers' or, alternatively, as a 'massive reduction of private autonomy' are both exaggerations.[80]

---

79. Pursuant to paragraph 3 of Article I.-1:102 DCFR, in the interpretation and development of the CFR regard should be had to the need to promote, among other things, good faith and fair dealing. Moreover, paragraph four states that issues within the scope of the rules, but not expressly settled by them, are, as far as possible, to be settled in accordance with the principles underlying them, one of which is the principle of good faith and fair dealing. One could argue (as was done during the conference by Hugh Beale) that this article could serve as an expansion clause that could also provide a basis for new obligations developed by the courts. However, presumably Article III.-1:103 (3), which is placed in Book III, is a lex specialis in relation to Art. I.-1:102, which is in Book I, and, therefore, has precedence over it (*see* Article I.-1:102 (5)).
80. *See* T. Wilhelmsson, 'Constitutional values and social justice', unpublished presentation at the ERA conference 'The Draft Common Frame of Reference' (Trier, 6-7.3.2008) and H. Eidenmüller, F. Faust, H. C. Grigoleit, N. Jansen, G. Wagner & R. Zimmermann, 'Der Gemeinsame

Now it is time for the stakeholders (i.e., all European citizens!) to give their critical views on the Draft. For the legitimacy of the final CFR it is crucial that they should not only be given the opportunity to speak, but it is also crucial that they should be listened to.

Referenzrahmen für das Europäische Privatrecht – Wertungsfragen and Kodifikationsprobleme –', *Juristenzeitung* 63 (2008): 529-584, respectively.

Chapter 7

The DCFR, Public Policy, Mandatory Rules, and the Welfare State

Jacobien W. Rutgers

1. INTRODUCTION

This paper will discuss public policy, mandatory rules, and the DCFR[1] from a multi-level perspective. At first sight, this title may seem rather odd, since neither the civil law notion of public policy or *ordre public* nor the common law concept of illegality or public policy appear in the DCFR. Instead, the DCFR provides that a contract which infringes 'fundamental values recognized as such in the Member States of the European Union', is void (Article II.-7:301 DCFR). In addition, a contract which is contrary to mandatory rules is void or valid or a court may adapt its content (II.-7:302 DCFR).

As is well-known, the DCFR is produced by a network of independent scholars, the Joint Network on European Private Law (CoPECL), that was invited thereto by the European Commission and has been financed within the sixth

---

1. C. von Bar et al. (eds), *Principles, Definitions and Model Rules of European Private Law, Draft Common Frame of Reference (DCFR)*, Interim Outline Edition (Münich: Sellier, 2008). Prepared by the Study Group on a European Civil Code, Research Group on EC Private Law (Acquis Group), based in part on a revised version of the PECL. I would like to thank Ruth Sefton-Green and the participants to a seminar of the Center of European Contract Law at the UvA, where an earlier draft of this paper was presented, for their comments. The usual disclaimer applies.

Alessandro Somma, *The Politics of the Draft Common Frame of Reference*, pp. 115-128.

Framework Research Programme.[2] The bulk of general contract law included in the DCFR is a modified form of the PECL,[3] which is combined with the work of the Study Group on a European Civil Code and of the Acquis Group.[4,5]

The DCFR will serve as the starting point of a political CFR, which will be established by the European Commission after consultation of the public. The tasks of this political CFR are manifold according to the Communications of the European Commission.[6] It may be a toolbox for future legislation of the EU and Member States, it may also provide the basis for a non-sector specific instrument, also known as the optional instrument, and it may be an interpretative instrument for the courts in the Member States and of the EU.[7] Missing in this list of CFR-functions is harmonization or even unification of private law.[8] The European Commission has repeatedly denied that this is its intention. However, considering the appearance of the DCFR, the proposal for a directive on consumer rights,[9] which the European Commission issued recently and which is linked to the CFR-project, it seems questionable whether further harmonization of contract law is not on the agenda of the European Commission.[10]

To structure the discussion in this paper, the presumption is that the DCFR is an instrument that applies to both cross-border contracts and national ones. In the case of the former, the DCFR applies without any reference or application of rules of private international law as for instance included in the Rome I Regulation on the law applicable to contractual obligations.[11]

---

2. Communication from the Commission to the European Parliament and the Council, 'European Contract Law and the revision of the acquis: the way forward', Brussels, 11.10.2004 COM (2004) 651 final, 9 et seq.
3. *Principles of European Contract Law* prepared by The Commission on European Contract Law; O. Lando & H. Beale (eds), *Principles of European Contract Law, Parts I & II* (The Hague: Kluwer Law International, 2000); prepared by The Commission on European Contract Law, O. Lando, et al. (eds), *Principles of European Contract Law, Part III* (The Hague: Kluwer Law International, 2003).
4. *Principles of the Existing EC Contract Law (Acquis Principles) Contract I, Pre-contractual Obligations, Conclusion of Contract, Unfair Terms*, Research Group on the Existing EC Private Law (Acquis Group) (München: Sellier, 2007).
5. DCFR (n. 1 above), 50 et seq.
6. Communication from the Commission to the European Parliament and the Council, A More Coherent European Contract Law, An Action Plan, OJ C 63/1-43 (2003), 1, 15, 16; Communication from the Commission to the European Parliament and the Council, European Contract Law and the revision of the acquis: the way forward, Brussels, 11.10.2004, COM (2004) 651 final, 3 et seq.; Report from the Commission, First Annual Progress Report on European Contract Law and the Acquis Review, Brussels, 23.09.2005, COM (2005) 456 final, 10; Report from the Commission, Second Progress Report on the CFR, Brussels, 25.07.2007, COM (2007) 447 final.
7. Communication the way forward, n. 2 above.
8. H. Collins, 'Review of the DCFR', *Modern Law Review* 71 (2008): 840.
9. Proposal for a Directive of the European Parliament and of the Council on Consumer Rights, Brussels 08.10.2008, COM (2008) 614 final.
10. *See* in this respect: Collins (n. 8 above).
11. Regulation (EC) No. 593/2008 of the European Parliament and of the Council of 17.06.2008 on the law applicable to contractual obligations (Rome I), OJ L 177/6-16 (2008).

As stated above, the DCFR provides rules concerning contracts which infringe 'fundamental values recognized as such in the Member States of the European Union' (Article II.-7:301 DCFR) and those which are contrary to mandatory rules (II.-7:302 DCFR). A distinction must be made between these two provisions concerning the origin of the fundamental principles on the one hand and that of mandatory rules on the other. With respect to both provisions, many issues arise. For instance, does this provision refer to fundamental principles which are merely recognized in one Member State or must it concern a genuinely European principle? Concerning mandatory rules, there is no reference within the DCFR as to their origin. They can be either European or national. If they are European, they can either be included in the DCFR itself or in any other European enactment. Thus, if the DCFR is enacted as a European instrument, it still leaves room for the application of national law. Moreover, especially in the situation of cross-border trade, those national rules and fundamental principles fall within the scrutiny of the free movements of goods (Article 28), services (Article 49), capital (Article 56) and persons (Article 39) as included in the EC-Treaty. Thus, the application of these provisions of the DCFR may involve three levels of regulation, which gives rise to all types of complications of a technical and normative nature. Moreover, these rules are open-ended and their meaning depends on the time, place, and society in which they perform their role.[12]

In order to show these complications, first the rules in the DCFR will be discussed and subsequently, they will be related to national contract law.

2. PUBLIC POLICY, MANDATORY RULES AND THE DCFR

The point of departure of the DCFR is freedom of contract, which is included in a provision entitled 'Party Autonomy' (Article II.-1:102 DCFR). The reason for this heading is that this rule not only applies to contracts but also to juridical acts. Parties are free to enter into any contract and to determine its content, provided that the rules on good faith and any other applicable mandatory rules are observed, nor is any form required (Article II.-1:107 DCFR).[13]

Despite the absence of the term public policy in the DCFR, it will be used nevertheless. As stated before, the rules concerning public policy and mandatory rules can be found in Section 3 of Chapter 7 (Invalidity) of Book II (Contracts and other juridical acts) headed 'Infringement of fundamental principles or mandatory

12. Cf. M. Fabre-Magnan, *Droits des obligations 1 – Contrat et engagement unilateral* (Paris: Thémis, Droit, Presses Universitaires de France, 2008), 153.
13. Cf. G. Alpa, *Manuale di diritto privato* (Milan: Cedam, 2005), 544; cf. H. Collins, *The Law of Contract* (London: Butterworths, LexisNexis, 2003), 22 et seq.; Fabre-Magnan (n. 12 above), 28; D. Medicus, *Schuldrecht I, Allgemeiner Teil*, 15, neubearbeitete Auflage (München: Verlag C.H. Beck, 2004) 64 et seq.; P. Schlechtriem & M. Schmidt-Kessel, *Schuldrecht, Allgemeiner Teil*, Sechste, neubearbeitete Auflage (Tübingen: Mohr Siebeck, 2005), 50; F. Terré, P. Simler & Y. Lequette, *Droit civil, Les obligations*, 9th edn (Paris: Dalloz, 2005) 23 et seq.

rules'. Thus, within the DCFR, contracts which are contrary to fundamental principles recognized in the Member States of the EU (Articles II.-7:301 DCFR) must be distinguished from contracts contrary to mandatory rules (Articles II.-7:302 DCFR).[14] Hereafter, first the rule concerning fundamental principles will be dealt with and subsequently, the situation that a contract is contrary to a mandatory rule. Since the comments and the notes to the DCFR are not yet available,[15] the comments to PECL will be used insofar as the provisions are similar.[16]

With respect to both instances, it must be remembered that European law provides the boundaries within which Member States may apply their own national mandatory rules or fundamental principles. In Arblade, the ECJ held that national rules concerning public policy fall within the scrutiny of the free movement of persons, goods, services, and capital.[17] Insofar as those national mandatory rules and fundamental principles constitute an infringement of the free movement of goods, services, capital, and persons, they must be set aside, unless they are justified because they concern one of the grounds mentioned in the Treaty or one of the overriding interests as developed in the case law of the ECJ, provided that these measures are proportional and necessary to achieve the result. Hereafter, this issue will not be discussed.

2.1. Fundamental Principles

Contracts contrary to 'principles recognised as fundamental in the laws of the Member States of the European Union' are void insofar as is dictated by the principle at stake (Article II.-7:301 DCFR). This provision does not specify the meaning of 'principles recognised as fundamental in the laws of the Member States of the European Union' nor is this notion present in the list of definitions included in the DCFR. When this provision is taken together with Article II.-1:102 DCFR, it is striking that a reference to fundamental principles is absent in the latter, since freedom of contract is also subject to those 'principles recognised as fundamental in the laws of the Member States of the European Union'.

At first sight, the meaning of Article II.-7:301 DCFR and in particular that of 'principles recognised as fundamental in the laws of the Member States of the European Union' is not crystal clear. Although the Introduction to the DCFR includes the words 'fundamental principles', it does not seem to answer the

14. Cf. Art. 15:101 PECL, Art. 15.102 PECL. *See* about these provisions included in PECL: H.L. Macqueen, 'Illegality and Immorality in Contracts', in *Towards a European Civil Code*, eds A. Hartkamp et al. (Nijmegen: Ars Aequi Libri; Kluwer Law International, 2004), 415, at 417 et seq.
15. DCFR, Introduction, n. 14.
16. DCFR, Introduction, n. 50 et seq.
17. Case C-363/96 and C-376/96 *Criminal proceedings against Jean-Claude Arblade and Arblade & Fils SARL and against Bernard Leloup and Others* [1998] ECR I-8453. It is submitted that in this case it concerned a public policy exception as it used as private international law. However, the definition which the ECJ gave also can be applied to substantive contract law.

question as to their meaning within the context of Article II.-7:301 DCFR, since in the Introduction they seem to be used in a different manner.[18] There, they are described as underlying principles and abstract basic values, of which a non exhaustive list is given.[19] Freedom, protection of human rights, economic welfare, solidarity and social responsibility, promotion of the internal market, preservation of cultural and linguistic plurality, rationality, legal certainty, predictability, and efficiency are provided as fundamental principles.[20] It is submitted that these abstract notions contradict each other, therefore concrete rules are needed in which these principles are balanced against each other.[21]

From the comments to Article 15:101 PECL, which employs the same concept, it follows that the words 'principles recognised as fundamental in the laws of the Member States of the European Union' are chosen to avoid the national notions of 'immorality, illegality at common law, public policy, *ordre public* and *bonos moros.*' Moreover, it is explicitly stated that this notion also includes European Community Law. Competition law and the free movements are given as examples thereof. In this respect, the issue arises as to what extent contracts may be contrary to the free movement of goods, services, capital, and persons, since this raises the question as to whether the free movements have a horizontal effect. This has only been accepted by the ECJ[22] with respect to the free movement of services, capital, and persons. With respect to the free movement of goods, the ECJ has explicitly rejected the horizontal effect.[23]

A mere national concept does not purport to be one of the fundamental principles within the meaning of Article 15:101 PECL, according to its Comments.[24] Thus, if it is understood correctly, the notion of fundamental principles concerns only those principles which are recognized in the EU at large. This raises the issue of how this relates to the discretion which the ECJ allows the Member States with respect to the concept of public policy to justify an impediment of the free

18. *See* about the values included in the Introduction: M.W. Hesselink, 'Common Frame of Reference & Social Justice', *European Review of Contract Law* 4 (2008): 258 et seq.
19. DCFR, n. 1 above; Introduction, n. 11, 19.
20. DCFR, n. 1 above; Introduction, n. 22.
21. DCFR, n. 1 above; Introduction, n. 11.
22. Case C-415/93 *Bosman* [1995] ECR I-4921; Case C-309/99 *Wouters* [2002] ECR I-1577; Case C-281/98 *Angonese* [2000] ECR I-4139. *See also*: C. Barnard, *The Substantive Law of the EU, The Four Freedoms* (Oxford: OUP, 2007), 94; D. Chalmers et al., *European Union Law* (Cambridge: CUP, 2006), 659-748; P. J. G. Kapteyn & P. VerLoren van Themaat, *Het recht van de Europese Unie en van de Europese Gemeenschappen* (Deventer: Kluwer, 2003), 498.
23. Case C-159/00 *Sapod Audic v Eco-Emballages SA* [2002] ECR I-5031. *See also*: P. Oliver, W.H. Roth, 'The Internal Market and the Four Freedoms', *Common Market Law Review* 41 (2004): 422; Barnard (n. 22 above), 94; Chalmers et al. (n. 22 above), 659; Kapteyn & VerLoren van Themaat, (n. 22 above), 499; P. Oliver & S. Enchelmaier, 'Free Movement of Goods: Recent Developments in the Case Law', *Common Market Law Review* 44 (2007): 649, at 662.
24. Article 15:101 PECL, Comment B, PECL, Part III (n. 3 above), 211 et seq.; Macqueen, (n. 14 above), 418. *See* for a critical analysis of this rule: M.E. Storme, 'Freedom of Contract: Mandatory and Non-Mandatory Rules in European Contract Law', *European Review of Private Law* (2007): 233, at 243 et seq.

movements. For instance, in Omega, the issue at stake was whether German police authorities could prohibit the running of a laser drome in Bonn, on the basis of protection of human dignity which is a fundamental right that is included in the German Basic Law (Article 1 paragraph 1 *Grundgesetz*).[25] This case is relevant, since a German rule which has a public policy character and is a fundamental principle, prevents an English importer of laser games and a German entrepreneur from entering into a franchise or supply contract. Thus, freedom of contract is restricted by a German fundamental principle. The ECJ held that this prohibition was contrary to the free movement of services. The next matter with which the ECJ had to deal was whether the German fundamental principle of human dignity could justify the free movement of services' infringement on the basis of public policy (Article 55 EC). The ECJ took a very balanced position. First, 'public policy' within the meaning of a justification ground of the free movement of services, had to be interpreted in a strict manner: that is to say only 'if there is a genuine and sufficiently serious threat to a fundamental interest of society'. Moreover, this could not be left unilaterally to the Member States. However, admitting that public policy differs from one country to another and from time to time, the ECJ granted the Member States 'a margin of discretion within the limits posed by the Treaty'. The ECJ reiterated that fundamental rights are part of the Community legal order. Moreover, the protection of human dignity is compatible with Community law, regardless of the fact that 'in Germany, the principle of respect for human dignity has a particular status as an independent fundamental right'.

It must be noted that in cross-border situations, it is not clear whether a court must merely take into account fundamental principles which are part of the lex fori or whether they should take into account, for instance, fundamental principles which prevail in any other Member State or only those which prevail in those Member States with which the contracts had links.[26] If the DCFR becomes an optional instrument that is applicable without reference to the Rome Regulation, it must include rules in this respect. Otherwise courts will be in the dark as to what fundamental principles to apply.

To sum up, some of the questions concerning Article II.-7:301 DCFR were discussed. Most attention was paid to the meaning of 'fundamental principles recognized as such in the Member States of the European Union'. Unlike what is stated in the Comments to the corresponding provision in PECL (Article 15:101 PECL), it was argued on the basis of ECJ case law that the Member States have a margin of discretion to determine whether there is a fundamental principle and that fundamental principle does not have to be recognized at large in the EU.

---

25. Case C-36/02 *Omega Spielhallen- und Automatenaufstellungs-GmbH v. Oberbürgermeisterin der Bundesstadt Bonn*, ECJ 14.10.2004, [2004] ECR I-9606. *See also*: Case C-275/92 *Her Majesty's Customs and Excise v. G. Schindler and J. Schindler*, ECJ 24.03.1994, [1994] ECR I-1039.
26. These problems are similar to those created by Art. 7 I of the Rome Convention on the law applicable to contractual obligations.

2.2. Mandatory Rules

Article II.-7:302 DCFR only concerns the effects of the instance that a contract is contrary to a mandatory rule. However, neither this provision nor the list of definitions include a description of a mandatory rule. In this respect, the DCFR differs from the PECL, since the reference in Article 15:102 PECL to Article 1:103 PECL, is absent in the DCFR. Article 1:103 PECL defines mandatory rules in cross-border context.[27]

The first section of Article II.-7:302 DCFR is superfluous in the sense that it states that this provision only applies when the mandatory rule, which is infringed by the contract, does not itself include the infringement's effects. In Section 2 of Article II.-7:302 DCFR, the consequences of such an infringement are provided. A court may declare the contract void or valid or may adapt the contract. The remedy chosen must be proportional and appropriate, taking into account all the relevant circumstances (Article II.-7:302 paragraph 3 DCFR).[28] From this provision it does not follow to what extent a court may do so of its own motion or whether it is bound by the plaintiff's claim or the defendant's counterclaim.

Concerning infringements of mandatory rules, many distinctions can be made. For instance, the rules can have a European or a national origin; the mandatory rule may belong to the realm of public law or private law or to both. The Comments to Article 15:102 PECL rather focus on the different elements of freedom of contract which may be restricted by a mandatory rule. The first category mentioned concerns the person that may enter into a contract.[29] A mandatory rule may provide that only a person that has a license for a certain activity can enter into a contract concerning that activity. For instance, under Finnish and Italian law, only companies that have a license may conclude gambling contracts with the public.[30] The second group of mandatory rules limits the manner in which a contract may be concluded.[31] For example, it is required that the contract is in writing in order to agree upon it validly.

The element of freedom of contract left that can be restricted, is the contract's content. In this respect, the Comments to Article 15:102 PECL discern a difference between an illegal purpose and the situation that a contract's performance is contrary to a mandatory rule.[32] In both instances, the same conditions must be fulfilled. Only when both parties to the contract had the intention that the object was contrary to the mandatory rule or that the performance infringes the mandatory

---

27. Article 1:103 PECL, Comment (n. 3 above), 100. The Comments to Art. 15:102 PECL seem to imply something different.
28. Cf. Macqueen (n. 14 above), 422 et seq.
29. Article 15:101 PECL, Comment C, Part III (n. 3 above), 212.
30. Case C-124/97 *Läärä*, ECJ 21.09.1999, [1999] ECR I-6067; Case C-67/98 *D. Zenatti*, 21.10.1999, [1999] ECR I-7289; Case C-243/01 *P. Gambelli*, ECJ 6.11.2003 [2003] ECR I-13031.
31. Article 15:101 PECL, Comment C, Part III (n. 3 above), 212.
32. *Ibid.*

rule, this infringement affects the contract.[33] Or at least, the illegal purpose was known or should have been known to the other party or the other party knew or should have known of the unlawful performance. Thus, an objective test is employed to assess whether the other party was aware of the illegal purpose or the performance contrary to a mandatory rule. Thus, when someone enters into a contract to deliver a box of wine to a friend and the contracted chauffeur drives drunk, which is forbidden by criminal law, the contract is not affected, since this performance was not intended by both parties.

So far the explanation in the Comments to Article 15:102 PECL. We will now make an attempt to apply these rules to a factual situation. The facts are partly taken from the ECJ case in *Munoz*.[34] EC Council Regulation 2200/96 includes a classification system for fruits and vegetables, according to which certain types of grapes of the highest quality are classified as table-grapes.[35] Pursuant to the Regulation itself and the ECJ case law, its aim is the encouragement of fair trade, market transparency, the quality of the products and the protection of the consumer. Let us presume that a certain type of grape is sold to consumers under the name of table-grapes, whereas according to Regulation 2200/96, the grapes sold do not fall within the category of table-grapes. The consumer is not aware of this mandatory rule, whereas the seller is. In other words, there is a contract which infringes a mandatory rule. Regulation 2200/96 itself does not provide for any contractual effects. Thus, the effects of the infringement must be established according to Article II.-7:302 paragraphs 2 and 3 DCFR. Circumstances which play a role in this respect is the aim of Regulation 2200/96, whether the violation is intentional or whether there is a category of persons that is protected by the rule concerned. Thus, a court must establish the effects of the rule considering that Regulation 2200/96 is intended, inter alia, to protect the consumer and that the seller sold the grapes knowingly under an incorrect label. When a Dutch court is confronted with this case, it will probably consider the contract voidable. In other words, only when the consumer herself invokes the rule will the court declare the contract void, since it is the consumer's protection that is at stake. However, the question is whether another court will come to a similar conclusion.

In the example of the table-grapes, it concerned a contract contrary to a mandatory rule of European origin, the situation is more complicated in the case of a cross-border contract which infringes a mandatory rule of a legal system other than the lex fori. When the DCFR applies in the form of an optional instrument without referring to the Rome I Regulation, insofar as contracts are concerned, specific rules should be included in that respect.

---

33. *Ibid.*
34. Case C-253/00 *Antonio Munoz y Cia SA, Superior Fruiticola SA v. Frumar Ltd.*, Redbridge Produce Marketing Ltd, ECJ 17.09.2002, [2002] ECR I-7289.
35. Council Regulation (EC) 2200/96 of 28.10.1996 on the common organization of the market in fruit and vegetables, OJ L297/1-28 (1996).

2.3. Conclusion

So far public policy and mandatory rules within the DCFR have been discussed. Within the context of the DCFR, the Member States still have the possibility of applying national mandatory rules as long as as they do not result in an infringement of one of the free movements and provided that they are not substituted by harmonization. With respect to 'fundamental principles recognized in the European Union' the situation is less clear. Taking into account the comments to PECL and the ECJ case law with respect to public policy, two different approaches can be discerned. The comments to PECL seem to follow the idea that a fundamental principle must be generally accepted in the EU, whereas the ECJ case law leaves a margin of discretion to the Member States. Considering that the free movements and ultimately its justifications establish to what extent there is room for a Member State to apply a fundamental principle and that this case law leaves the Member States a margin of discretion, it does not necessarily involve a fundamental principle that is widely recognized in the Member States. Thus, also the application of the rules which are included in the DCFR have a multi-level aspect. There are rules which are included in the DCFR, which refer to national mandatory rules and possibly national fundamental principles.

3. PUBLIC POLICY, MANDATORY RULES WITHIN THE NATIONAL LEGAL SYSTEM AND THE WELFARE STATE

Within the national legal systems, the debate on freedom of contract and its restraints also has another dimension. For instance, more attention is given to the role of contract law within the welfare states. This element seems to be ignored in the European-Commission-documents on contract law, as has been pointed out by the Manifesto on Social Justice. However, this was not always the case.

In the course of the twentieth century, the role of contract law has changed. When the codifications were introduced on the European continent in the nineteenth century, there was a strict distinction between public law on the one hand and private law on the other. The idea was that public law dealt with issues of general interest and the organization of society, whereas private law focused on the individual and its relations with others and objects.[36] With respect to contract law, the role of the State was limited, since the underlying idea had been that a person

36. M. Bagheri & C. Nakajima, 'Ex Ante and Ex Post Allocation of Risk of Illegality: Regulatory Sources of Contractual Failure and Issues of Corrective and Distributive Justice', *European Journal of Law and Economics* 18 (2002): 15-26; M. Weber, 'Wirtschaft und Gesellschaft', in *Grundriss der verstehenden Soziologie*, ed. J. Winckelman, (Tübingen: J.C.B. Mohr, 1956), 389 et seq.; H. Collins, The Voice of the Community in Private Law Discourse, *European Law Journal* 4 (1997): 407-421.

entered freely into a contract, which the State should facilitate.[37] The role of the courts was to enforce contracts.[38] Only the legislator could restrict freedom of contract by mandatory rules, which would only come into play when a party had entered into a contract involuntarily, for instance when a party had concluded a contract under threat.[39] In addition, there has been the notion of public policy, *ordre public* or illegality, according to which contracts are void, when they are contrary to these notions.

However, after the Second World War, contract law has become increasingly important within the Welfare State, which can be characterized as a capitalist society in which the market economy plays an important role.[40] The market economy in turn is characterized by the exchange of goods, services, and capital.[41] Contract law facilitates these exchanges and in addition to property and company law, is one of the elements of the market economy's legal infrastructure.[42] Moreover, contract law is also used as an instrument to achieve certain ends of the Welfare State which were originally reserved for public law.[43] For instance, a mandatory rule which controls rent prices in landlord and tenant contracts is intended to protect the tenant, who is regarded as a weaker party.[44] In addition, it also serves the public interest, since it provides housing at affordable prices.

---

37. Collins (n. 13 above), 7.
38. *Ibid.*
39. *Ibid.*
40. Cf. A.S. Hartkamp, *Mr. C. Asser's Handleiding tot de beoefening van het Nederlands burgerlijk recht, Verbintenissenrecht, Deel II, Algemene Leer der overeenkomsten* (Deventer: Kluwer, 2005), 43 et seq.; Collins (n. 13 above), 10 et seq.; G. Esping-Andersen, *The Three Worlds of Welfare Capitalism* (Cambridge: Polity Press, 1990), 4; Lurger (n. 43 above), 190.
41. Collins (n. 13 above), 1 et seq.; Alpa (n. 13 above), 10.
42. Cf. Medicus (n. 13 above), 72.
43. Cf. Alpa (n. 13 above), 21; Bagheri & C. Nakajima (n. 13 above), 9; M. W. Hesselink, 'The Structure of the New European Private Law', in *The New European Private Law*, ed. Hesselink (Kluwer Law International, 2002), 228 et seq.; T. Koopmans, 'Vrijheden in beweging', in *Juridisch Stippelwerk* (Deventer: Kluwer, 1991), 37-66; O. Lando, 'The Structure and the Legal Values of the Common Frame of Reference', *European Review of Contract Law* 3 (2007): 251; B. Lurger, 'The Common Frame of Rerence/Optional Code and the Various Understandings of Social Justice in Europe', in *Private Law and the Many Cultures of Europe*, eds T. Wilhemsson, E. Paunio & A. Pohjolainen (The Hague: Kluwer Law International, 2007), 187 et seq.; T.H. Marshall, *Class, Citizenship and Social Development, Essays* (New York: Anchor Books, Doubleday & Company, Inc. Garden City, 1965), 122; M.R. Mok, *Pacta sunt servanda; ja toch? Afscheidrede RUG* (Zwolle: W.E.J. Tjeenk Willink, 1997), 9 et seq.; T. Wilhelmsson, 'Welfarism in European Contract Law', *European Law Journal* (2004): 712-733; Contra: H. Collins, 'The Voice of the Community in Private Law Discourse', *European Law Journal* 4 (1997): 407-421.
44. Cf. T.H. Marshall, *Class, Citizenship and Social Development, Essays* (New York: Anchor Books, Doubleday & Company, Inc. Garden City, 1965), 122-124. Mok (n. 43 above), 9 et seq. *See also*: H. Collins, 'Does Social Justice Require the Preservation of Diversity in the Private Laws of Member States of Europe', in *Private Law and the Many Cultures of Europe*, eds T. Wilhemsson, E. Paunio & A. Pohjolainen (The Hague: Kluwer Law International, 2007), 159 et seq. *See* about the protection of weaker parties in the DCFR: Hesselink (n. 18 above), 262 et seq.

However, not only purely economic aims, but also moral and social values are the object of contract law.[45] Contract law is by all means not the only instrument to perform those welfare ends.[46] For instance, taxation and also social security play a very important role. Thus, the notion of public policy and mandatory rules reflect societal choices in the different Member States.[47] If this conclusion is correct, it must also follow from the different national legal systems.

When the notion of public policy and mandatory rules in different Member States are considered superficially, different approaches can be perceived. For instance, French (Article 6 *Code civile*)[48] and Italian law (Article 1343 *Codice civile*) distinguish between public policy and good morals, whereas under English law the overall-term is illegality, although the notion of public policy is also employed. An Italian commentator writes that it is one of the most frequently used general clauses in Italian law. Under English law, however, another attitude can be perceived: 'obviously a doctrine of public policy is somewhat open-textured and flexible, and this flexibility has been the cause of judicial censure of the doctrine'.[49]

As to the content of public policy, under French law a distinction is made between the *ordre public contemporain/économique de protection* and the *ordre public traditionnel* or *classique*.[50] The latter is described as including the fundamental values of the State, whereas the former is considered to be more protective of one contracting party towards to the other.[51] In English literature, different classifications of contracts contrary to public policy can be found. Regular headings to come across are: the objects of the contract are contrary to common law or legislation, contrary to good governance/proper administration, interference with the proper machinery of justice, against public and sexual morality and restraint of trade clauses.[52] When this list is compared to those in French law, the conclusion can be drawn that the headings within English legal literature mainly involve traditional public policy concerns and less societal ones in the meaning of the *ordre public contemporain*. An Italian commentator draws again another distinction with respect to Italian law. He distinguishes between public policy that concerns family relations (*rapporti di famiglia*) on the one hand and public policy that concerns economic relationships (*rapporti di natura economica*) on the other

45. Collins (n. 44 above), 161 et seq.; Lurger (n. 43 above), 189; R. Sefton-Green, 'Social Justice and European Identity in European Contract Law', *European Review of Contract Law* 2 (2006), 277.
46. Collins (n. 44 above), 159 et seq.
47. Asser-Hartkamp (n. 40 above), 42 et seq. Cf. C.H. Sieburgh, *Tertium Datur, de niet uitgesloten derde in het burgerlijk recht* (Deventer: Kluwer, 2004) 27.
48. Fabre-Magnan (n. 12 above), 153.
49. Chitty on Contracts, 29th edn, vol. I, 16-003. In German textbooks little attention is paid to the notion of public policy (*Sittenwidrigkeit* § 138 BGB); Schlechtriem & Schmidt-Kessel (n. 13 above), 59 et seq.
50. Fabre-Magnan (n. 12 above), 153; Simler & Lequette (n. 13 above), 376 et seq.
51. *Ibid.*
52. Chitty on Contracts, 29th edn, vol I, 16-005; Collins (n. 13 above), 53 et seq.; P. Birks (ed.), *English Private Law*, vol. II (Oxford: OUP, 2000), 8.218 et seq.

hand.[53] Under German law, distinctions are made with respect to mandatory rules (§ 134 BGB). In the textbooks, mandatory rules that apply to adhesion contracts are discerned from those that apply to contracts which are individually negotiated.[54] Thus, a superficial look at the notion of public policy and mandatory rules within some national legal systems show differences.

As explained above, contract law and the market are part of the national institutional frameworks that constitute the Welfare State.[55] Within the EU, the Welfare State and its arrangements, also referred to as the social order, are a national matter.[56] Nevertheless, the Member States have increasingly fewer instruments to develop their own social policy due to European interference in other areas. Member States are, for instance, restricted by the Economic and Monetary Union (EMU) and as a consequence they cannot develop their financial policy on an individual basis anymore.[57] Another example which shows that the Member States have less discretion to organize their Welfare States concerns the national health schemes.[58] The free movement of services (Article 49 EC-Treaty) provides patients with the possibility to travel abroad and receive treatment in another Member State, which must be reimbursed under the national health schemes.[59] In other words, the Welfare State within the EU is also indirectly arranged in a multi-level manner.

Despite these incremental convergences, the Welfare State's institutional frameworks in the Member States still differ.[60] These divergences can be traced back to the evolution of the Welfare State in the different Member States according to political science. Within this scholarship, following Esping-Andersen, different types of Welfare States in the European Community are distinguished.[61] They are

53. Alpa (n. 13 above), 134.
54. Medicus (n. 13 above), 86 et seq.
55. F.W. Scharpf, 'The viability of advanced welfare states in the international economy: vulnerabilities and options', *Journal of European Public Policy* (2000): 190-228, at 192; id., 'The European Social Model: Coping with the Challenges of Diversity', *Journal of Common Market Studies* 40 (2002): 650. Cf. W. Streeck, 'Competitive Solidarity: Rethinking the "European Social Model"', Working Paper no. 99/8 given at Max Planck Institut für Gesellschaftsforschung, MPIfG, 4.
56. *See* for instance with respect to public health: Case C-141/07 *Commission v. Germany, ECJ*, 11.09.2008; G. De Búrca, 'Towards European Welfare?', in *EU Law and the Welfare State, in search of solidarity*, ed. G. de Burcà (Oxford: OUP, 2005), 1-9.
57. A. Hemerijck, 'The Self-Transformation of the European Social Model(s)', in *Why We Need a New Welfare State*, eds G. Esping-Andersen et al. (Oxford: OUP, 2002), 176, 190 et seq.
58. *See* in this respect: G. Davies, 'The Effects of Mrs Watts trip to France on the national health service', *King's Law Journal* (2008): 158-167; V. Hatzopoulos, 'Health Law and Policy: The Impact of the EU', in *EU Law and the Welfare State, In search of solidarity*, ed. G. de Burcà (Oxford: OUP, 2005), 111-168.
59. *See* e.g., Case C-158/96 *R. Kohll v. Union des Caisses de Maladie*, ECJ 28.04.1998 [1998] ECR I-1931; Case 157/99 *Smits and Peerbooms* 12.07.2001 [2001] ECR I-5473.
60. G. Teubner, 'Legal Irritants: Good Faith in British Law or How Unifying Law Ends Up in New Divergences', *The Modern Law Review* 61 (1998): 24 et seq. However, it should be noted that Teubner discusses different types of capitalism rather than different types of the welfare state.
61. *See* for other classifications of the welfare state: Kleinman (n. 63 below), 28 et seq.

the Scandinavian, the Anglo-Saxon, Mediterranean, other continental Welfare States and the new Member States.[62] Each type of Welfare State is characterized by its own interaction between the State, the market, and civil society or the family.[63] Very generally speaking, the Anglo-Saxon system is market-biased, in the southern-European States the family is strongly emphasized, and in the Scandinavian countries the State provides welfare.[64] Moreover, in the other continental European countries, the idea is that the State should only interfere if other communities or groups such as the family or other elements of civil society fail to achieve those aims.[65] With respect to the last group, France seems to be the odd one out, since the State has a very strong and central position.[66]

When these different types of the Welfare States are considered together with mandatory rules and the notion of public policy, then the interaction between the State and the market within each type of Welfare State is also reflected in the use of mandatory rules and the notion of public policy. For instance, within English law, public policy is a notion that is not very frequently used in contrast to France. In common law it is in principle left to the market to solve issues and only in exceptional situations, the State will interfere, whereas within the French model the State is present. This is also reflected in the French legal system. For instance, a distinction is made between the *ordre public classique* and *contemporain*, as discussed above. By means of the latter the French State interferes in contractual relationships, for instance, to protect weaker parties.

It is submitted that a model is a simplification of reality and does not do justice to all the characteristics of each Member State.[67] However, when it is accepted that there are different types of Welfare States which are characterized by their own interaction between the market, the State, and civil society or the family and secondly, that national contract law is part of the institutional framework of the market and consequently of the national Welfare State, then harmonization of contract law, one of the institutional framework's elements, will have consequences for the Welfare State on a national level or even may create frictions

62. G. Esping-Andersen, *The Three Worlds of Welfare Capitalism* (Cambridge: Polity Press, 1990), 26 et seq. Cf. F.W. Scharpf, 'Legimitate Diversity: The New Challenge of European Integration', in *The State of the European Union, Law, Politics and Society*, eds T.A. Börzel & R.A. Cichowski, vol. 6 (Oxford: OUP, 2003), 79-104. Cf. Esping-Andersen, *Social Foundations of Postindustrial Economies* (Oxford: OUP, 1999), 5.
63. Esping-Andersen, 'Towards the Good Society, Once Again?', in *Why We Need a New Welfare State*, eds G. Esping-Andersen et al. (Oxford: OUP, 2002), 11 et seq. Esping-Andersen refers to the family, whereas other authors also refer to civil society; *see* M. Kleinman, *A European Welfare State*? (New York: Palgrave, 2002), 37.
64. Esping-Andersen, *Social Foundations of Postindustrials Economies* (n. 62 above), 5. Cf. F.W. Scharpf, 'Introduction: the problem-solving capacity of multi-level governance', *Journal of European Public Policy* 4 (1997): 530.
65. Kleinman (n. 63 above), 37.
66. *Ibid.*, 40. *See also* V.A. Schmidt, *The Futures of European capitalism* (Oxford: OUP, 2002), 109. It should be noted though, that she deals with different types of capitalism rather than with different types of the welfare state.
67. Scharpf (n. 55 above), 192.

on a national level.[68] This discussion raises the question about to what extent it is possible to harmonize contract law without harmonizing the European social model.[69]

4. CONCLUSIONS

The rules concerning mandatory rules and public policy as included in the DCFR enhance a multi-level approach, since they refer to mandatory rules which may be either national or European. Moreover, the rule concerning public policy refers to fundamental principles recognized as such in the Member States of the EU. From the text itself, it is not self-evident whether it concerns merely principles which are recognized at large within the EU or whether it also may concern fundamental principles which are merely recognized in one Member State.

The application of mandatory rules and the notion of public policy also has another dimension which has a multi-level character as well. It concerns the role of national contract law within the Member States and in particular within the national Welfare States. Contract law and the market belong to the institutional framework of the Welfare State. From political science literature it follows that various types of Welfare States can still be distinguished within the EU, even though convergence is taking place. Each type is characterized by its own interaction between the market, the State, and civil society or the family. Moreover, in general, the Welfare State and social policy still belong to the competence of the Member States. When one of the elements of the Welfare State's institutional framework is harmonized on a European level, it has consequences with respect to the social order within a Member State. Given that contract law plays a role within the Welfare State, this raises the question as to what extent contract law should be harmonized on a European level without having a European social order or Welfare State, or at least it raises more thoughts about such a model. Otherwise, a European social order is created in a creeping manner.

68. W. Streeck (n. 55 above), 4. Cf. Teubner (n. 60 above), 11-32.
69. Cf. Lurger (n. 43 above), 192 et seq.

Part Three

Consumer Protection

Chapter 8

Much Ado About (Almost) Nothing: The Integration of the So-Called 'Consumer Acquis' in the Draft Common Frame of Reference

Brigitta Lurger

1. THE DCFR AND THE EUROPEAN CONSUMERS' RESULTING QUESTIONS

The history of the so-called 'CFR' or DCFR in the area of European Contract law does not have to be repeated here.[1] When looking at the DCFR 'Interim Outline

1. *See* instead C. von Bar, E. Clive & H. Schulte-Nölke (eds), *Principles. Definitions and Model Rules of European Private Law. Draft Common Frame of Reference (DCFR)*, Interim Outline Edition (München: Sellier, 2008), 29 et seq.; M. Hesselink, *CFR & Social Justice* (München: Sellier, 2008), Ch. 2; B. Lurger, 'The Common Frame of Reference/Optional Code and the Various Understandings of Social Justice in Europe', in *Private Law and the Many Cultures of Europe*, eds T. Wilhelmsson, E. Paunio & A. Pohjolainen (Netherlands: Kluwer International, 2007), 177 et seq.; R. Schulze, 'The Academic Draft of the CFR and the EC Contract Law', in *Common Frame of Reference and Existing EC Contract Law*, ed. R. Schulze (München: Sellier, 2008), 3, 5 et seq.; H. Beale, 'The Future of the Common Frame of Reference', *European Review of Contract Law* 3 (2007): 257; N. Reich, 'A Common Frame of Reference (CFR) – Ghost or Host for Integration?', ZERP discussion paper 2006 no. 7, 6; N. Reich, 'Der Common Frame of Reference und Sonderprivatrechte im "Europäischen Vertragsrecht"', *Zeitschrift für Europäisches Privatrecht* (2007): 161, 162 et seq.; T. Pfeiffer, 'Methodik der Privatrechtsangleichung in der

Alessandro Somma, *The Politics of the Draft Common Frame of Reference*, pp. 131-150.

Edition' published in January 2008,[2] as formulated by the SGECC and the Acquis Group (Research Group on EC Private Law), from a consumer's perspective it might, however, be helpful to mention once again that the whole project started off as a large academic codification project covering almost all areas of 'patrimonial' private law (contract law, tort law, unjust enrichment, movable property, and so forth). This project was welcomed and supported by the European Parliament[3] and initially also by the Commission which concluded an FP 6 Contract with the researchers (SGECC, Acquis Group and others) in 2005, thus providing them with substantial financial support until the completion of their work in 2009 (CoPECL Network of Excellence).[4]

On the other hand, the policy of the DG Health and Consumer Protection (DG SANCO) of the Commission gradually moved in a position that was quite in opposition to the tasks that had to be performed under the FP 6 project: it kept repeating that its main purpose was little more than improving the so-called 'Consumer Acquis' (a narrow set of eight particular EC directives leaving out a lot of other directives and regulations also shaping consumer contract law).[5] It intended in particular to render it more 'coherent' with the help of a non-binding – or only inter-institutionally binding – 'Common Frame of Reference'.[6] No 'European

---

EU. Der gemeinsame Referenzrahmen zum europäischen Vertragsrecht', *Archiv für die Civilistische Praxis* 208 (2008): 227, 228 et seq.; W. Ernst, 'Der, Common Frame of Reference' aus juristischer Sicht', *Archiv für die Civilistische Praxis* 208 (2008): 248, 249 et seq.; H. Eidenmüller et al., 'Der Gemeinsame Referenzrahmen für das Europäische Privatrecht', *Juristenzeitung* (2008): 529 et seq.; N. Jansen & R. Zimmermann, 'Grundregeln des bestehenden Gemeinschaftsprivatrechts', *Juristenzeitung* (2007): 1113-1115; id., 'Restating the *Acquis Communautaire*? A Critical Examination of the Principles of the Existing EC Contract Law', *Modern Law Review* 71 (2008): 505 et seq.; O. Remien, 'Zweck, Inhalt, Anwendungsbereich und Rechtswirkung des Gemeinsamen Referenzrahmens: Eine erste Analyse des Standpunktes des Justizministerrates vom 18.4.2008', *Zeitschrift für Gemeinschaftsprivatrecht* (2008): 124.

2. C. von Bar, E. Clive & H. Schulte-Nölke (eds), *Principles. Definitions and Model Rules of European Private Law. Draft Common Frame of Reference (DCFR)*, Interim Outline Edition (München: Sellier, 2008).
3. *See* Lurger (n. 1 above), 177-178.
4. The *Common Principles of European Contract Law* (CoPECL), 'Network of Excellence' was established under the Sixth Framework Programme for Research and Technological Development (Decision No. 1513/2002/EC, OJ L 232, 29.8.2002, 1).
5. Doorstep Selling Directive (85/577); Package Travel Directive (90/314); Unfair Contract Terms Directive (93/13); Timeshare Directive (94/47); Distance Selling Directive (97/7); Price Indication Directive (98/6); Injunctions Directive (98/27); Consumer Sales Directive (99/44). For the other regulations and directives concerning consumer contracts, but as yet excluded by the Commission *see* Section 4.1. below.
6. Communication from the Commission to the European Parliament and the Council – A more coherent European contract law – An action plan, 12 Feb. 2003, COM (2003) 68 final; Communication from the Commission to the European Parliament and the Council, European Contract Law and the revision of the *acquis*: the way forward, 11 Oct. 2004, COM (2004) 651 final; First Annual Progress Report on European Contract Law and the Acquis Review, 23 Sep. 2005, COM (2005) 456 final; Green Paper on the Review of the Consumer Acquis, 8 Feb. 2007, COM (2006) 744 final; Second Progress Report on the Common Frame of Reference, 25 Jul. 2007, COM (2007) 447 final.

Contract Code' or even 'Civil Code' would be realized. The only thing the DG SANCO could imagine beyond such improvement measures in the consumer law area was the so-called 'optional horizontal instrument'. This optional instrument was envisaged to provide a set of contract law rules that could be chosen by the parties, even in consumer (business-to-consumer (b2c)) contracts.[7]

On 18 April 2008, the Council adopted a report that narrowed the project down even more:[8] the future CFR (which will be developed out of the DCFR by the Commission) shall be a 'better law making tool' used on a facultative basis by Community law makers. No complete set of contract law rules that could be used as an 'optional instrument' will be developed. The CFR will cover general issues of contract law and consumer contract law (limited to the eight directives = 'Acquis') and nothing more.[9] The 'better law making tool' (CFR) will not be binding in any respect (not even inter-institutionally). Its main purpose will be to serve the process of the revision of the 'Acquis'.

In some of its recent documents and press releases, the DG SANCO revealed its plans to formulate a 'Framework Directive on Consumer Contractual Rights' that will harmonize certain key elements of consumer contract law. The directive shall merge some of the existing EC consumer directives (The Doorstep Selling Directive (85/577), Unfair Contract Terms Directive (93/13); Distance Selling Directive (97/7) and the Consumer Sales Directive (99/44)) into 'one fully harmonized coherent legislative instrument'.[10] The DG SANCO understands this framework directive as the main outcome of the 'Acquis' revision process.[11] Some sector-specific directives, like the current Consumer Credit Directive and the Package Travel Directive may, in addition, eventually be amended.

On 8 October 2008, the Commission finally issued its Proposal for a 'Directive on Consumer Contractual Rights'.[12] Its content will be discussed below together with the respective consumer protection devices in the DCFR (see Section 4.2). Surprisingly enough, the proposal states that no external expert knowledge was

---

7. Lurger (n. 1 above), 177, 180 et seq.; J. Rutgers, 'An Optional Instrument and Social Dumping', *European Review of Contract Law* 2 (2006): 199 et seq.; Hesselink (n. 1 above), Ch. 2.2.; S. Leible, 'Was tun mit dem Gemeinsamen Referenzrahmen für das Europäische Vertragsrecht? – Plädoyer für ein optionales Instrument', *Betriebs-Berater* (2008): 1469; H. Schulte-Nölke, 'EC Law on the Formation of Contract – from the Common Frame of Reference to the "Blue Button" ', *European Review of Contract Law* 3 (2007): 332; H. Beale, 'The Future of the Common Frame of Reference', *European Review of Contract Law* 3 (2007): 257, 269 et seq.
8. Council of the European Union, 3 Mar. 2008, 6718/08 JUSTCIV 30 CONSOM 24; Rat der Europäischen Union, Pressemitteilung vom 18 Apr. 2008, 8397/08 (Presse 96); Remien (n. 1 above), 124.
9. The published DCFR of 2008 also contains rules for particular types of contracts, unjustified enrichment, torts, *negotiorum gestio*, and a general law of obligations. An expanded 2009 edition will additionally contain rules on movable property, proprietary security rights, and trusts.
10. M. Kuneva, 'Opening Speech at the Bi-Annual Meeting of ECTAA' (Sofia 27 May 2008), SPEECH/08; Consumers: Commission sets out five priorities for consumer policy in a digital age, press release, 20 Jun. 2008, IP/08/979.
11. Green Paper on the Review of the Consumer Acquis, 8 Feb. 2007, COM (2006) 744 final.
12. COM (2008) 614 final.

needed. The Acquis Group Principles (AcqP)[13] and the resulting DCFR consumer protection rules[14] are not mentioned at all. The proposal's main arguments for the positive effects of the new directive are derived from the directive's nature as a maximum harmonization instrument:[15] the simplification and radical unification of legal rules shall considerably lower the costs for the trade sector all over Europe. But, for the consumer, it will also considerably lower the standard of protection as compared to the status quo in many Member States:[16] a fact that is not mentioned by the proposal.

As some authors already remarked:[17] was this not 'Much Ado' about relatively small results? There is a certain disproportionality to be observed between the years, if not decades, of man/woman/power that have been invested by so many researchers all over Europe[18] in the elaboration of a comprehensive set of black-letter rules, comments, and comparative notes in the areas of contract law, torts, unjust enrichment, trust, and property law, already before and recently under the FP 6 project of the Commission, and the final outcome: some changes in already existing consumer directives in the area of contract law – mainly situated in a proposal for a directive that does not even mention the DCFR, the Commission's network project on European Contract law (CoPECL) or the Acquis Group.

From the perspective of the European consumer, the most important question is: what have all these investments done to my legal situation as a consumer or as an EU citizen? Will I be better off as a consequence of the use of the future CFR/present DCFR? Is this huge investment in me – as a consumer and citizen – equaled by its positive effects on my life, my chances, my welfare, or well-being?

---

13. H. Schulte-Nölke, C. Twigg-Flesner & M. Ebers (eds), *EC Consumer Law Compendium. The Consumer Acquis and Its Transposition in the Member States* (München: Sellier, 2008); Research Group on the Existing EC Private Law (Acquis Group) (eds), *Principles of the Existing EC Contract Law (Acquis Principles), Contract I: Pre-contractual Obligations, Conclusion of Contract, Unfair Terms* (München: Sellier, 2007); id., *Contract II: Performance, Non-performance, Remedies* (München: Sellier, 2008).
14. For a thorough comparison of the AcqP and the respective DCFR rules *see* C. Twigg-Flessner, 'Pre-contractual duties – from the Acquis to the Common Frame of Reference', in *Common Frame of Reference and Existing EC Contract Law*, ed. R. Schulze (München: Sellier, 2008), 97 et seq.
15. For the Commission's declared belief in maximum harmonization see the Commission's Consumer Policy Strategy 2002-2006, COM (2002) 208 final, 12; EU Consumer Policy Strategy 2007-2013: Empowering consumers, enhancing their welfare, effectively protecting them, COM (2007) 99 final, 7.
16. For justified critique of maximum harmonization in consumer law *see* Reich (n. 1 above), 171 et seq.; *ibid.*, 33 et seq.; Lurger (n. 1 above), 177, 185 et seq. Against maximum harmonization with respect to the DCFR consumer protection rules: Hesselink (n. 1 above), Ch. 5.1.; O. Lando, 'Liberal, Social and "Ethical" Justice in European Contract Law', *Common Market Law Review* 43 (2006), 817, 827.
17. J. Smits, 'The Draft Common Frame of Reference for a European Private Law: Fit for Purpose?', *Maastricht Journal of European and Comparative Law* 15 (2008): 145-146; Remien (n. 1 above), 124-127; Ernst (n. 1 above), 248, 275 et seq.
18. von Bar, Clive & Schulte-Nölke (eds) (n. 2 above), 41 et seq.

2. COMPETENCES AND OTHER FORMAL ISSUES

What seems positive in the DCFR is the integration of consumer protection rules into general contract law.[19] Whereas in the Lando Principles of European Contract Law (PECL) and in former PEL drafts of the SGECC the consumer was practically non-existent, the SGECC (providing about 90% of the DCFR rules) and the Acquis Group were now asked by the Commission to merge their draft rules.[20] The integration of the two sets of rules took place at the very last minute before the publication of the DCFR (January 2008). This integration does not only render the contract law rules more practicable[21] and reflects the reality of contract practice,[22] but it additionally has the function of a signal relating to the underlying values of a particular set of contract law rules: consumer protection is no longer treated as the rare exception to the principle of unrestricted private autonomy, but as normality. The protection of weaker parties, in particular of consumers, is emancipated from a side issue to an important element – if not a principle – of general contract law.

While integration as such appears as an important signal and a positive step forward for consumer protection, the way the integration was carried out is far from ideal:[23] at the center of every systematic integration of consumer protection rules into general contract law you have to place a thorough examination of the particular need for protection and the effectiveness and appropriateness of the protective means employed by a certain rule. The final question of the examination should be: is the need for protection limited to contract parties that are consumers, or is it also present for business parties in similar situations? The Acquis texts and the DCFR integrated texts reveal that these examinations, which should result in evaluations, corrections, restrictions, or generalizations where necessary and appropriate, were not undertaken most of the time. The Acquis/DCFR texts strongly adhere to the original texts of the directives, in many cases generalizations or changes seem rather arbitrary.[24]

---

19. For more details on this topic *see* B. Lurger, 'The "Social" Side of Contract Law and the New Principle of Regard and Fairness', in *Towards a European Civil Code*, eds A. Hartkamp, et al., 3rd edn (Nijmegen: Ars Aequi Libri, 2004), 273, 275 et seq.; B. Lurger, 'Integration des Verbraucherrechts in das ABGB?', in *ABGB – auf dem Weg in das 3. Jahrtausend, Reformbedarf und Reform*, eds C. Fischer-Czermak & M. Schauer (Wien: Manz, 2003), 111 et seq.; B. Lurger, 'The Future of European Contract Law between Freedom of Contract, Social Justice and Market Rationality', *European Review of Contract Law* 1 (2005): 442, 454 et seq.
20. H. Micklitz, *The Visible Hand of European Regulatory Private Law*, EUI Working Paper LAW no. 2008/14, 2.
21. Every time one of the parties is a consumer, you now have to search for the particular legal instruments outside the general contract law rules which apply to your case in many Member States.
22. The high percentage of consumer contracts on the market and the daily routine of contracting between consumers and businesses.
23. Eidenmüller et al. (n. 1 above), 529, 544; N. Jansen & R. Zimmermann, 'Grundregeln des bestehenden Gemeinschaftsprivatrechts', *Juristenzeitung* (2007): 1113, 1120 et seq.
24. For details, *see* Section 4.2. below.

From the point of view of EU competences, the integration approach encounters some problems, as well. The EC's power to regulate contract law as a whole is unclear and disputed.[25] If it exists at all, it is certainly a competence shared between the EC and the Member States. As confirmed by the ECJ Tobacco Advertising decision,[26] the Community legislature enjoys no general power to regulate the internal market.[27] The subsidiarity principle (Article 5 EC) has to be observed. Existing legislative measures in contract law are limited to particular vertical fields of regulation and, in the main, they provide only a minimum level of protection which can be raised by national laws. The CFR is conceived as a vague and flexible creature: a non-binding soft law, a framework to refer to. The 'optional instrument' has been buried.[28] Such a CFR will not constitute a problem for restricted EC competences.

The situation is considerably different for the Commission's recent Proposal for a 'Directive on Consumer Contractual Rights'[29] and the idea of a further codification of European contract law on the basis of the DCFR integration rules. What makes the proposed directive problematic is its maximum harmonization nature.[30] This approach will have a negative impact on the level of consumer protection in the Member States, which in turn is a violation of Article 95 paragraph 3 and Article 153 EC, binding the EU to ensure a high level of consumer protection. The directive will harmonize rather 'horizontal' areas of contract law, namely issues not restricted to particular contract types, and it will deprive Member States of their power to regulate these areas completely. Whether such a sharp intrusion into the competences of the Member States for the sake of a better functioning of the Internal Market may be justified under the subsidiarity principle of Article 5 EC is doubtful. Such a change of policy should not be underestimated in its weight and consequences, it must be preceded by (a thorough academic and above all) a comprehensive *political* debate which has not been initiated by the Commission so far.[31]

---

25. S. Weatherill, 'Recent Developments in the Law Governing the Free Movement of Goods in the EC's Internal Market', *European Review of Contract Law* 2 (2006): 90, 100 et seq., with further references; N. Reich, 'A European Contract Law, or an EU Contract Law Regulation for Consumers?', *Journal of Consumer Policy* 28 (2005): 383; id. (n. 1 above), 172 et seq.; E. Truilhé-Marengo, 'Towards a European Law of Contracts', *European Law Journal* 10 (2004): 463, 476 et seq.; B. Lurger, *Grundfragen der Vereinheitlichung des Vertragsrechts in der Europäischen Union* (Wien. New York: Springer, 2002), 104 et seq.
26. *Ibid.*
27. Weatherill (n. 25 above), 104 et seq.
28. Report of the Council: Council of the European Union, 3 Mar. 2008, 6718/08 JUSTCIV 30 CONSOM 24; Rat der Europäischen Union, Pressemitteilung vom 18 Apr. 2008, 8397/08 (Presse 96); Remien (n. 1 above), 124.
29. COM (2008) 614 final.
30. For justified critique of maximum harmonization in consumer law, *see* Reich (n. 1 above), 33 et seq.; Lurger (n. 1 above), 185 et seq.; against maximum harmonization with respect to the DCFR consumer protection rules: Hesselink (n. 1 above), Ch. 5.1.; Lando (n. 16 above), 817, 827.
31. G. Kathrein, 'Europäisches Vertragsrecht – Österreichische Haltung', in *Common Frame of Reference and Existing EC Contract Law*, ed. R. Schulze (München: Sellier 2008), 285, 290; Lurger (n. 1 above), 185 et seq.

Further harmonization of contract law in the sense of the DCFR integration approach – beyond the now practised consumer contract approach – would not only encounter competence problems, but – what appears much more serious to me – also the problem of a lacking common understanding among the Member States on the guiding values and principles of contract law, or in particular of a 'European' contract law (see also Section 3 below).[32]

The evaluation of the quality and impact of the consumer protection rules formulated in the DCFR strongly depends on the future nature of the (D)CFR:[33] how are its rules meant? How are they to be implemented or otherwise used? Without assuming some kind of impact on consumer contract law and thus the lives of consumers, the attempt of an evaluation is senseless from the outset: if the DCFR will be ignored, a legal nothing, the non-effect on consumers is obvious.

As evidenced by the Commission's recent proposal for a 'Directive on Consumer Contractual Rights',[34] at least in the area of consumer contract law, the (D)CFR is likely to be used as a model, or at least a source of inspiration for the EU legislator. And: where the legislator – or rather the Commission – takes over a text from the (D)CFR, it will have the intention to present it as a maximum harmonization instrument. It is presently still unknown whether the Commission will find the necessary support for its maximum harmonization plans. There is still hope that it will not. The following evaluation of the DCFR consumer rules will, therefore, proceed from the assumption that the EU legislator will adopt texts of the DCFR in its legislative instruments (directives, regulations), whether horizontal or vertical, punctual or comprehensive, and will determine them as either maximum or minimum harmonization.

3. THE LEVEL OF PRINCIPLES AND VALUES

The codification project of the SGECC and also the FP 6 Project on Common Principles of European Contract law (CoPECL)[35] suffer from the constant denial and down-playing of the political dimensions of contract law. This holds true for the Commission as well as for the researchers involved. A rather neutral and technical so-called 'academic CFR' (= DCFR) shall be turned into a so-called 'political CFR' by the Commission and other EU institutions.[36] But how can a text that contained no political aspects from the outset suddenly become a political text once it is simply used as a model or source of inspiration by the European legislator? Obviously, this miracle will never occur. Every set of contract law rules (once in force) is political in so far as it shapes our markets and societies, changing

32. Lurger (n. 1 above), 186 et seq.; id. (n. 19 above), 442, 447 et seq.
33. R. Sefton-Green, 'The DCFR, the *Avant-projet Catala* and French Legal Scholars: A Story of Cat and Mouse?', *Edinburgh Law Review* 12 (2008): 351, 361.
34. COM (2008) 614 final.
35. *See* Section 1 above.
36. von Bar, Clive & Schulte-Nölke (eds) (n. 1 above), 5-19.

them in one or the other direction. Different rules support different views of our societies: more freedom of contract or more restrictions, more regard for the counter-party or more egotism, more trust or more caution? Will only the 'fittest' survive, or will the State help the weaker parties, and in what manner?

It has been amply explained in literature that the illusion of academic neutrality is an as inappropriate concept for European contract law as is the narrow goal of market functionalism.[37] In all its communications on European contract law and on the revision of the Acquis,[38] the Commission concentrates on the functioning of the Internal Market more than on any other goal.[39] Harmonized consumer protection rules first and foremost have to contribute to market functioning. That they shall also realize a certain concept of justice and fairness in contract law is not mentioned at all. Consumers are not perceived as citizens whose lives are – amongst others – shaped by contract law rules, but simply as demand factors on cross-border and national markets.[40] The EC's narrow market-oriented approach fundamentally differs from the continental private legal orders which are built on more comprehensive models of social justice which also include aspects of distributive justice.[41] This dominance of the economic efficiency doctrine and of a 'market access justice' has also been explained as an 'Americanization' of European private law which goes along with a process of 'de-'politization' of law making.[42]

During the whole process of preparation of the DCFR texts, which took more than one decade, the underlying principles, values and policy choices of the proposed rules were mainly swept under the carpet. Officially the endeavour was non-political, technical, neutral, and academic. This also explains why the DCFR

---

37. Study Group on Social Justice in European Private Law, 'Social Justice in European Contract Law: A Manifesto', *European Law Journal* (2004): 653 et seq.; Lurger (n. 32 above), 442-447 et seq.; C. Schmid, 'The Instrumentalist Conception of the Acquis Communautaire in Consumer Law and its Implications on a European Contract Law Code', *European Review of Contract Law* 1 (2005): 211, 226; M. Hesselink, 'The Politics of a European Civil Code', *European Law Journal* (2004): 675 et seq.; O. Lando, 'The Structure and the Legal Values of the Common Frame of Reference', *European Review of Contract Law* 3 (2007): 245, 251; id. (n. 16 above), 817, 822; R. Sefton-Green, 'Social Justice and European Identity in European Contract Law', *European Review of Contract Law* 2 (2006): 275, 278; all with references to many others. Eidenmüller et al. (n. 1 above), 529, 534 also explain that the DCFR as almost every 'Gesetzeswerk' is not merely technical, but the expression of concrete value concepts, that the underlying legal political goals matter.
38. *See* the references in Chapter 1, footnote 6, as well as the Commission's Consumer Policy Strategy 2002-2006, COM (2002) 208 final, 12; EU Consumer Policy Strategy 2007-2013: Empowering consumers, enhancing their welfare, effectively protecting them, COM (2007) 99 final, 7.
39. Schmid (n. 37 above), 211 et seq.; Lurger (n. 1 above), 181 et seq.
40. M. Hesselink, 'European Contract Law: A Matter of Consumer Protection, Citizenship, or Justice?', *European Review of Private Law* (2007): 323, 328 et seq.
41. H. Micklitz, 'The Visible Hand of European Regulatory Private Law', EUI Working Paper LAW no. 2008/14, 9; Lurger (n. 25 above), 370 et seq.; id. (n. 19 above), 464 et seq.; id. (n. 1 above), 192.
42. Micklitz, *ibid.*, 8 et seq., 14.

contract law excludes almost all contracts that are of real importance for the lives of consumers (at least more important than distance selling and timesharing): consumer credit, other financial services, tenancy, services of public interest (like the postal service, public transport, energy and telecommunications), and labour contracts.[43] It does not come as a surprise that in these areas every attempt to pretend political neutrality would be ridiculous.

However, the academic groups drafting the DCFR were asked by the Commission to present not only definitions and model rules, but also 'principles' that would reflect its underlying values.[44] In the introduction of the DCFR interim outline edition 2008, the authors (von Bar, Clive, Beale and Schulte-Nölke) express 'fundamental principles' as 'core aims' of European private law and contract law:[45] 'justice, freedom, protection of human rights, economic welfare, solidarity and social responsibility'. Specific European aims are the 'promotion of the Internal Market' and the 'preservation of cultural and linguistic plurality'. A set of 'formal aims' includes 'rationality, legal certainty, predictability and efficiency'.[46] In the closer description of those aims or values, the authors seem to offer something for everyone: 'corrective justice' will be most important, but 'distributive justice' will sometimes also play a role.[47] Freedom of contract is a basic value of contract law, but it will have to be restricted where this seems justified and proportionate or where there is an unacceptable discrimination.[48] The general clause of good faith[49] is seen as an expression of the principle of solidarity but also as the standard of 'good commercial practice'.[50]

The considerable vagueness of these principles leaves the reader without any clear idea where the DCFR really stands.[51] The DCFR catalogue of values is certainly a step forward considering the narrow set of values the Commission has previously been operating within this context: the enumeration of principles seems quite comprehensive, they are not restricted to the functioning of the Internal Market; there seems to be no – at least no massive – (anachronistic) neo-liberal tendency to overestimate the principle of freedom of contract.[52]

However, the 'fundamental principles'/'core aims' were formulated by the authors after most of the texts of the DCFR had already been drafted by the various academic groups and sub-groups. It is, therefore, not surprising that these texts sometimes reveal underlying value choices that are not predicted or described by

43. *See also* Section 4.1. below.
44. von Bar, Clive & Schulte-Nölke (eds) (n. 1 above), 8 et seq., Introduction, 10 et seq.
45. *Ibid.*, 12 et seq., Introduction, 19.
46. *Ibid.*, 13, Introduction, 22.
47. *Ibid.*, 14, Introduction, 24.
48. *Ibid.*, 14 et seq., Introduction, 25 et seq.
49. *See also* Section 4.2. below.
50. *Ibid.*, 17, Introduction, 32 et seq.
51. Eidenmüller et al. (n. 1 above), 535 call the explanations concerning the 'core aims', practically worthless'. Hesselink (n. 1 above), Ch. 8.1, on the contrary, thinks that they will play an important role in interpreting the DCFR rules.
52. Hesselink (n. 1 above), Ch. 8.3; Eidenmüller et al. (n. 51 above), 537, 549 are, however, wrong when they conclude that the DCFR contains a 'massive reduction of private autonomy'.

the introduction. These value choices rather frequently depend on the composition of the groups of researchers that have drafted the respective books, parts, or chapters of the DCFR. One example is the treatment of the principle of freedom of contract in the black-letter text in relation to the solidarity principle:

(a) Solidarity, regard and fairness, on one hand, and freedom of contract, on the other, are the often conflicting core values of contemporary contract law. None of the two principles is hierarchically superior to the other.[53] But in the general contract law rules of the DCFR only 'party autonomy' (contractual freedom) is mentioned as an important principle in the black-letter text (Article II.-1:102), not the principle of regard and fairness. Article II.-1:102(2) only states that the freedom of contract may be restricted by the rules on good faith and fair dealing and by other mandatory rules. That these rules are the expression of an independent principle itself is left in the dark.
(b) Even though the introduction acknowledges that restrictions of freedom of contract may be necessary not only to protect consumers, but also to protect small businesses that lack expertise in a certain field,[54] the DCFR general contract law rules (Book II) limit most of their mandatory protection to consumers.[55] As compared to the PECL[56] and to the Acquis Principles[57] the DCFR black-letter rules are in many aspects more liberal and less protective. Some parts of Book IV (specific contracts), however, seem to be very concerned about weaker (business) parties, like commercial agents, franchisees, distributors, and clients of service providers and realize the principle of contractual solidarity to a much larger extent than the general contract law rules in Book II.

The DCFR's approach to consumer protection on the level of principles must, therefore, be summarized as being rather inarticulate or undecided: the authors of the introduction and its catalogue of 'core aims' (von Bar, Beale, Clive, Schulte-Nölke) are not identical with the authors of the black-letter rules of the DCFR. The former seem to be torn between the Commission's narrow liberal concept of market functionalism and the neo-liberal tendencies of a number of members of the SGECC, on one hand, and academic and political voices, on the other hand, that point out that contemporary contract law in most Member States enshrines a comprehensive notion of justice, including the principle of solidarity and the protection of human rights. The authors of the introduction, thus, mention all existing principles without giving any clear indication in which direction a modern future European contract law would have to go. Contrary to the Commission's narrow

53. B. Lurger, *Grundfragen der Vereinheitlichung des Vertragsrechts in der Europäischen Union* (Wien New York: Springer, 2002), 370 et seq.; id. (n. 19 above), 452; id. (n. 1 above), 273, 287 et seq.; *ibid.*, 177, 188; Hesselink (n. 1 above), Ch. 8.3 a 8.10.
54. Bar, Clive & Schulte-Nölke (eds) (n. 1 above), 15, Introduction, 25, 27.
55. Hesselink (n. 1 above), Ch. 5.3.
56. Lando (n. 37 above), 245, 251 et seq.
57. *See* the rule by rule comparisons by Twigg-Flesner et al. (n. 14 above), 97 et seq.

plans to use the (D)CFR (for the revision of the Consumer Acquis), about 90% of DCFR rules stemming from the SGECC were not drafted with the aim of protecting consumers or weaker parties (with some exceptions in Book IV). In the SGECC, political discussions were generally avoided, the diverging views of the Member States' legal systems on the core values of contract law were not bridged by the provision of a unified coherent system of policy choices for a European contract law.

In order to find out whether the DCFR contains firm support of consumer interests or rather a tendency to lower the general standard of protection for consumers in favour of the interests of businesses (or neither), one will have to look at the particular black-letter rules themselves.

4. PARTICULAR DCFR RULES

4.1. Absent Rules

What is striking is that the EU Commission, the Acquis Group, and finally the drafters of the DCFR consumer provisions reduced their project and endeavours from the very beginning to eight EC consumer protection directives: the Doorstep Selling Directive (85/577); the Package Travel Directive (90/314); the Unfair Contract Terms Directive (93/13); the Timeshare Directive (94/47); the Distance Selling Directive (97/7); the Price Indication Directive (98/6); the Injunctions Directive (98/27) and the Consumer Sales Directive (99/44). Some of them – the Package Travel, Timesharing, Injunctions, and Price Indication Directives – even had little or no impact on the content of the DCFR. What was finally left in the project and the DCFR were the same four directives that are dealt with in the recent Commission Proposal for a 'Directive on Consumer Contractual Rights':[58] Doorstep Selling, Distance Selling, Unfair Contract Terms, and Consumer Sales Directives.

It is hard to find a reasonable justification for that extreme restriction. It is neither true that EC law covers only these areas of consumer law, nor that these directives are of particular importance for the protection of consumers as compared to other EC law. On the contrary: the following list will show that the majority of EC consumer law can be found outside the areas covered by the DCFR and that especially areas that are of vital importance for consumers are not dealt with in the DCFR or the related Commission project on consumer law.

What is missing in the DCFR: financial services (consumer protection on financial and capital markets), consumer credits, tenancy, payment systems, funds transfers, protection of consumers granting personal or real security in favour of another person as debtor, e-commerce (in part in the DCFR), public (network) services (electricity, gas, water, public transport, postal services, and telecommunication), regulation of services, and labour law. The Commission and the DCFR

58. COM (2008) 614 final.

also failed to see that many EC private law rules outside the area of contract law have a considerable impact on consumers: human rights, EC antitrust law (Articles 81, 82 ET) and block exemption regulations, public procurement law, the Unfair Commercial Practices Directive (2005/29), the protection of intellectual property rights, product safety, and food safety law.

This leads me to conclude that the Commission's declared commitment to the improvement of consumer protection in the EU – as found in its communications related to the contract law project[59] – must be read with caution. This commitment was obviously not very strong, at least less strong than its commitment to other goals: particularly the protection of the interests of businesses engaging in cross-border trade and the improvement of the functioning of the Internal Market (whatever this may mean in the eyes of the Commission).

The DCFR does not mention the controversial standard ('Verbraucherleitbild') of the 'average consumer, who is reasonably well informed and reasonably observant and circumspect'. This concept has been justifiably criticized for its failure to protect the most vulnerable consumers, for its disregard of the cultural differences that exist in the Member States, and for its obvious effect of lowering the standards of protection in many Member States.[60] This silence, however, does not necessarily mean that the DCFR relies on a different or better concept. Mere silence cannot be interpreted as a clear departure from EC law's well known 'average consumer'. The DCFR simply leaves open which role model a court or lawyer should use when interpreting the DCFR consumer protection rules. And there is no indication that the Commission when making use of the (D)CFR rules will modify the present consumer role model; it is rather likely that it will adhere to it, as before.

4.2. Present Rules

The Commission's and the Acquis Group's plans to render the above mentioned eight consumer protection directives ('Acquis')[61] more coherent were mainly based on the idea that contradictions and incoherencies could be eliminated by the use of principles that somehow already exist in the 'Acquis'. The Acquis Group's attempt to partly *generalize* the existing rules, the results of which

59. *See* the references in Chapter 1, footnote 6, as well as the Commission's Consumer Policy Strategy 2002-2006, COM (2002) 208 final; EU Consumer Policy Strategy 2007-2013: Empowering consumers, enhancing their welfare, effectively protecting them, COM (2007) 99 final.
60. Lurger (n. 1 above), 193; B. Lurger & S. Augenhofer, *Österreichisches und Europäisches Konsumentenschutzrecht*, 2nd edn (Wien, New York: Springer, 2008), 43 et seq.; T. Wilhelmsson, 'The European Average Consumer – A Legal Fiction?', in *Private Law and the Many Cultures of Europe*, eds T. Wilhelmsson, E. Paunio & A. Pohjolainen (Netherlands: Kluwer International, 2007), 243 et seq.; H. Micklitz, *The Visible Hand of European Regulatory Private Law*, EUI Working Paper LAW no. 2008/14, 7; Hesselink (n. 1 above), Ch. 5.1.
61. For a list *see* Section 4.1.

were later incorporated into the DCFR, encountered serious criticism.[62] And indeed, any generalization of a particular rule in the sense of an extension of its scope of application to additional cases implies a policy choice and a change of law. This step cannot be said to lie already in the present 'Acquis'.

However, the authors of the AcqP do not explain where the basis for their 'generalizations' really lies: unlike the SGECC, the Acquis Group never undertook comparative research to gather information about the autonomous contract law rules of the Member States outside the directives, and thus could not use these rules as a basis for their Principles. Another possible basis for their proposals would be a critical evaluation of the existing EC rules resulting in amended rules that cure the discovered defects. As explained in Section 2, the required examination of the need for protection, the appropriateness of the means, and the justification for the restriction of a particular rule to the class of consumers hardly can be found. The proposed rules often adhere very closely to their originals in the directives and reproduce, for instance, every detail of the lists of exemptions from the Doorstep and the Distance Selling Directives, even though many of the exemptions seem to lack a reasonable justification.

The notions of *consumer* and *business* can be found in the list of definitions in Annex I of the DCFR.[63] As in present EC law, consumers can only be natural persons. In the consumer definition, the word 'primarily' in front of 'for purposes which are not related to his or her trade, business or profession' extends the notion beyond the existing EC law notions (dual use cases).[64] In the definition of business, the 'primarily' is lacking. Does this mean that it may not be used here? If so, a third category of actors would have been created: persons primarily acting for business purposes would neither qualify as businesses nor as consumers. The word 'self-employed' in the business definition excludes persons who are employees. If these persons act for the purposes of their profession (primarily) and not primarily for non-business purposes, they are also excluded from the consumer definition and belong to a third category as well.[65]

The recently proposed 'Directive on Consumer Contractual Rights'[66] in its respective definitions (Article 2(1) and (2)), however, has dropped the two problematic words 'primarily' and 'self-employed'. The negative message for consumers is that, thus, employees contracting for purposes of their job, but in their own name, seem to be part of the notion of business, and not – as presently in many Member States – of the consumer notion.

62. T. Wilhelmsson, 'The Contract Law *Acquis*: Towards More Coherence Through Generalisation?', in *4th European Jurist's Forum* (Wien: Manz, 2008), 111 et seq.; Eidenmüller et al. (n. 1 above), 529, 533, 544 et seq.; Jansen & Zimmermann (n. 1 above), 1113, 1117 et seq. In defense of the AcqP: F. Zoll, 'Die Grundregeln der Acquis-Gruppe im Spannungsverhätnis zwischen acquis commun und acquis communautaire', *Gemeinschaftsprivatrecht* (2008): 106 et seq.
63. von Bar, Clive & Schulte-Nölke (eds) (n. 1 above), 328, 329.
64. ECJ 20 Jan. 2005, case C-464/01, ECR 2005, I-439 (*Gruber/Bay Wa AG*).
65. Eidenmüller et al. (n. 1 above), 548.
66. COM (2008) 614 final.

The notion of *good faith and fair dealing* is used many times in the DCFR.[67] It is, however, not defined in Annex I.[68] The general duty to cooperate in the performance of a contract is found in Article III-1:104 DCFR. It is accompanied by duties to cooperate in particular contracts.[69] Duties to act in good faith and to cooperate are of particular importance for the protection of the interests of consumers, but they are also relevant on a more general level: they are an expression of the principle of solidarity (regard and fairness) which sometimes conflicts with the principle of private autonomy.[70] Or as Ole Lando described it: 'a contract should be regarded as an instrument of cooperation, not as a confrontation of adversaries each seeking his advantage at the expense of the other'.[71] This seems to be a frightening message for some authors,[72] but it is the absolutely correct assessment of contemporary European contract law and contract theory,[73] which differs from the liberal contract theory of the nineteenth and early twentieth centuries.

However, the DCFR in some of its parts seems to be uncertain about the desirability of good faith, cooperation, fairness, and solidarity. Unlike in the PECL, it does not contain a general duty of good faith, but only a particular duty to *negotiate* in good faith (Article II.-3:301(2)) and a duty to *perform* in good faith (Article III.-1:103(1)) instead. The duty in Article II.-3:301(2) DCFR (negotiation) is narrower than its parallel provisions in Articles 2:101-2:103 AcqP. The 'legitimate expectations of consumers' of Article 2:102 AcqP are omitted altogether. The duty in III-1:103(1) is limited in its paragraph (3) by excluding remedies of non-performance as a consequence of its breach.[74]

The *pre-contractual information duties*[75] of the DCFR reveal that they are a product of the same exercise: the authors of the DCFR took the text of the respective AcqP rule and reduced the scope or intensity of its protection – to a smaller or larger extent. Articles II.-3:101, 3:102 DCFR as compared to Articles 2:201, 2:202 AcqP can serve as an example. The general information duty in the DCFR applies only to contracts for goods or services and requires a business as seller or provider. Article II.-3:101 paragraph 2 DCFR was added which suggests that among businesses 'no information' is the rule: information must only be provided if a failure to

67. *See* Arts I-1:102 (3) b: interpretation of CFR; II-1:102 (1): party autonomy subject to the rules of good faith; II-3:301 (2): duty to negotiate in good faith; II-8:102 (1) g: interpretation of contract; II-9:404-406: unfair contract term is contrary to good faith and fair dealing; III-1:103 (1) performance of an obligation; III-1:104: related duty to cooperate.
68. In Annex I 'good faith and fair dealing' are only described as an 'objective standard of conduct'.
69. Arts IV-C-2:103 (service contracts); IV-C-3:102 (construction); IV-C-4:102 (processing); IV-D-2:101 (mandate); IV-E-2:201 (commercial agency, franchise and distributorship).
70. *See* Section 3 above.
71. Lando (n. 37 above), 245, 251.
72. Eidenmüller et al. (n. 1 above), 538.
73. *See also* Lurger (n. 25 above), 370 et seq., 448 et seq.; id. (n. 19 above), 442, 449 et seq.
74. Criticized by Lando (n. 37 above).
75. *See also* C. Twigg-Flesner, 'Pre-contractual Duties – From the Acquis to the Common Frame of Reference', in *Common Frame of Reference and Existing EC Contract Law*, ed. R. Schulze (München: Sellier, 2008), 97 et seq.

inform would deviate from 'good commercial practice'.[76] The specific information duty for consumers in Article II.-3:102 DCFR was also slightly limited in scope, and the duty to provide information about delivery charges, taxes, and other costs was eliminated altogether.[77] The ensuing information duties (Articles II.-3:103 and II.-3:105 DCFR) are simply implementations of the Distance Selling and the E-Commerce Directive.

The idea expressed in Article II.-3:107 DCFR – the already existing right of withdrawal in distance selling contracts is prolonged where the information given is insufficient – is not really new. Unlike in Article 2:207 AcqP, this right of withdrawal was not extended to other breaches of duties to inform under this chapter. The specific information duties of the Package Travel, the Timesharing and other Directives were left outside the Draft. The language issue which is already addressed in some directives is missing in the DCFR. The same is true for the question of burden of proof, and the permissibility of charging the costs for providing information to the other party.

The Proposal for a 'Directive on Consumer Contractual Rights'[78] applies only to contracts between businesses and consumers. The information duties apply only to B2C contracts for goods and services. The general information duty of Article 5 contains a list of information, including information about costs. The sanctions for the breach of information duties have to be provided by the contract law of the Member States (Article 6(2)). Additional costs on which no pre-contractual information was given are not owed to the business (Article 6(1)). A specific list of information for distance contracts and contracts concluded away from business premises is formulated in Article 9. The proposed Directive's information duties differ from the respective DCFR and AcqP provisions in so far as they stick closer to the text of the existing directives and avoid generalizations as well as extensions of scope to non-consumer contracts.

The *right of withdrawal*[79] covers a whole chapter in the DCFR (Articles II.-5:101 and II.-5:202). In a general part, exercise of the right, withdrawal period, information, and effects of withdrawal are regulated. The intention to withdraw can be communicated in any manner, without any form requirements (Article II. 5:102), which is a consumer-friendly rule. The 'ordinary' withdrawal period was prolonged to fourteen days, which is, of course, also positive for the consumer. The rule that the withdrawal period ends in all cases where not all required information were provided (including the information on the right of withdrawal itself) after one year after the conclusion of the contract (Article II.-5:103(3)) constitutes a departure from the ECJ decision in the *Heininger* case:[80] thus the DCFR rule is less favorable to the consumer than the present EC law in that respect. The rule on

76. The latter is a term not explained by the list of definitions in Annex I.
77. There is such a duty, however, for distance selling contracts in Art. II-3:103 DCFR.
78. COM (2008) 614 final.
79. *See also* E. Terryn, 'The Right of Withdrawal, the Acquis Principles and the Draft Common Frame of Reference', in *Common Frame of Reference and Existing EC Contract Law*, ed. R. Schulze (München: Sellier, 2008), 145 et seq.
80. ECJ 13 Dec. 2001, case C-481/99, ECR 2001, I-9945 (*Heininger*).

'linked contracts' (Article II.-5:106) is formulated rather narrowly. The rules of unjustified enrichment applying after the withdrawal from the contract are considerably less favorable to the consumer than the present implementations of many Member States.

The general part shall apply to some of the rights of withdrawal existing under EC law, but not to all: contracts concluded away from business premises, distance contracts for goods or services (including financial services and personal security provision by a consumer), and timeshare contracts are included. Insurance contracts concluded personally on the business' premises are excluded. Unfortunately, Article II.-5:201 repeats the long lists of exceptions of the Doorstep and Distance Selling Directives, even though only a few exceptions can be rationally justified, many of them seem to be the result of lobbying.

The withdrawal chapter is a good example for the failure of the AcqP and the DCFR to undertake a critical revision and sytematization of the punctual, disperse, and non-homogenous rules of the EC directives.[81] No assessment of the exact need for protection was made: consumers contracting away from business premises are in need of protection *only if* they are taken by surprise. According to Article II.-5:201 DCFR, the consumer has a right of withdrawal even where she/he contacted the business her/himself (and thus no surprise attack can have occurred). And where is the need for protection in timeshare contracts? It is the particularly 'dangerous' nature of a certain category of contracts, including timeshare contracts, for customers: these contracts involve a long-term commitment for the consumer or customer, as well as a considerable investment of money and they provide a complicated structure of rights and duties which is hard to comprehend for the consumer or customer.[82] It would have been necessary to determine which types of contracts belong to this category, apart from timeshare contracts (consumer credit,[83] insurance contracts, capital investment and other financial services, and so forth). In some cases, protection would have to be extended even to business customers, because they are significantly less experienced and less informed than the providers of particular services. This idea has already been realized by the rights of withdrawal (and other protective provisions in favour of customers) in the EC Insurance Directives (92/49/EEC; 2002/83/EG). Thus, it is part of existing EC contract law.

The proposed Directive on Consumer Contractual Rights only 'centralizes' the rules for distance contracts (with the exception of financial services) and doorstep contracts. Unlike the DCFR (Article II.-5:201), Article 12 of the proposed directive defines distance selling contracts (Article 2(6)) and contracts concluded or negotiated away from business premises (Article 2(8)) separately. As in the DCFR, in the latter category no attention is paid to the necessary surprise attack by

81. For such an endeavour undertaken with respect to the numerable Austrian rights of withdrawal, *see* S. Kalss & B. Lurger, *Rücktrittsrechte* (Wien: Verlag Österreich, 2001), 74 et seq.
82. *Ibid.*
83. Even the right of withdrawal of the recent Consumer Credit Directive (2008/48/EC) was ignored by the DCFR.

the business. Contracts concluded at the consumer's initiative are excluded only in a very special situation (Article 19(2)(c): consumer contacts business by means of distance communication and requests the business' visit at her/his home, contract must be for repair or maintenance of consumer's property).

As in the DCFR, there is an 'ordinary' withdrawal period of fourteen days (Article 12(1)). Where the consumer was not informed of her/his right of withdrawal, the 'extraordinary' period of withdrawal ends three months after the business has complied with all of her/his duties under the contract (Article 13).[84] The intention to withdraw must be expressed on a durable medium (Article 14). Article 18 provides for the termination of 'accessory' contracts without explaining which contracts are supposed to be 'accessory'. Two long lists of exceptions follow (Articles 19 and 20), some of which were even extended or added as compared to the present directives.

It is certainly an innovative and positive step to introduce a prohibition of *discrimination*[85] to the DCFR's general rules on contracts (see Articles II.-2:101 and II.-2:105). Chapter 2 does not cover all types of discriminations that are prohibited by Article 13 ET, but only discrimination on grounds of sex, ethnic, or racial origin. The provision on remedies (Article II.-2:104) refers to Book VI (torts) and to Book III Chapter 3 (remedies for non-performance of an obligation), which may mean that even a right to specific performance exists.[86] The victim has a slightly alleviated burden of proof (Article II.-2:105). The proposed Directive on Consumer Contractual Rights contains no provisions on discrimination.

The DCFR rules on *unfair contract terms* (Articles II.-9:401 and II.-9:411)[87] follow the Unfair Contract Terms Directive (93/13) when they exclude the main performances of the contract from their scope (Article II.-9:407(3)). There is no DCFR rule sanctioning the inequality of main performances as such (like *laesio enormis* under § 934 Austrian ABGB). The consumer (and any other party) may avoid a contract only when there is a situation of unfair exploitation by the other party resulting in an 'excessive benefit or grossly unfair advantage' of the latter (Article II.-7:207).

The rule on the inclusion of standard terms in a contract in Article II.-9:103 DCFR does not require a real opportunity of the consumer to get acquainted with the terms and thus falls back behind what is the basis of present EC and Member States' law.[88] Point (i) of the grey list of the directive's Annex concerning the binding nature of terms which the consumer had no real opportunity to become acquainted with is omitted by the DCFR as well (see Article II.-9:411).

---

84. This rule is in line with the ECJ's Heininger decision (13 Dec. 2001, case C-481/99, ECR 2001, I-9945). In the Heininger case, the credit contract was not yet fully performed and the business had not yet informed the consumer of its right of withdrawal.
85. *See also* S. Leible, 'Non-discrimination', in *Common Frame of Reference and Existing EC Contract Law*, ed. R. Schulze (München: Sellier, 2008), 127 et seq.
86. Leible (n. 85 above), 141.
87. *See also* T. Pfeiffer, 'Non-negotiated Terms', in *Common Frame of Reference and Existing EC Contract Law*, ed. R. Schulze (München: Sellier, 2008), 177 et seq.
88. *Ibid.*, 181.

The basic rule about the 'unfairness' of a contract term is split into three different rules: (a) Article II.-9:404 – B2C, (b) Article II.-9:405 – C2C, and (c) Article II.-9:406 – B2B contracts. 'Unfairness' is generally a contradiction to 'good faith and fair dealing'. In rule (a) no agreement could be reached on whether the unfairness test should also apply to individually negotiated terms of a contract (which were 'supplied by the business' in the first place). Present Austrian consumer protection law also includes individually negotiated terms (§ 6(1) Consumer Code) and had some rather good experiences with this rule. The b2b-test comprises only standard terms and is additionally restricted to 'gross deviations from good commercial practice'.[89] Even though many Member States successfully practice a fairness control of standard terms in b2b-contracts, the narrow wording of Article II.-9:406 seems to reflect the serious doubts of some of the drafters that such a provision is necessary. The grey list of unfair terms of the directive was turned into a 'presumed unfairness' list applying only to b2c-contracts.

Thus, there can be seen no general improvement of the situation of the consumer in the DCFR unfairness control of pre-formulated terms. Recent ECJ decisions on the interpretation of the directive are not reflected in the text of the rules. The proposed Directive on Consumer Contractual Rights (Articles 30-39) does not change much in the old directive, either. Only the list of unfair clauses in the Annex is amended: now two lists shall exist – a black list of prohibition and a grey list of presumption (the business must prove that the clause is not unfair).

In the DCFR rules on *sales contracts* (Book IV Part A), which cannot be dealt with here in detail, some smaller changes in favor of consumers are suggested: the Member States are no longer allowed to exclude second-hand goods sold at a public auction. Digital content and software are defined as 'goods' (Article IV.-A-1:101(2)). The consumer is not restricted in the choice of remedies anymore (Article IV.-A-4:201). The risk does not pass until the consumer takes over the goods (Article IV.-A-5:103). The proposed Directive on Consumer Contractual Rights also adds this new consumer-friendly risk (and delivery) rule. But the other improvements suggested by the DCFR cannot be found in the proposal of the Directive. For most questions, the proposal reproduces the text of the old directive but now turns it into a maximum harmonization text.

5. CONCLUSION

The main achievement of the DCFR is certainly not the improvement of consumer protection. The 'core aims' of the DCFR include the consumer-friendly principles of 'solidarity', 'social responsibility' and 'cultural diversity'. But the descriptions of these principles are extremely vague, and they are not sufficiently reflected in the particular contract law rules of the DCFR (see Section 3). The positive results for consumers are meagre and punctual and are accompanied by a rather long list of caveats for consumers and consumer protection organizations (see Section 4.2).

89. A notion not defined in Annex I.

If taken as a basis for *minimum* harmonization in consumer contracts, the DCFR rules would not improve much and would also not do much harm.

However, a dramatic reduction in consumer protection would be achieved by transposing the DCFR rules to a *maximum* harmonization instrument. The Commission's Proposal of a 'Directive on Consumer Contractual Rights'[90] of 8 October 2008 is already waiting out there to turn this consumer nightmare into reality (see Sections 1, 2 and 4.2). Little or no comfort lies, of course, in the fact that the Commission's contract law project (CoPECL) and its resulting (D)CFR are limited to a very small number of EC directives leaving the majority of EC consumer law still out of their reach (see Section 4.1). I dare to suggest that the Commission – in its contract law and consumer protection policy – is currently heading into the wrong direction.

What should be done to improve this situation? First, it is important to acknowledge the fact that the recommendation and choice of a particular set of contract law rules always implies political choices that have a considerable impact on our markets and societies, and to act accordingly: the question of which policy choices have to be made for a truly common European contract law has to be discussed openly on all levels of law making and society.

Additionally, a more comprehensive view of contract law and of consumer protection is needed: the principle of protection, solidarity and fairness is not restricted to consumer protection issues. It also operates in favour of other categories of weaker parties and of parties in a particular situation of vulnerability. Its realization or non-existence is an important factor for every market behaviour and every market actor. Contract law has to be seen in its inter-relation with other areas of market law, such as unfair commercial practices and antitrust law. The scope of the analysis also should be expanded beyond what is now covered by the DCFR: to all types of contracts in which EC regulation is present and consumer protection is needed. Only such a comprehensive view will enable us to fully understand the operation of contract law, national as well as European.

Finally, a high level of consumer protection should be guaranteed in all these areas, whether by EU or by national law. In EU law, the concept of minimum harmonization should be kept. If we want to expand EC contract law beyond its present scope, first and foremost we need common political views on the basic principles underlying contract and market law that can be called 'European'.

If there is anything in our legal and political systems we can be particularly proud of as Europeans – as compared to countries like the USA, Japan, China, India, Brazil, and the like – it is the Member States' and the Union's concern for the social security of all its citizens. Vital interests of citizens, such as health care, food and product safety, economic welfare, age and retirement, or public infrastructure, are not left to private initiative or to charity but are seen as important elements of the State's responsibility for its citizens.

The markets have two sides, a liberal one and a social one: it is, of course, legitimate and important to strive primarily for your own profit and benefit on the

90. COM (2008) 614 final.

market. But it is beneficial for the whole system to act *also* with respect for the other market participants, their legitimate interests, and with respect for important public goals and human rights (no child labor, protection of the environment, and so forth). Other market systems tend to overemphasize the liberal side of markets. It is the strength of Europe to cherish also the other, the social side of our market societies. We should be aware of this strength and defend it against neo-liberal trends, also in contract law.

Chapter 9

Unfair Terms and Unfairness Test in Contracts between Businesses and Consumers

Marisa Meli

1. THE COMMISSION REPORT ON THE IMPLEMENTATION OF THE DIRECTIVE ON UNFAIR TERMS IN CONSUMER CONTRACTS

Directive 1993/13 on unfair terms has to be considered the most important communitarian intervention on consumer contracts. Indeed for the first time European Communities, instead of regulating specific contracts, devote their attention to all kinds of business-to-consumer contracts, setting out a new aim: contracts concluded with consumers must not contain unfair terms; unfair terms must be eliminated, for the internal market to function smoothly.

To underline the importance of the aim, the same Directive obliged the Commission to present a Report to the European Parliament and the Council concerning the implementation of the Directive five years after the deadline of its transposition. The Report was published in 2000,[1] and it is a very important document, because it raises a number of questions with a view to improving the existing situation.

1. COM (2000) 248 final.

Alessandro Somma, *The Politics of the Draft Common Frame of Reference*, pp. 151-161.

The basic consideration it contains is not very encouraging. Notwithstanding whatever efforts are made, businesses continue to use unfair terms in their contracts. It could therefore be said that the Directive failed its aim. According to the Commission, this happened for a number of reasons.

Some critical remarks concern the field of application of the Directive. The Commission considers incorrect both the idea of excluding contractual terms which have been individually negotiated by the consumer, and the choice of limiting the intervention to business-to-consumers contracts.

The Report focused above all on ways of determining if a contractual term is unfair. Firstly, the Commission disagrees with some of the limitations of the unfairness test; like the exclusion concerning mandatory provisions, which is dangerous for contracts related to general interest services, and the exclusion regarding the price and the subject matter of the contract, which can raise interpretative problems that can compromise the proper application of the directive itself. Moreover, criticism concerns the general criterion for the unfairness test. Both because it has been transposed in different ways by the Member States, and because it does not define in a clear way the relationship between the two elements required: good faith and significant imbalance.

Even the second way of assessing the unfairness of contractual terms, that is the indicative list annexed to the Directive, is not very satisfactory. Firstly because the list is indicative and a contractual term corresponding to a point is not automatically deemed unfair; secondly because the list is not compulsory, and certain countries have refused to transpose it as it stands.

The Commission emphasizes also that as well as the unfairness test, the Directive has introduced another important principle: the principle of transparency. Contractual terms offered to the consumer must always be drafted in plain, intelligible language. Transparency also means that the consumer should be able to obtain, prior to conclusion of the contract, the information he needs to consciously make his decision. For the Commission, however, the principle of transparency is not affirmed strongly enough. The infringement is not penalized in the strict sense of the word, because contractual terms which do not comply with transparency criterion are neither removed from the contract nor regarded as unfair. The only consequence provided is that in such a case the most favourable interpretation to the consumer shall prevail.

Lastly, the Report considers the inadequacy of the Directive with regard to the unfairness consequences. The only prescription is that the unfair term used in a contract shall not be binding to the consumer, but the contract shall continue to bind the parties, if it is capable of continuing in existence without the unfair term.

The Directive leaves it to the Member States to ensure that adequate and effective means exist to prevent the continued use of unfair terms. These means include provisions for taking action before the courts or before competent administrative bodies.

Even if in some States there exists an administrative body, the chosen way to implement the Directive in each Member States is judicial power. The Commission underlines that regarding the court system, many problems arise. Procedures are time-consuming, and the unfair terms continue to have their effects until the decision is taken. Moreover, the res judicata has effects only between the parties and other undertakers can continue to use the same term in their contracts.

So, there is a contradiction between the goal of legislation on unfair terms and the result of its enforcement. For that reason, the Commission looks towards a 'positive' system for eliminating unfair terms, for example, through the creation of a European Authority, something like what already exists in antitrust law. In other words, the new aim posed by the Commission is not only to harmonize substantial law in consumer transactions, but also to discover new implementation measures so consumers can become *more confident* in transnational transactions.

We have to keep in mind this scenario for evaluating the forward steps undertaken by the Commission.

2. THE STEPS FORWARD: THE REVISION OF THE *ACQUIS*, THE COMMON FRAME OF REFERENCE, AND ITS DRAFT

To properly understand what the steps forward are, we have to begin from the development of European private law. The Commission intervened with the Communication 'European Contract law and the revision of the *acquis*: the way forward',[2] which follows up the 2003 Action Plan.

According to these documents, the new aim becomes improving the quality and consistency of the *acquis* in the area of contract law. The Commission considers the necessity for proposals to amend the existing directives while, in the meantime, affirming the need for a Common Fame of Reference which must be developed to improve, inter alia, the coherence of the existing *acquis*.

The work started with the Green paper on the review of the consumer *acquis*[3] and thereafter with the publication of the Principles of the Existing EC contract law, edited by the Research Group on the Existing EC Private law,[4] which was entrusted with it by the European Commission.

This work is a sort of restatement of the existing EC law, also in the field of unfair terms.[5] While in other sectors of consumer law restatement means to

2. COM (2004) 651 final.
3. COM (2006) 744 final; C. Twigg-Flesner, 'No Sense of Purpose or Direction? The Modernisation of European Consumer Law', *European Review of Contract Law* 2 (2007): 198.
4. Research Group on the Existing EC Private Law (ed.), *Principles of the Existing EC Contract Law (Acquis Principles) Contract I, Pre-contractual Obligations, Conclusion of Contract, Unfair Terms* (München: Sellier, 2007). For the preliminary work *see* H. Schulte-Nölke, C. Twigg-Flesner & M. Ebers (eds), EC *Consumer Law Compendium – Comparative Analysis* (München: Sellier, 2008). For a first comment of the ACQP *see* R. Schulze (ed.), *Common Frame of Reference and Existing EC Contract Law* (München: Sellier, 2008).
5. On the *acquis*'s restatement *see*: R. Schulze, 'Der Acquis Communautaire und die Entwicklung des Europäischen Vertragsrechts', in *Informationspflichten und Vertragsschluss im Acquis Communautaire*, eds R. Schulze, M. Ebers & H. C. Grigoleit (Tubingen: Mohr Siebeck, 2003), 3;

reorganize and put together many different European directives in a more coherent way, in unfair terms it is not very clear what restatement means, because there is only one community intervention for regulating it.

The Acquis Group explains that it worked from the inside, analyzing each point of the directive, trying to eliminate some of the contradictions and deficiencies in the text. Moreover, it has introduced some modifications, but only those allowed by community law, looking not only to the European legislator but also to the contribution of the Court of Justice.

This kind of work made it possible to intervene with some amendments, for example extending application to business-to-business contracts, but without the possibility of radically modifying the choices that the directive contains.

In the meantime, the Acquis Group with others academic groups took part in the project to elaborate a Draft Common Frame of Reference.

It represents a possible model for a political CFR that contains Principles, Definitions, and Model Rules of European Private Law. It is a vast work, following the idea that the CFR must, at any rate, cover the field of application of existing Directives that are under review, and any others that are likely to be reviewed in the foreseeable future. Thus all consumer law should be included.

The ambition is also to cover the material in the existing principles of European Contract Law: this means general rules on contracts and other judicial acts, with the aim of developing clear and consistent concepts and terminology. The idea, in other words, is to make a Draft that can meet all the functions required by the Commission. These functions are numerous; they include increasing the coherence of the *acquis*, for the Draft to serve as a kind of legislators' guide or 'toolbox', and for it to be used as an optional instrument.

What it is not very clear is how all these functions can be put together; the result is in fact a bulky work that cannot be seen as the best solution for any of the multiple functions it was designed for.

It is my opinion that the different aims of European private law cannot converge in a unique and common instrument, like the CFR. So, for example, the optional instrument needs some specific requirements, above all in the field of mandatory provisions related to business-to-business contracts, and it has nothing to do with the harmonization of existing contract law. The optional instrument has to contain modern and efficient rules for regulating transnational contracts; it cannot become heavier by rules concerning consumers' transactions or other civil matters that the DCFR actually contains.[6]

M. Ebers, 'La revisione del diritto europeo del consumatore: l'attuazione nei Paesi della direttiva sulle clausole abusive (93/13/CEE) e le prospettiva d'ulteriore armonizzazione', *Contratto e impresa, Europa* 12 (2007): 696. On the development of the Consumer Protection Policy in Europe *see* R. Howells & T. Wilhelmsson, *EC Consumer Law* (Aldershot/Dartmouth: Ashgate, 1997); B. Pasa & G. Benacchio, *The Harmonization of Civil and Commercial Law in Europe* (Budapest, New York: Central European University Press, 2005); P. Nebbia, *Unfair Contract Terms in European Law* (Oxford: Hart, 2007).

6. In this sense also the last Recommendation, 3 Sep. 2008, where the European Parliament welcomes the presentation of the DCFR, but it points out that the Commission should bear in mind

Neither is it possible to believe that the massive work will serve only as an instrument for better-lawmaking, like the Commission pointed out. It would be a very poor function in comparison with the work done.

On the other side, the harmonization of existing contract law must reflect principles and values on which communitarian law is based,[7] but must also be able to reconsider the choices contained in each directive with the aim of reaching better results. This kind of work cannot be done by academics; it needs a new legislative intervention, and my impression is confirmed by the new directive proposal on consumer rights,[8] which is much more incisive and innovative than the academic projects developed until now.

Let us start to verify this point, analyzing the unfair terms discipline contained in the DCFR leaving from our starting point: Directive 1993/13 failed to comply with its aims; shall we consider the new DCFR's regulation more efficient in eliminating unfair terms from b2c-contracts?

3. UNFAIR TERMS: BLACK AND GREY LIST

The answer would seem a positive one, looking at the list of unfair terms contained in the Draft, because it simplifies the way of determining unfair terms and makes it equal in each Member State. The anterior instrument contained only an indicative list of terms which may normally be regarded as unfair, but it was contained only in the annex and it was not transposed in each Member State. Now the list is contained in the text and it is a double one.

On one side we find a sort of black list. The black list is a good solution in itself, because it is very useful for setting apart contract terms that are surely unfair. The problem is that in the DCFR there is no real black list, because it contains only one term that has to be considered unfair: exclusive jurisdiction clauses, i.e. terms conferring exclusive jurisdiction for all disputes arising under the contract on the court for the place where the business is domiciled.[9]

Indeed, the list could be integrated when it is certain that there are other terms that can be considered unfair. The drafters in fact explain that the list is meant to be extended if and as soon as there is a sufficient basis for doing so. But who shall integrate the list? And how? Is it conceivable that we have to wait for future interventions of the Court of Justice? Of course it would be a very complex

---

that the CFR could go well beyond a mere legislative tool and could result in an optional instrument.

7. In the first (dated 23 Mar. 2006) the Parliament calls on the Commission to distinguish between legal provisions applicable to b2b and b2c-transaction, underlying the importance of taking into account the European social model when harmonizing contract law.
8. COM (2008) 614 final.
9. The sources are the judgments C-240/98 to C-244/98 *Oceano Grupo Editorial SA v. Marciano Quinterno*, 27 Jun. 2000 and Case C-168/05 *Mostaza Claro v. Centro Movil Millenium SL*, 26 Oct. 2006.

procedure. From this point of view, the rule contained in the directive proposal on consumer rights appears much more convincing. Contract terms which are in all circumstances considered unfair are already much more than one, and overall the procedure for reviewing the terms contained in the list is already regulated.

It is the same for the so called grey list. The content of the list is quite the same as the previous one contained in the annex of the Directive. The problem is, again, the lack of any procedure to amend or integrate it in the future.

This means, in other words, that a work based on the restatement of the *acquis* is a very limited one and only a new legislative intervention with innovative solutions would be capable of significant modifications.

4. UNFAIRNESS TEST: SIGNIFICANT IMBALANCE, GOOD FAITH, AND LIST OF FACTORS

The main provision for unfairness test states that in a contract between a business and a consumer, a term (which has not been individually negotiated) is unfair if it is supplied by the business and it significantly disadvantages the consumer, contrary to good faith and fair dealing.

It is very surprising that the concept of unfairness is formulated in the same way as it was in the Directive: there is again the 'contrary to good faith' criterion as well as the 'significant imbalance' criterion. And so even if it was clear enough that the complicated structure of the rule arises only problems: it was immediately not clear if the two requirements are requested together or one by one.

Even the directive proposal on consumer rights confirms that a contract term is unfair if, contrary to the requirement of good faith, it causes a significant imbalance in the parties' rights and obligations. We cannot therefore give up this definition, requirement of good faith is a central one for the unfairness test, which must be added to the significant imbalance; if so, we have to give careful consideration to this requirement and definitively try to understand what it means.

Let us start with the way in which the expression is used by the European legislator in the original directive on unfair terms. Recital 16 states that the 'assessment, according to the general criteria chosen, of the unfair character of terms, in particular in sale or supply activities of a public nature providing collective services which take account of solidarity among users, must be supplemented by a means of making an overall evaluation of the different interests involved'.

This explains quite clearly that for the unfairness test it is not sufficient to check the imbalance of rights and obligations, to the detriment of the consumer, that a contractual term contains, but a supplementary inquiry that makes an equitable comparison of the interests involved is necessary. This kind of assessment is devolved to the good faith criterion.

It could be surprising that an equitable assessment is devolved to a criterion that is not very well defined, making use of a general clause as usually occurs in some civil law systems, like the German one.

My impression is indeed that the use of the expression 'good faith' by the European legislator is quite different from the use of the same expression in civil law systems. The European legislator doesn't want to use a general clause devolving to the judge, in each different country, the task of filling up the clause's content. On the contrary, through the good faith criterion, the European legislator would like to impose on all Member States a constrained way for conducting the unfairness test and for balancing the different interests involved.

If we look at the same recital 16, it goes on: 'in making an assessment of good faith, particular regard shall be had to the strength of the bargaining position of the parties, whether the consumer had an inducement to agree to the term and whether the goods or services were sold or supplied to the special order of the consumer. Thereafter: the requirement of good faith can be satisfied by the seller or supplier where he deals fairly and equitably with the other party whose legitimate interests he has to take into account'.

So it seems clear that through the good faith criterion the comparison of the interests involved has to be made following the benchmarks described by the legislator himself. This is true even if the legislator uses apparently indefinite concepts, like 'fair and equitable' conduct. What in fact we have to understand is that these expressions are used to describe the conduct of a precise undertaking. Businesses have to interact with the counterpart in a fair and equitable way if they want to interact with each other in a safe and smoothly functioning market.

If so, good faith, fair dealing, and equitable conduct are not only relational concepts, describing the way in which each undertaking acts with the counterpart; they also characterize the way in which economic agents must behave in the market, practising honest commercial practices. For evaluating if a business is doing so, it is necessary to look at the particular kind of activity involved and to verify if the business behaviour corresponds to professional standards. So even the unfairness test is related to the market behaviour and through this kind of control it is possible to grant a fair trade and the correct functioning of the market.

Sometimes (for example in the Directive concerning liability for defective products) the European legislator uses the concept of 'reasonableness'. But it is always the same. The central point is balancing the producer's conduct with the consumer interest and also with the market interest.[10]

This is confirmed in the common text on unfair terms elaborated by the two English and Scottish Law Commissions.[11] The expression good faith is definitively put away, *pro* the more familiar one 'reasonableness'. The new formula is: 'where a term of a consumer is detrimental to the consumer, the business cannot rely on the term unless is fair and reasonable'. And it is possible to agree with Hugh Beale when he says that the new formula is more similar to the meaning awarded by the

---

10. On the relationship between *good faith* and *reasonableness* criteria *see* C. Amato, *Per un diritto europeo dei contratti con i consumatori* (Milano: Giuffré, 2003), 120 et seq.
11. Law Commission – Scottish Law Commission, 'Unfair Terms in Contracts', <www.lawcom.gov.uk/docs/cp166.pdf>.

European legislator, than have been the different meanings awarded to the good faith criterion by commentators.[12]

The point in fact is not to evaluate if a contractual term is equitable in itself, but if it is equitable and reasonable that a business puts it into the contract. It is of course not very simple to make this kind of assessment. For that reason, the legislator points out a list of factors. So the central point becomes: is the list of factors satisfactory enough to assess the unfairness of contractual terms?

I do not think that the point was explored in enough depth by the drafters. England and Scotland, for example, are going to adopt a much more analytical list of factors,[13] and it is not conceivable that this point is left to the different evaluations of Member States. Finland points out that the assessment can be made 'in view of the price of the good or service or other relevant circumstances'.[14] And this is very surprising because this kind of evaluation can encourage the fall of the market, through the so-called market for lemons.[15]

In comparison with these different solutions, the DCFR dogmatically confirms almost all the provisions contained in the previous directive. The only innovation it contains is that regard is to be had to the duty of transparency. Indeed, this is a good change, because at the beginning the role of transparency in unfairness terms discipline was not very clear.[16]

The only consequences provided by legislator were that in the case of unclear terms the most favourable interpretation for the consumer shall prevail, so that the contractual term may be maintained despite its irregularities. And also that the unfair nature of the terms will not be related to the definition of the main subject matter of the contract or to the adequacy of the price, in so far as these terms are put into the contract according to the principle of transparency. But the infringement of the principle was not sanctioned in the strict sense of the word, because contractual terms which do not comply with the criteria of

12. H. Beale, 'Unfair Terms in Contracts: Proposal for Reform in the UK', *Journal of Consumer Policy* 27 (2004): 289.
13. Beale (n. 12 above), 297.
14. *See* Schulte-Nölke, Twigg-Flesner & Ebers (n. 4 above).
15. I refer to G. A. Akerlof, 'The Market for "Lemons": Quality Uncertainty and the Market Mechanism', *Quarterly Journal of Economics* 84 (1970): 488; S. Grundmann, 'L'autonomia privata nel mercato interno: le regole di informazione come strumento', *Europa e Diritto Privato* (2001): 270; A. Gambaro, 'Perché si vessa il cliente? Note ed appunti di un itinerario tra i modelli occidentali', *Quadrimestre* (1991): 386; R. Pardolesi & A. Pacces, 'Clausole vessatorie e analisi economica del diritto: note in margine alle ragioni (ed alle incongruenze) della nuova disciplina', *Diritto Privato* (1996): 377; F. Gomez, 'EC Consumer Protection Law and EC Competition Law: How Related Are They? A Law and Economics Perspective', in *The Forthcoming EC Directive on Unfair Commercial Practice*, ed. H. Collins (The Hague/New York: Kluwer Law International, 2004), 187.
16. *See* M. Wolf, 'Party Autonomy and Information in the Unfair Contract Terms Directive', in *Party Autonomy and the Role of Information in the Internal Market*, eds S. Grundmann, W. Kerber & S. Weatherill (Berlin: De Gruyter, 2001), 313. *See also* V. Rizzo, *Le 'clausole abusive' nell'esperienza tedesca, francese, italiana e nella prospettiva comunitaria* (Napoli: ESI, 1994).

clarity and intelligibility are neither removed from the contract nor regarded as unfair.

In the Draft it is specified that terms which have been supplied by the business in breach of the duty of transparency may on that ground alone be considered unfair and it is also provided that regard is to be had to the duty of transparency when assessing the unfairness of a contractual term. The Draft states also that it is necessary to analyze the circumstances prevailing during the conclusion of the contract, including the extent to which the consumer was given a real opportunity to become acquainted with the terms before the conclusion of the contract. This is again a proper provision, but only looking at the specific relationship between business and consumer.

Looking at the business' market strategies in a more general sense, the Draft confirmed that in an unfairness test, regard is to be had to the 'nature of goods and services to be provided under the contract and to the circumstances prevailing during the conclusion of the contract'. This represents the core aspect of the unfairness test, which resumes the assessment of conflicting interests and means a control of business strategy. In the future, the drafters or even the European legislator should pay much more attention to it. On the contrary, until now it has not been very well specified. Even the reference to the circumstances prevailing during the conclusion does not seem very useful, because it is already defined that the control concerns only terms not individually negotiated.

On these points, the DCFR has nothing to add to the original Directive, and it definitively cannot make any contribution to a better elimination of unfair terms in Europe.

5. MARKET REGULATION AND ENFORCEMENT MEASURES

It remains to be checked if the DCFR would have a stronger incidence on the unfairness consequences.

Even in this respect it cannot be said that the DCFR has achieved any result. It does not go beyond the inefficiencies of Directive 1993/13. It states again that one term which is unfair is not binding on the party who did not supply it, and that if the contract can be reasonably maintained without the unfair term, the other terms will remain binding for the party.

Putting aside the civil effects of unfairness, the main problem is that the DCFR maintains the traditional approach to eliminating unfair terms. The removal of unfair terms is devolved to private enforcement, even if the Report of the Commission underlined that private action, even in the form of collective action for injunctions, is not adequate or sufficient.

Indeed, the use of unfair terms and also the vagueness of certain terms are an obstacle for the orderly functioning of the market, and they require a business strategies control that cannot rely only on private initiative and judicial power. It becomes necessary to analyze if in this sector would be useful a form of market regulation with some form of public implementation devoted to an independent authority,[17] as already exists in some legal systems.

Of course it could be said that the drafters couldn't introduce new enforcement measures, because the work is based on the restatement of the consumer *acquis*. That is another way to say that this kind of work is not very useful and only a new intervention of the European legislator can modify the traditional approach in a radical manner.

In addition, I have to underline that, even with a communitarian intervention, it is not actually possible or useful to proceed to a review of consumer *acquis* without covering the Directive 2005/29 on unfair commercial practices. The Directive has to be considered the second pillar in consumer law. Like Directive 1993/13, it does not concern specific contracts but rather all kinds of business behaviours. The aim is to protect consumer economic interests from unfair business-to-consumers commercial practices.

If we look at the two communitarian interventions together, it can be said that business behaviours must be based on two fundamental rules: businesses cannot introduce unfair terms in contracts and cannot relate on unfair commercial practices for promoting or executing contracts. Indeed, I think it is possible going on and looking to these duties as if they represent only one rule: Businesses cannot relate on unfair commercial practices, whereas also the use of unfair terms in contracts can be seen as an example of unfair practice.

The text of the Directive 2005/29 supports this interpretation. It is addressed to commercial practices directly related 'to influencing consumer's decisions in relation to products'. So it mainly concerns commercial communications, including unfair advertising but also other kinds of misleading and aggressive commercial practices.

More generally speaking, however, the Directive describes its scope referring to any act, omission, course of conduct or representation, commercial communication including advertising and marketing, by a trader, 'directly connected with the promotion, sale or supply of a product to consumer' (Article 2(d)). More precisely, the field of application is defined by looking at all business-to-consumer commercial practices 'during or after a commercial transaction in relation to a product' (Article 3). The formula therefore is wide enough to comprise also the use of unfair terms in consumer contracts.

Directive 2005/29 also asks Member States to ensure that adequate and effective means exist to combat unfair commercial practices. Unlike the case of unfair terms, each Member State has chosen public implementation measures.

This means that if we consider unfair terms as an example of unfair commercial practice, it will be simple to find new implementation measures based also on public enforcement. And it is an interesting result because the Directive on unfair commercial practices mainly concerns control on business strategies. Commercial practices are defined unfair when they are contrary to the requirement

17. In this sense, see also G. Monti, 'The Revision of the Consumer Acquis from a Competition Law Perspective', *European Review of Contract Law* 3 (2007): 295.

of professional diligence. Professional diligences, like the good faith criterion in unfair terms, means the standard of special skill and care which a trader may reasonably be expected to exercise towards consumers, commensurate with honest market practice.

According to this statement, the control of unfair terms is not only devoted to the balancing test made by judicial power in a conflict between one business and one consumer, but also to a public authority that can better evaluate business strategy.

This is in one sense considered by the European legislator in the proposal for a directive on consumer rights. Again, it leaves it to Member States to ensure that their courts or administrative authorities have at their disposal adequate and effective means of preventing the continued application of unfair terms in consumer contracts. But it points out also that Member States lay down effective, proportionate and dissuasive penalties for infringements of the Directive. This means that private action is not still considered sufficient enough and that the development of European private law must mainly concern business commercial practices, looking at implementation measures that can efficiently combine private and public enforcement measures.

Chapter 10

'Technical Harmonization' versus Substantive Differences: Termination and Withdrawal in the Draft Common Frame of Reference

Peter Rott

1. INTRODUCTION

EC law has a reputation for its lack of coherence and consistency, and one example of incoherence are the details of the various rights of withdrawal included in EC Directives, namely the Doorstep Selling Directive 85/577/EEC,[1] the Timesharing Directive 94/47/EC,[2] the Distance Selling Directive 97/7/EC[3] and Directive 2002/65/EC on the Distance Marketing of Financial Services,[4] that appear to be the paradigm for bad law-making. The European Commission has taken the academic critique as an impetus for a major reform of EC consumer law, aiming for a coherent set of rules.[5] In parallel to the process of reforming EC consumer law,

1. OJ 1985, L 372/31.
2. OJ 1994, L 280/83 now replaced by Directive 2008/122/EC.
3. OJ 1997, L 144/19.
4. OJ 2002, L 271/16.
5. *See* only the EC Commission's Communication 'A More Coherent European Contract Law – An Action Plan', COM (2003) 68 final, at 8, the Green Paper on the Review of the Consumer Acquis,

Alessandro Somma, *The Politics of the Draft Common Frame of Reference*, pp. 163-175.

the Common Frame of Reference is being developed, with a much broader programme to cover. It deals with the whole of contract law, including the remedy of termination, but it also tries to integrate EC consumer contract law. Input on the latter has come from the so-called Acquis Group, which has tabled proposals on how to bring more coherence into EC consumer law.[6] The Study Group on European Contract Law, however, has modified the Acquis Group proposals when it integrated them into its Draft Common Frame of Reference that was published in early 2008.[7]

The effect on the regulation of the right of withdrawal is twofold: first, the DCFR – following the Acquis Group – seeks consistency of the various rights of withdrawal, and second, perhaps even more importantly, it tries to integrate the right of withdrawal into the set of the other remedies available. In particular, it attempts to streamline the right of withdrawal with the right of termination, which is available in a number of different situations, including a fundamental breach of contract by one party. This far-reaching harmonization approach is of striking similarity to what the German legislator has done in its reform of the law of obligations that came into effect on 1 January 2002, and the DCFR even applies the same regulation technique when it comes to the consequences of the withdrawal, which is a reference to the respective rules on the consequences of the termination of the contract. Thus, a strong German influence on this particular part of the DCFR is plain.[8]

This triggers the question as to whether the wish for coherence and consistency of the law has had too much influence on the DCFR, thereby neglecting differences between the various rights of withdrawals as such and even more the differences between the right(s) of withdrawal emanating from consumer law and the general contract law right(s) of termination. In other words, justice considerations that had been reflected in the piecemeal approach of the EC and in the rules of national consumer laws and national laws of obligation might have been washed away in order to achieve, for political reasons or otherwise, harmonization in the law. The respective approach of the German legislator has been heavily criticized by some authors at the time,[9] and their criticisms and German experience with the

---

COM (2006) 744 final, at 21 and the proposal for a Directive on Consumer Rights, COM (2008) 614 final, at 3.

6. *See* Acquis Group (ed.), *Principles of the Existing EC Contract Law – Contract I* (Munich: Sellier, 2007).
7. *See* the contributions to R. Schulze (ed.), *Common Frame of Reference and Existing EC Contract Law* (Munich: Sellier, 2008).
8. *See also* E. Terryn, 'The Right of Withdrawal, the *Acquis* Principles and the Draft Common Frame of Reference', in *Common Frame of Reference and Existing EC Contract Law*, ed. R. Schulze (n. 7 above), 168, and generally O. Lando, 'The Structure and the Legal Values of the Common Frame of Reference (CFR)', *European Review of Contract Law* 3 (2007): 250.
9. *See* for the various rights of termination that have been collected under one heading J. Kohler, 'Rücktrittsrechtliche Bereicherungshaftung', *Juristenzeitung* 57 (2002): 684, and for the various rights of withdrawal P. Rott, 'Harmonising Different Rights of Withdrawal: Can German Law Serve as an Example for EC Consumer Law?', *German Law Journal* 7 (2006): 1109 et seq. For an

new law, in particular case-law, are considered in the following assessment of the proposed rules of the DCFR.

2. TECHNICAL HARMONIZATION VERSUS DIVERSITY IN SUBSTANCE

Obviously, not all rules of law reflect considerations of justice. There are technicalities such as the calculation of periods that merely require a decision to be made, and that decision should indeed be the same for situations that are alike. To that extent, no one would doubt the merits of harmonizing the different rights of withdrawal. In contrast, the duration of the period of withdrawal is certainly not a technicality, and harmonizing the periods of different rights of withdrawal would only be useful if these rights of withdrawal serve the same purpose. Even more, the usefulness of a right of withdrawal stands and falls with the consequences that its exercise triggers. If they are highly unfavourable to the consumer, they may act as a deterrent that devalues the right of withdrawal. Here, a balance must be found between the consumer's interests and the interests of the trader, and it is anything but obvious that this balance is the same with all rights of withdrawal. It is even less obvious that the balance would be the same with respect to the various rights of termination enshrined in the DCFR, and between the rights of withdrawal and the rights of termination. Before going into the details of the regulation of both the right of withdrawal and the right of termination, it is therefore necessary to step back and revisit the purposes of the various rights that are meant to be largely streamlined.

The right of withdrawal is a speciality of consumer law, and the different rights of withdrawal may all be brought under one broad goal: they aim at securing the consumer's free and self-determined decision.[10] That free and self-determined decision, however, may be in peril for different reasons.[11] In doorstep selling, it is the surprise, the pressure, and the lack of comparison of goods or services and prices that may make the consumer make an unreasonable decision to contract.[12] In distance selling, the reason – at least with respect to the delivery of goods – is that the consumer cannot see them in reality, inspect or test them before the purchase, and may therefore be disappointed when they are delivered.[13] The justification

account of the streamlining of the right of withdrawal with the right of termination under German law *see* P. Rott, 'Die einseitige Vertragsbeendigung im deutschen Recht', in *Neue Entwicklungen im französischen, deutschen und polnischen Zivilrecht aus der Perspektive des europäischen Rechts*, ed. M. Pyziak-Szafnicka (Łodz: Łodz University Press), 165 et seq.

10. *See* G. Reiner, 'Der verbraucherschützende Widerruf im Recht der Willenserklärungen', *Archiv für civilistische Praxis* 203 (2003): 9 et seq.
11. For an overview, *see* S. Kalss & B. Lurger, *Rücktrittsrechte* (Vienna: Manz, 2001).
12. *See* only recital (4) of the Doorstep Selling Directive 85/577/EEC.
13. *See* recital (14) of the Distance Selling Directive 97/7/EC. That this argument also holds true for the distance marketing of financial services has been recently rejected by Terryn (n. 8 above), 151.

for the right of withdrawing timesharing contracts and consumer credit contracts[14] is that these contracts can be very complex and difficult to understand and may therefore require an additional period of reflection;[15] although timesharing contracts often have a situational element as well since they tend to be concluded on holidays, in a very particular mood that may vanish quickly on return to everyday life.[16]

Even more, one could question whether it is always the same consumer who is protected. The doorstep selling consumer is typically passive, and it is also well-known that doorstep sellers use certain communication systems through which they identify and mark easy victims, or particularly vulnerable consumers. These consumers are undoubtedly different from consumers who are experienced in shopping on the Internet, or in terms of consumer law, in distance selling. And Internet shoppers may again be different from other distance purchasers, namely those who order (offline) from a catalogue, or as a reaction to a mail advertisement. It may therefore be necessary also to make distinctions as to their legal treatment between the different kinds of consumers involved in certain transactions.

With regard to the right of termination, the variety is even greater, although the common denominator may be seen in problems in the performance by the other party to the contract. Such problems may be, e.g., the fundamental non-performance of the contract (Article III.-3:502 DCFR), or delayed performance, if the contracting partner has still not delivered after the setting of an additional period for performance (Article III.-3:503 DCFR), or anticipated non-performance (Article III.-3:504 DCFR), or inadequate assurance of performance (Article III.-3:505 DCFR), or the lack of conformity in a consumer sales contract (Article IV.A.-4:202 DCFR). Moreover, the right of termination may be agreed upon contractually, with or without the prerequisite of a breach of contract, under Article III.-1:109 DCFR.

3. THE HARMONIZED APPROACH OF THE DCFR, ITS LIMITS, AND ITS INJUSTICES

3.1. A Short Overview of the Right of Withdrawal in the DCFR

The right of withdrawal is dealt with in the second book of the DCFR, in Articles II.-5:101 et seq. The common rules of the Articles II.-5:101 et seq. apply if the consumer is granted a right of withdrawal elsewhere, e.g., in Article II.-5:201 on

14. The Consumer Credit Directive 87/102/EEC had not introduced a right of withdrawal at EC level, but many Member States have done so. The new Consumer Credit Directive 2008/48/EC has now filled this gap in its Art. 14. For an account, *see* P. Rott, 'Die neue Verbraucherkredit-Richtlinie und ihre Auswirkungen auf das deutsche Recht', *Wertpapier-Mitteilungen* 62 (2008): 1104 et seq.
15. In some legal systems, in particular in France, that period of reflection must be expired before the conclusion of the contract.
16. *See*, e.g., A. Ehrhardt-Rauch, 'Der Teilzeit-Wohnrechtevertrag', *Verbraucher und Recht* 17 (2002): 119 et seq.

'Contracts negotiated away from business premises', which includes doorstep selling and distance selling, or in Article II.-5:202 on timeshare contracts.[17] The right of withdrawal in consumer credit contracts may be integrated now that the new Consumer Credit Directive has been adopted.

The common rules deal with the exercise of the right of withdrawal, the period of withdrawal, adequate information on the right of withdrawal, the legal consequences of the withdrawal, and linked contracts. Some of these issues had been dealt with in the above-mentioned Directives, and the Acquis Group has distilled the relevant rules from these Directives and proposed to extend them to those types of contracts where they were regulated differently or not at all. In other cases, the Directives had left considerable freedom to the Member States, requiring them merely to find solutions that do not undermine the effectiveness of the right of withdrawal. These gaps have been filled by the Acquis Group and the Study Group as well.[18] In the following, I will single out two essential aspects of the right of withdrawal and discuss the issue of harmonization versus substance: the period of withdrawal and the consequences of withdrawal as streamlined with the consequences of the termination of the contract.

3.2. THE PERIOD OF WITHDRAWAL

3.2.1. The Duration

As in German law, the uniform period of withdrawal has been set at two weeks. In principle, a uniform period of withdrawal appears to make sense, and it is of importance to the Commission that the period of withdrawal is easy to calculate.[19] The question is, however, whether two weeks is always sufficient.

While there should be no doubt that a two-week period allows the consumer to recover from the surprise or psychological stress of a doorstep situation[20] and also enables the consumer to inspect goods bought on the Internet, this is more questionable in the case of timeshare contracts. In this field, the period of ten days has perceived to be too short by a number of authors.[21] The reason is of a psychological nature, and it is twofold. First, timeshare contracts are usually concluded when the consumer is on holidays, and indeed in a holiday mood of euphoria. This mood will frequently persist until the consumer returns home, to everyday life. Therefore, authors have suggested to either let the period of withdrawal only begin on return

17. For a critique of this provision, *see* H. Eidenmüller et al., 'Der Gemeinsame Referenzrahmen für das Europäische Privatrecht', *Juristenzeitung* 63 (2008): 545.
18. For an analysis of the differences between the proposals of the Acquis Group and the DCFR, *see* Terryn (n. 8 above).
19. One problem of EC law to date is that some periods of withdrawal are expressed in the term 'working days', whose meaning differs between the Member States.
20. *See also* G. Monti, 'The Revision of the Consumer *Acquis* from a Competition Law Perspective', *European Review of Contract Law* 3 (2007): 301 et seq.
21. *See* Ehrhardt-Rauch (n. 16 above), 119 et seq.

from holidays or to extend it to a period in which the 'normal' consumer would be back, e.g., to four weeks. Linking this back to the aim of the right of withdrawal to allow the consumer a free and self-determined decision, consumer psychology would necessarily have to be taken into consideration, and holiday euphoria may have a role to play. Whether or not this really requires a four-week period is difficult to assess, but the point is made that the question is not one of harmonization but of achieving the results that the right of withdrawal is meant to achieve.

The second difference between the right of withdrawal in timeshare contracts and also in consumer credit contracts, on one hand, and the situational rights of withdrawal in doorstep and distance selling on the other, lies in the different effects of the respective contracts. In timeshare and consumer credit contracts, the negative effect of having to pay the price is less immediate, since the price must only be paid over time.[22] Now, the consumer usually only reconsiders the contract once it produces noticeable effects. In the case-law of the ECJ, this was considered in the case of *Cofidis*.[23] This demonstrates at least that the right of withdrawing from the contract within two weeks may be of limited use in fighting market failure in the fields of timeshare and consumer credit contracts, and in fact the withdrawal of a consumer credit contract within that period of time occurs rarely in practice.

3.2.2. The Beginning of the Period of Withdrawal

With a view to the beginning of the period of withdrawal, EC law has always made a difference between the distance selling of goods and all the other rights of withdrawal. While in most contracts, the period of withdrawal begins to run with the conclusion of the contract (provided that the consumer has been informed of his or her right of withdrawal), the additional requirement in the case of the distance selling of goods is that the goods have been delivered to the consumer.[24] The reason is of course that the whole idea of the right of withdrawal in distance selling is that the consumer cannot see and inspect the goods that he or she purchases and that the consumer may therefore have an incorrect idea of it. Some goods, in particular, clothes, the consumer will need to 'test' anyway before purchasing them. Here, EC consumer law has already set the relevant benchmark.

Remarkably, Article II.-5:103(2)(c) DCFR extends this rule to doorstep selling cases in which goods are not immediately handed over. In fact, doorstep sellers also work with catalogues and the like that may give an incorrect picture to the consumer of what to expect. To that end, the consumer's interest is therefore the same as in distance selling, and this is well-reflected in the DCFR.

22. *See also* Eidenmüller et al. (n. 17 above), 546.
23. ECJ, Case C-473/00, *Cofidis SA v. Jean-Louis Fredout* [2002] ECR I-10875, with a comment by P. Rott, 'Effektiver Rechtsschutz vor missbräuchlichen AGB – Zum Cofidis-Urteil des EuGH', *Europäische Zeitschrift für Wirtschaftsrecht* 14 (2003): 5 et seq.
24. *See* Art. 6(1) sub-para. 2 of the Distance Selling Directive 97/7/EC.

3.2.3. The Extended Period of Withdrawal

Under all the current EC Directives that provide for a right of withdrawal, the period of withdrawal only begins to run once the consumer has received adequate information on this right, and this is also the rule provided by Article II.-5:103(2)(b) of the DCFR. Consequently, where no information, or inadequate information, is provided, the period of withdrawal does not run and cannot end. This has been made utterly clear for doorstep selling cases in the ECJ case of *Heininger*.[25] This principle has a practical background but is also based on considerations of justice. The practical background was set out by the ECJ in the following words: 'if the consumer is not aware of the existence of the right of cancellation, he will not be able to exercise that right'.[26] The ECJ held that it was the trader's own fault to have come into this situation of legal certainty, since under the regime of the Doorstep Selling Directive the trader had the duty to inform the consumer of his right of withdrawal, and by doing so, he would have triggered the start of the regular period of withdrawal.

In other cases, in particular in the Timesharing Directive 94/47/EC and in the Distance Selling Directive 97/7/EC, the EC legislator itself has introduced limitation periods. The period of withdrawal is extended by three months, to a total of three months and seven or ten days respectively. The DCFR proposes a compromise solution:[27] the maximum period is set at one year.

Of course, the decision which level of consumer protection should be provided is first and foremost a political decision. One could, however, ask the question whether or not harmonization of the extended periods is justified at all. First, one could argue that distance selling consumers are more likely to be aware of their right of withdrawal than doorstep selling consumers. The argument that the 'average' distance selling consumer has a general idea that he has a right of withdrawal shines through in other parts of EC legislation. Article 3(1) No. 3 lit. a) of Directive 2002/65/EC on the Distance Marketing of Financial Services requires the trader to inform the consumer not only of the existence of a right of withdrawal but also of its non-existence. This reflects the increased awareness of consumers of the right of withdrawal and is meant to prevent unjustified expectations in a situation where the right of withdrawal is excluded.[28] Does this argument hold true for doorstep selling as well? Is the doorstep seller the same consumer as the distance seller? To point here at a general concept of the 'average consumer' would mean to

25. Case C-481/99, *Georg Heininger and Helga Heininger v. Bayerische Hypo-und Vereinsbank AG* [2001] ECR I-9945.
26. *Ibid.*, para. 45.
27. Which again recalls German law where the compromise was fixed at a six months period before the law was changed in order to implement the *Heininger* judgment. For a critique *see* P. Mankowski, 'Zur Neuregelung der Widerrufsfrist bei Fehlen einer Belehrung im Verbraucherschutzrecht', *Juristenzeitung* 56 (2001): 748 et seq.
28. *See also* H.-W. Micklitz & M. Schirmbacher, 'Duties to Inform Contained in Directive 2002/65/EC Concerning the Distance Marketing of Consumer Financial Services', *European Banking and Financial Law Journal (EUREDIA)* 5 (2003): 473.

ignore that doorstep sellers especially target vulnerable consumers (in particular elderly people) who are not aware of such more recent developments. Thus, whereas a limitation of the extended period of withdrawal in cases of lack of information of the right of withdrawal is debateable for distance selling, it is an invitation to the breach of the same information obligation in doorstep selling cases.

3.3. The Consequences of Termination and Withdrawal

The provisions related to the consequences of termination and of withdrawal are almost all new. This paragraph provides a brief overview[29] before it turns in more detail to issues where different situations have been regulated differently, or where they might require more distinctions than the harmonized approach of the DCFR allows for. The basic structure is this: Article III.-3511 et seq. DCFR deal with the consequences of termination. The provisions apply to all sorts of rights of termination provided by law, and also to the contractually agreed right to termination if the contract does not specify otherwise. Article II.-5:105(1) provides for the consequences of withdrawal that Articles III.-3511 et seq. DCFR apply unless there are specific provisions for the consequences of withdrawal so that the provisions on the consequences of termination and of withdrawal are generally streamlined, as long as there are no explicit deviations provided in Article II.-5:105(2)-(4).

3.3.1. Brief Overview

Obviously, in all cases in which the contract is terminated or withdrawn from, the parties have to return what they have received, Article III.-3:511(1). Goods that have to be returned must be transferred, under Article III.-3:511(3) DCFR. The DCFR also provides for a number of rules under which the party that has received goods or services may incur liability for their use, for loss or damage, or for the devaluation of goods. Under Article III.-3:514(1), to which Article II.-5:105(1) refers, the recipient of goods must pay a reasonable amount to the supplier for the use made of the goods before returning them. Moreover, the recipient is liable for loss of or any damage to the goods that has occurred before the termination or withdrawal, under Article III.-3:513(1)(b), to which Article II.-5:105(1) refers for the right of withdrawal. Here, the law on the right of withdrawal explicitly deviates from the law on the right of termination by making an exception in cases where the consumer took reasonable care to prevent such destruction, loss, or damage. The recipient of a service has to pay compensation for that service, under Articles III.-3:511(4) and III.-3:513(1)(a), and Article II.-5:105(1) also refers to that rule for the consequences of withdrawal. Finally, the law deals with compensation for

29. For a detailed analysis see P. Rott, 'The right of withdrawal in the Common Frame of Reference', *European Business Law Review*, 20 (2009): 219 et seq.

the devaluation of new good by turning it into a second-hand good, but this is a heading that only applies to the right of withdrawal.[30]

3.3.2. The Return of Payment

If one party has already paid, such payment has to be returned under Article III.-3:511(2) DCFR. For the right of withdrawal (only), Article II.-5:105(2) section 2 DCFR requires the trader to return any payment made by the consumer without undue delay, and in any case not later than thirty days after the withdrawal becomes effective, i.e., after the notice or the returned goods have been received, as described in Article I.-1:106(3) DCFR. This provision extends Article 6(2) section 3 of the Distance Selling Directive to all consumer contracts. Consequently, the trader's performance is delayed if the payment is returned after more than thirty days, which may trigger damages and the like.

3.3.3. The Return of Goods

The rule of Article III.-3:511(3) DCFR applies to the termination of a contract and to the exercise of the right of withdrawal likewise: goods that have to be returned must be transferred. While the notion of 'transfer' would not seem to require necessarily that goods are sent to the trader's place of business, nothing in the DCFR appears to prevent such an agreement to be made by contract, and in particular in the trader's standard terms.[31]

This is the normal rule in cases of distance selling, and it is justifiable there, since the goods were sent by the trader to the recipient in the first place. This is entirely different in doorstep selling cases. In fact, in doorstep selling cases, the goods would not be with the consumer at all had the consumer not been surprised at home. For this reason, a number of Member States, including Finland and the United Kingdom, have enacted specific rules under which the trader has to collect the goods at the consumer's house if the latter withdraws from the contract, and this was also good law in Germany until 2000.[32] A consumer who does not wish to meet the trader again can still send the goods by mail.

3.3.4. Compensation for Use

In principle, it is fair to make the recipient of goods pay for the use of these goods if he had an advantage from using the goods. This is true where the party that has sold

30. Again, this is in line with German law where the liability for turning a new good into a second-good is also limited to the right of withdrawal but excluded for the right of termination (*see* § 346 para. 2 s. 1 No. 3 BGB). The provision is not discussed here since it is not relevant for the topic of this chapter. For detailed critique from a consumer protection point of view *see* Rott (n. 29 above).
31. For more details *see* Rott (n. 29 above).
32. *See* the comparative overview by P. Rott, *Die Umsetzung der Haustürwiderrufsrichtlinie in den Mitgliedstaaten* (Baden-Baden: Nomos, 2000), 140.

the goods terminates the contract because the other party does not pay, and it is also true where a consumer withdraws from a contract because he changed his mind. In the latter case, it is even said to be necessary to ask the consumer to compensate the trader for the use made since the consumer might otherwise 'buy' goods only to return them after two weeks of use, therefore abusing his right of withdrawal. And even if a consumer had an (unintended) advantage from using goods that he purchased on the doorstep, he should be liable for compensation, although in this case, the argument of abuse certainly does not hold. Of course, the obligation to compensate the trader for use made also constitutes a disincentive to exercise one's right to withdrawal, or to termination. This was just confirmed by the ECJ in the *Quelle* case,[33] for the right to replacement under the Consumer Sales Directive 1999/44/EC, and it has also been put forward by academics who argue that Article 6(2) of the Distance Selling Directive 97/7/EC therefore prohibits the consumer from being charged with the obligation of compensation for use.[34] Although it is in the end the legislator's decision as to whether or not the use of received goods should be compensated, this obligation on the user's part should at least not be excessive in amount so as to act as a deterrent to making use of one's legal rights at all.[35]

The further problem is that Article III.-3:514(1) DCFR always applies once the recipient of goods has made use of them, independently of whether or not he had any benefit from such use. For example, a consumer may have bought electronic equipment at the doorstep and may have used it for a day but has then decided that he does not need it at all. In such a case, the consumer has to pay compensation, although it was merely due to the surprise at the doorstep that he obtained and used the good. The responsibility for such useless use ultimately lies with the seller. Therefore, there should be a restriction for doorstep selling according to which the consumer merely has to return an unjustified enrichment.

3.3.5. Liability for Loss and Damage

The grounds of liability. The allocation of the risk of innocent loss or damage has always been a core issue in the regulation of the right of termination. There is no higher justice to that issue. In contrast, the legislator simply has to make a decision. At best, one could argue that the benefits and the risk should be on the same party. Thus, the party who obtains the benefits reaped during the time between the conclusion and the termination of the contract should also bear the risk. This is,

---

33. ECJ, Case C-404/06 *Quelle AG v. Bundesverband der Verbraucherzentralen und Verbraucherverbände*, [2008] ECR I-2865; on which see P. Rott, 'The *Quelle* Case and the Potential of and Limitations to Interpretation in the Light of the Relevant Directive', *European Review of Private Law* 16 (2008): 119 et seq.
34. *See*, e.g., H.-W. Micklitz, 'Die Fernabsatzrichtlinie 97/7/EG', *Zeitschrift für Europäisches Privatrecht* 7 (1999): 887. *See also* AG Trstnjak, 18 Feb. 2009, Case C-489/07, *Pia Messner v. Firma Stefan Krüger*, not yet reported.
35. For more details on the problem of calculating the compensation for use, *see* Rott (n. 29 above).

however, not the solution of the DCFR, and it is not the solution of German law either. While the supplier of the good can claim compensation for the use of the goods, as explained above, the risk of loss or damage through force majeure lies with the party who has received the goods. Exceptions apply in particular, according to Article III.-3:514(3), where the reason for the impossibility to return the goods lies in a non-performance of the other party of the contract, including non-conformity with the contract.

The law on the right of withdrawal explicitly deviates from the law on the right of termination by stating an exception, in Article III.-3:513(1)(b), for cases where the consumer took reasonable care to prevent the destruction of, loss of, or damage to the good. In doorstep selling cases, this is justifiable on the above-mentioned grounds that goods often come into the consumer's possession because of the surprise aspect of the visit or even the pressure exercised over the consumer, in other words, they should not be in the consumer's possession in the first place. In distance selling cases, one could argue that the consumer should not be disadvantaged when ordering goods in this way. If the consumer had tested and inspected goods in a shop, he would not be strictly liable for their loss or damage. Thus, he should not be strictly liable for the loss or damage under distance selling law either.[36]

The calculation of damages. If the recipient of goods is liable for loss of or damage to goods before the termination of the contract, the amount of compensation corresponds to the payment that was agreed upon, under Article III.-3:513(2). The same applies to the consequences of the right of withdrawal, see Article II.-5:105(1).

The idea behind this rule appears to be that the contracting parties have agreed upon the specific value of the good that should then also be relevant for calculating damages.[37] Exceptions only apply in cases of non-conformity of the goods with the contract, since in such cases it would be obviously unfair if the trader benefited by receiving the full agreed price of a defective good.[38] In this case, the rules on reduction in price apply, which is expressed in the formula that the value of the benefit is that proportion of the price which the value of the actual performance bears to the value of the promised performance, under Article III.-3:513(2) sentence 1 DCFR.

Still, the rule is not sufficiently flexible, and the most striking example is again doorstep selling. One particular danger of doorstep selling lies in overpricing goods or services.[39] The argument of the free agreement on the value of the goods is not valid in this situation since the right of withdrawal is the very instrument with

36. *See also* P. Rott, 'Widerruf und Rückabwicklung', in *Verbraucherschutz und Schuldrechtsmodernisierung*, eds H.-W. Micklitz et al. (Baden-Baden: Nomos, 2001), 265.
37. *See* E. Schmidt & G. Brüggemeier, *Grundkurs Zivilrecht*, 7th edn (Neuwied: Luchterhand, 2006), 333.
38. *See also* R. Gaier, 'Das Rücktritts(folgen)recht nach dem Schuldrechtsmodernisierungsgesetz', *Wertpapier-Mitteilungen* 56 (2002): 9, on German law.
39. *See also* A. Arnold & W. Dötsch, 'Verschärfte Verbraucherhaftung beim Widerruf?', *Neue Juristische Wochenschrift* 56 (2003): 188; Terryn (n. 8 above), 170 et seq.

which the free and self-determined decision is meant to be achieved in doorstep selling cases. Therefore, in such cases, the consumer should merely have to compensate the trader for the objective value of the goods.[40]

Compensation for received services. Under Article II.-5:105(1) with Art. III.-3:511(4) and III.-3:513(1)(a), the recipient of a service who has terminated or withdrawn from a service contract has to compensate the service provider for the value of services that were already rendered because services are obviously benefits that cannot be returned as such.[41] As in the case of the destruction or deterioration of goods, it is the agreed price that must be paid unless the services were defective. In other words, the recipient has to pay the agreed price for a service although he or she has terminated or withdrawn from the contract. The reason for this rule is that the trader should be protected from rendering services without being paid. At the same time, it is obvious that this rule completely devalues the right of termination or withdrawal. Thus, the drafters of the DCFR decided the dilemma in favour of the service provider.

This decision is, however, not justified, or just, in those cases in which the service provider could have protected himself against the dilemma, and has therefore created the dilemma in the first place. The first example is distance selling. Under Article II.-5:201(3)(b) DCFR, the right of withdrawal ceases to exist once the supply of services other than financial services if performance has begun, at the consumer's express and informed request, before the end of the withdrawal period. Thus, the described dilemma can only arise if the service provider has rendered a service without the consumer's express and informed request. In such a case, however, there is no reason to protect the trader against loss. He could have protected himself by asking for the consumer's express and informed request.[42]

The second example is doorstep selling. A trader who concludes a service contract at the doorstep can protect himself by simply working under the condition that the service will only be rendered after the expiry of the right of withdrawal.[43] Generally, the service will not be urgent; otherwise there would not have been a doorstep sale in the first place but the consumer would have taken the initiative of concluding a service contract.

Both situations are therefore fundamentally different in that the trader's dilemma is self-induced so that the decision to tip the balance in favour of the trader is simply unjust.

---

40. On the other hand, the consumer should benefit from the discount agreed upon. In such cases, the agreement should indeed be relevant in calculating the compensation. For more details, *see* Rott (n. 36 above), 270 et seq. *See also* H. C. Grigoleit, 'Besondere Vertriebsformen im BGB', *Neue Juristische Wochenschrift* 55 (2002): 1154, and the critical comments by Gaier (n. 38 above), 9.
41. *See also* Terryn (n. 8 above), 169.
42. *See also* B. Schinkels, 'Die Wertersatzverpflichtung des Verbrauchers bei Widerruf von Fernabsatzverträgen – Rechtsfortbildungsvorschläge', *Zeitschrift für das gesamte Schuldrecht* 2 (2005): 181.
43. *See also* H. Roth, 'Das Fernabsatzgesetz', *Juristenzeitung* 55 (2000): 1017, on the equivalent provision of German law.

4. CONCLUSIONS

There are some instances where the drafters of the DCFR have indeed adjusted the rules on the different rights of withdrawal in such a way that similar situations with identical needs of protection are answered with identical rules. The prime example for this is the new rule in doorstep selling under which the period of withdrawal only begins with the delivery of goods.

Otherwise, the DCFR largely focuses on a technical form of harmonization or streamlining of rules that neglects the variety of situations and needs of protection addressed by the different rights of withdrawal, thereby devaluing the right of withdrawal, in particular in doorstep selling, in parts. Harmonization of the rules by abolishing justified protection for those who legitimately wish to get rid of a contract and of what was delivered under that contract is, however, entirely unnecessary. Neither does such harmonization make the law more comprehensible, nor more just. Maybe it is the intention of the drafters of the DCFR to reduce consumer protection, in particular in doorstep selling cases. Otherwise, this type of harmonization somehow recalls the 'better regulation' approach pursued by Commissioner Verheugen, who seems to think that 'better' regulation is equivalent to the decrease of the number of pages that are filled with EC legislation.[44]

44. *See* the Commission's Working Document Second progress report on the strategy for simplifying the regulatory environment, COM (2008) 33 final: 3: 'Overall, since October 2005, the Commission has already put forward about 400 legal acts for repeal, modification or replacement. As a result, about 300 legal acts representing about 5 000 pages of the Official Journal will be deleted from the Community statute book.'

Part Four
Other Specific Issues

Chapter 11

Non-contractual Liability Arising Out of Damage Caused to Another: The Making of a Hybrid

Gert Brüggemeier

1. PRELIMINARY REMARKS

A spectre is haunting Europe once again. This time it is the 'Spectre of the Common Frame of Reference' (CFR).[1] The other authors of this volume have already contributed to demystifying this phenomenon. But instead of focusing on contract law like the others, this piece critically scrutinizes Book VI on non-contractual liability. Book VI[2] is the most prominent representative of the three books on legal obligations (*obligations de plein droit*). While the books on contract law will probably be published as an official EU Frame of Reference, this is unlikely for Books IV-VI. If published, the function of the CFR would then be that of a toolbox

1. Metaphor used by N. Reich, 'A European Contract Law', *Journal of Consumer Policy* 28 (2005): 383.
2. The preparation of Book VI lay exclusively within the competence of the Study Group. The overall control has been assigned to C. von Bar. Comments are not as yet available. Its publication is scheduled for March 2009. For working papers, *see* C. von Bar, 'Konturen des Deliktsrechtskonzepts der Study Group on a European Civil Code', *Zeitschrift für Europäisches Privatrecht* (2001): 515 and J. Blackie, 'Principles of a European Law of Delict according to the Study Group on a European Civil Code', in *Grundstrukturen des Europäischen Deliktsrechts*, ed. R. Zimmermann (Baden-Baden: Nomos, 2003), 133.

Alessandro Somma, *The Politics of the Draft Common Frame of Reference*, pp. 179-198.

for the preparation of new EU legal acts searching to increase the coherence of European (consumer) contract law (*Acquis*).

Even though the practical importance of Book VI appears to be less significant, a critical discussion of it in a collection of analyses on the DCFR is nevertheless fully justified. This is so because it is – like the Principles of European Tort Law (PETL)[3] – a sophisticated draft model for a European law of delict/torts, addressing basic problems of liability law.

In my contribution, I will present the contents and structure of the draft model followed by a critical discussion. Given the limited space, the views expressed cannot claim to be exhaustive. The focus is on the essential issues. The contribution will conclude with a brief summary.

2. CONTENT AND STRUCTURE OF DCFR: BOOK VI

Book VI contains fifty-seven articles in seven chapters and can be divided into two parts. Part 1 consists of four chapters and could be described as the core of the draft model. Chapter 1 (fundamental provisions) mainly contains a 'basic norm' whose three central elements are the basic prerequisites of all liability: legally relevant damage, accountability, and causation. They are discussed individually in Chapters 2-4, respectively. This structure is essentially the same as that of the PETL. Also included in Chapter 1 are rules on preventive protection, comprising injunctions and compensation for salvage costs.

Part 2 contains three chapters: Chapter 5 (defences), Chapter 6 (remedies), and Chapter 7 (relationship between these rules and national legal systems).

2.1. Part One: The Basic Norm and Its Elements

'A person who suffers legally relevant damage has a right to reparation from a person who caused the damage intentionally or negligently or is otherwise accountable for the causation of the damage'. This is what the basic norm of Article VI-1:101 is all about.[4] The passive construction was deliberately chosen to emphasize the victim's perspective. The advantage of this approach over that from a tortfeasor's perspective is not readily apparent. In comparison with fault and/or

---

3. European Group on Tort Law (ed.), *Principles of European Tort Law – Text and Commentary* (2005); for more information on this, *see* G. Alpa, 'Principles of European Tort Law: A Critical View from the Outside', *European Business Law Review* 16 (2005): 957; G. Wagner, 'The Project of Harmonizing European Tort Law', *Common Market Law Review* 42 (2005): 1269; R. van den Bergh & L. Visscher, 'The Principles of European Tort Law: The Right Path to Harmonization?', *European Review of Private Law* (2006): 511; M. Schulz, 'Disharmonization: A Swedish Critique of Principles of European Tort Law', *European Business Law Review* 18 (2007): 1305.
4. The characteristic Roman numeral VI of Book VI, has consequently been omitted in the articles of this book.

one's own misconduct,[5] other legal causes of accountability appear to be secondary. Where legally relevant damage has not been caused intentionally or negligently, a party will only be accountable for causing such damage if this is stipulated in Chapter 3 (accountability).[6]

The Study Group was faced with the fundamental choice between two approaches: to focus on the injury of a legally protected interest or to adhere to the plain requirement of damage, i.e., whether to adopt the German (§ 823 I BGB) or the French model (Article 1382 *Code civil*), and it appears to have found a compromise by following the Italian *Codice Civile* of 1942.[7] It is not the injury of a protected interest *and* damage resulting thereof that triggers liability; the causation of a damage is sufficient. However, plain damage, as stipulated in Article 1382 *Code civil (dommage)*, will not do – what is necessary is qualified damage: *danno ingiusto*[8] or 'legally relevant damage'!

2.1.1. Legally Relevant Damage

What is a legally relevant damage? This issue is addressed in Chapter 2. The fundamental first article (2:101) attempts to provide a definition. For this purpose, two new categories are introduced: loss and injury. The concept of damage comprises three categories: *economic loss, non-economic loss* and *injury (as such)*.[9] The first two concepts are internationally recognized categories of damage. Nevertheless, both are properly explained, whereas the third concept, although new in this context, remains largely ambiguous.[10]

Legally relevant is one of these three forms of damage under three alternative conditions: (i) if it is listed in the subsequent Articles 2:201-211; furthermore (ii) if it results from the violation of a right or (iii) if it results from the violation of an interest which is worthy of legal protection. The last two variants are default rules for cases which are not listed under Articles 2:201-211.

Paragraph 3 addresses – in what seems to me a somewhat concealed manner – relational torts, i.e., the indirect or remote damages whose legal imputation is accomplished through the duty of care in Anglo-American common law,[11] and

5. The DCFR Book VI, has meticulously avoided the concept of fault. Supposedly, one started originally with intentional torts and negligence as the basic forms of a tort. The present version sees a reversion to the concepts of intent and negligence as forms of fault or types of one's own misconduct. For more on this, see the text below (2.1.2.).
6. *See* Art. 1:101 para. 2. Two other forms of legal accountability are considered in Ch. 3: Basically it involves vicarious liability and strict liability.
7. Corresponding evidence can be found in von Bar (n. 2 above), 520. *See* also Blackie (n. 2 above), 137.
8. Art. 2043 it. c.c. With *danno ingiusto*, however, the problem of unlawfulness (!) of the damaging behaviour lies in the foreground.
9. Article 2:101 para. 1 is so far, unclear. It only speaks of 'injury' but the category 'injury as such' arises in the in both Arts 2:201 and 2:203 and particularly (and subsequently) in Art. 6:204.
10. 'Injury as such' (c), is simply missing. *See* Art. 2:101 para. 4.
11. The English Law of Torts speaks of the threshold function of the duty of care. For further information, *see* the text below.

(often) through *Verkehrspflichten* under German law of delict.[12] Remarkably, all references to the category of duty have eventually been omitted from the Draft. Instead, it focuses on proximity, reasonableness, and policy considerations. We will return to this aspect in the section on causation and in Part 2.

Hereafter, the most important cases of legally relevant damage are listed under Articles 2:201 and subsequent sections, starting with losses which result from personal injury: wrongful death, injury to body, and health. Here, Article 2:201 paragraph 1 introduces, apart from economic and non-economic loss, 'injury as such' as an equally compensable relevant damage. Once again, recognized phenomena (loss which includes costs of treating personal injury; impairment of mental health by a medically diagnosable illness) are explained;[13] but 'injury as such' remains blurred. This framework with injury to the body and health, however, suggests that the ulterior concern may be the reception of the *danno biologico* concept as it has developed under Italian law over the last thirty years.[14]

The legal consequences arising from the death of a person are concurrently regulated in a separate article.[15] Then follows loss as a result of infringement of a person's right to dignity, liberty, and privacy.[16] In this case, too, 'injury as such' is considered a third category of loss. Next is loss resulting from infringement of property and lawful possession,[17] followed by relevant loss which is to be considered as pure economic loss.[18] This concerns economic torts. In fact, they are listed individually in a manner similar to that of the English 'torticles':[19] breach of trust, incorrect information and interference in the business enterprise, and so forth.[20] Cases of loss caused through anti-competitive practices fall under the last category (unlawful impairment of business – Article 2:208).

Environmental damage (Article 2:209) can also be found on this extensive list of pure economic losses. Albeit in an obscured form, namely as the costs incurred by State Authorities through the financing of measures aimed at remedying environmental impairments (damage to biodiversity and contamination of sites). Per se damage or injury as such does not apply to these situations.

---

12. *See* C. von Bar, *Verkehrspflichten. Richterliche Gefahrsteuerungsgebote im Deutschen Deliktsrecht* (Köln: C. Heymanns Verlag, 1980); G. Brüggemeier, *Deliktsrecht* (Baden-Baden: Nomos, 1986).
13. Article 2:201 para. 2 a) and b).
14. For further information, *see* below in Text (5).
15. This concerns the subrogation of claims of the victim, the consequential damages to relatives (loss of maintenance) and the payment of a *pretium mortis* (Art. 2:202).
16. Article 2:203.
17. Article 2:206.
18. von Bar however emphasizes that the draft totally refrains from the category of pure economic loss. This category allegedly opposes Europeanization. C. von Bar (n. 2 above), 523.
19. For a full list, *see* B. Rudden, 'Torticles', *Tulane Civil Law Forum* 6/7 (1991-1992): 105.
20. Articles 2:204 (incorrect information), 2:205 (breach of confidence), 2:208 (unlawful impairment of business), 2:210 (fraudulent misrepresentation), 2:211 (inducement of non-performance). For further information, *see* T. Weir, *Economic Torts* (Oxford: Clarendon Press, 1997).

Regarding terminology, the *de minimis* rule from the rear section[21] belongs to this context. Legally relevant damages are, in other words, solely non-minor losses!

2.1.2. Chapter 3: Accountability

It is basically still in the tradition of the nineteenth century that the principal reason for accountability in Book VI is *fault*, although this term is purposely not used in Chapter 3. Liability arises for the intentional and negligent infliction of a legally relevant damage.

After lengthy discussions in the Study Group, it appears that they have abandoned the difference between trespass torts and negligence as general types of tortious wrongs, which was originally adopted from the English common law of torts. What remains are two forms of personal misbehaviour: *intent* is appropriately defined as willingly and knowingly committing the damaging act.[22] *Negligence* means non-observance of the standard of required behaviour.

The standard applied is objective, taking into account the specific circumstances of the case or in line with a statutory provision.[23] The category of unlawfulness is not employed at all,[24] in contrast to the prominent position accorded to it in the Germanic and other civil law legal systems.[25] In principle, this is to be welcomed, although non-contractual liability for intentional wrongs cannot do without the sub-category of unlawfulness.[26] The DCFR tries to tackle this problem in the manner adopted by common law in relation to defences (Chapter 5).

If one applies an objective standard of negligence, it seems obvious that exceptions must be made for those incapable of committing torts.[27] Children under the age of seven are not accountable for damage occasioned intentionally or negligently. Children/minors between the age of seven and eighteen are judged according to the standard of their age group. Apparently, discernment

---

21. Article 6:102.
22. Article 3:101 – In contrast, the PETL seem to restrict the intentional tort to the violation of a duty of care and defines intent therefore as 'conscious negligence' (Art. 4:101 PETL: 'intentional violation of the required standard of conduct'). The conscious and wilful injury no longer constitutes the focal point.
23. Article 3:102. That a protective statute itself decides the standard of required conduct, is rather unusual. (Art. 3:102(a)).
24. An exception is contained in Art. 2:208: 'unlawful impairment of business'.
25. According to Art. 46 of the Swiss draft reform bill on the Law of non-contractual Liability, every injury of a legally protected interest should be unlawful, even if this, regardless of human behaviour, occurs through a specific hazard – dog bites, for example. For information on Austrian Law, *see* H. Koziol, *Österreichisches Haftpflichtrecht, Allgemeiner Teil*, vol. 1, 3rd edn (Wien: Manz, 1997), 138.
26. For further information, *see* G. Brüggemeier, *Haftungsrecht. Struktur, Prinzipien, Schutzbereich. Ein Beitrag zur Europäisierung des Privatrechts* (Heidelberg: Springer, 2006), 32 et seq.
27. *See* Art. 3:103.

is no prerequisite for the minor to be held accountable for damaging acts. However, children above the age of seven appear to be fully responsible for acts committed intentionally.[28] Furthermore, non-accountable minors are in exceptional cases liable for damage according to the principles of equity.[29] Surprisingly, the category of adults considered not accountable for legally relevant damage is not discussed here, but it is discussed at a later point under the heading of defences (Chapter 5).[30]

Parents are liable for losses occasioned by minors under the age of 14 who are considered not to be accountable for legally relevant damage. This surprising limitation to the age of 14 appears to have originated from the law of the Dutch *Burgerlijk Wetboek*.[31] What would then apply to 14-18-year olds who are considered incapable of committing torts? Would the rules which govern incapable adults apply accordingly in this case? The provisions relating to supervisory liability of homes and institutions for non-accountable minors and adults are complex. Both groups of supervisors are, however, liable only if they have neglected their supervisory duties.

In the second part of this chapter of Book VI, the Study Group turns its focus on industrial society, based on the division of labour. This sections deal with the principal's liability and forms of strict liability[32] for classic cases of hazards and industrial-technological risks. Article 3:201 contains firstly the traditional case of liability of the employer for torts committed by his employees and the legal person/ corporation for torts of its organs.[33] This is different from the odd law in Germanic civil law regimes where liability still derives from the additional fault of the employer himself. A provision on general enterprise liability for organizational fault (*défaut d'organisation*), which exists in most national drafts for reform and in the PETL,[34] is missing.

Once again in accordance with the Dutch model,[35] owners of buildings are liable for damages resulting from the unsafe condition of the building.[36] The keeper of an animal is also liable without fault.[37]

28. *See* Art. 3:103 para. 1 (restriction on negligence).
29. Article 3:103 para. 3.
30. Article 5:301.
31. Article 6:169 para. 1 BW.
32. The term of 'strict liability' has been avoided entirely. It is said to confuse more than it helps. Instead, 'liability without misconduct' is referred to von Bar (n. 2 above), 515, at 520.
33. For information on this 'classic' topic of legal comparison, *see* G. Eörsi, 'Private and Governmental Liability for the Torts of Employees and Organs', in *International Encyclopaedia of Comparative Law*, ed. A. Tunc, vol. XI (Tübingen: J.C.B. Mohr, 1976), Ch. 4 and J. Spier (ed.), *Unification of Tort Law: Liability for Damage Caused by Others* (Wien: Springer, 2003).
34. *See* Art. 49a of the Swiss Draft, § 1304 of the Austrian Draft, Art. 1353 of the French Avant-Projet 2005 and Art. 4:202 PETL.
35. *See* Art. 6:174 para. 1 BW.
36. Article 3:202.
37. Article 3:203.

Product liability is considered at great length (nearly one and a half pages) in Article 3:204. Essentially the entire provisions of the EC Directive on product liability of 1985[38] have been compressed into this one article.[39] The Directive's restriction of the scope of protection in cases of property damage to consumer assets and the exclusion of liability for development risks have been adopted. A post-marketing duty of the manufacturer to monitor his products has not been introduced. The limitation to the recovery of property damage not exceeding a value of EUR 500 has been dropped.[40]

Article 3:205 contains the strict liability of keepers of motor vehicles in line with the German and French (*Loi Badinter*)[41] models. But what about the strict liability of operators of railways, airplanes, and motor vessels in a European law of non-contractual liability?[42]

Not only is general enterprise liability missing, but also a general strict liability for 'particularly dangerous activities', similar to that existing in US law, from the (*First*) *Restatement of Torts* onwards.[43] In Germanic legal systems, scholars have long demanded a similar general strict liability rule concept to do away with the patchwork law of diverse statutory rules.[44] This topic has also been on the agenda of the Study Group.[45] However, it is not considered in the present version of Book VI. Instead, Article 3:206 contains a cautious quasi-strict rule on environmental liability. It concerns only commercial activities. Liability requires a high probability that organizational defects will result in damages of the type in question (paragraph 1(a)). This does not apply if State safety regulations (threshold values etc.) have been observed. An extension of liability is, however, possible if this is in accordance with liability rules under Member States' law.[46]

Generally, it must be stressed that this sub-chapter refers to a different scope of protection and uses different terminology. 'Legally relevant damage' is neglected.[47] Instead, the focus is on *personal injury* and consequential loss, loss within VI-2:202,[48] and loss resulting from *property damage*.

---

38. Council Directive of 25 July 1985 ... concerning liability for defective products (85/374/EEC), OJ L 210/29-33 (1985); *see* further H. C. Taschner, *Produkthaftung* (München: C. H. Beck, 1986); amended through Directive 1999/34/EC, OJ L 141/20 (1999). For information on European product liability, *see* G. Howells, *Comparative Product Liability* (Aldershot: Dartmouth, 1993).
39. Article 3:204 para. 3 contains a misleading narration of Art. 3 para. 3 of the Directive on Product Liability.
40. An editorial error?
41. *See* further A. Tunc, 'Loi Badinter – On Traffic Accidents and Beyond', *Tulane Civil Law Forum* 6/7 (1991-1992): 27.
42. For further information, *see*, e.g., H. Kötz, 'Gefährdungshaftung', in *Gutachten und Vorschläge zur Überarbeitung des Schuldrechts*, ed. Bundesminister der Justiz, vol. 2 (Köln: Bundesanzeiger, 1981), 1779.
43. § 520 Restatement of Torts, 1938.
44. *See* Kötz (n. 42 above), ibid.; M. Will, *Quellen erhöhter Gefahr* (München: C.H. Beck, 1980).
45. *See* von Bar (n. 2 above), 527.
46. Article 3:207(b).
47. Except for vicarious liability under Art. 3:201.
48. Losses of dependants in cases of fatalities.

2.1.3. Causation

The legally relevant damage must have occurred through one of the above reasons for accountability. Causation is a central prerequisite of liability. However, in contrast to the PETL,[49] the DCFR seems to consciously refrain from introducing the causation concept of *conditio sine qua non* or any alternative concept. According to Article 4:101 paragraph 1, a person causes damage if such damage is considered a consequence of his/her conduct or a consequence of a source of danger for which he/she is responsible. Here, as with other previously discussed situations, the failure to clarify is evident. To me, it appears that by using this vague definition the Study Group wants to cover both internationally recognized concepts: the *cause in fact* and the *legal cause*. This means that the concept of causation provided by Book VI of the DCFR comprises also the normative imputation of remote damages in so-called relational torts cases.[50] As a result, legal questions and questions of fact are intermingled. Paradigmatic cases illustrating this inclusion and exclusion of legal questions in common law are the American case *Palsgraf v. Long Island R.R.Co*[51] and the Australian-English case *Wagon Mound*.[52]

Meanwhile, in German Law,[53] the non-causation related terms *Haftungszusammenhang* or *Zurechnungszusammenhang* have been established to cope with this normative question of imputation.

This interpretation of Article 4:101 paragraph 1 is supported by the fact that paragraph 2 also deals with a normative problem of imputation – the so-called thin skill rule. Here the party who caused an unforeseeably substantial loss cannot wholly or partly relieve him/herself of responsibility by showing that the victim's vulnerability contributed to the severity of the damage.

The other two articles under the heading 'causation' involve cases of joint and several torts: joint tortfeasors, including participation by instigating and assisting, and alternative causes. The classic alternative causation is actually an unidentifiable case of single causation among a multitude of occurrences. The legal consequence in the case of alternative causation is highly controversial: joint liability or several proportionate liability according to the causation probabilities? The PETL decided in favour of proportionate liability.[54] Article 4:103 of Book VI chooses to continue with the traditional solution of joint liability which can also be found in most national civil codes.[55]

49. Article 3:101 PETL.
50. For further information, *see* Art. 2:201 para. 3 and the text above.
51. 162 N.E. 99 (N.Y. 1928).
52. *Overseas Tankship (UK) Ltd v. Marts Dock & Engineering Co. Ltd* (*The Wagon Mound No. 1*) [1961] AC 388; *Overseas Tankship (UK) Ltd v. The Miller Steamship Co. Pty Ltd* (*The Wagon Mound No. 2*) [1967] 1 AC 617.
53. *See*, e.g., BGH, 5.2.1985, BGHZ 93, 351 (Haftungszusammenhang); BGH, 14.2.1989, BGHZ 106, 391 (Zurechnungszusammenhang).
54. Article 3: 103 para. 1 PETL.
55. *See* § 830 (1) (ii) BGB, Art. 6:99 Dutch BW; *see* also Art. 1348 French Avant-Projet 2005.

2.2. Part Two: Chapters 5-7

2.2.1. Chapter 5: Defences

If the basic conditions of liability are fulfilled – a legally relevant damage has attributably been caused – reasons for excluding or limiting liability could then come into play. This issue is addressed in Chapter 5. The organization of the individual defences stands in contrast to systematic civil law reasoning. Instead, it follows rather the logic of common law. The comprehensive list of defences, however, is not very common in Anglo-American tort law.

The defences are mostly dealt with in connection with the respective nominate tort.

Consent and acting at one's own risk (assumption of risk) are covered.[56] Both exclude liability. Comparative/contributory negligence would result in a proportionate reduction of liability. Insubstantial contributory negligence is irrelevant.[57] In the case of injuries by a traffic accident, the victim must accept responsibility only when considerable contributory negligence is present,[58] in line with the French model. Noteworthy is the fact that in strict liability the German model is applied, i.e., the injured must accept responsibility for his/her own contribution by keeping a car or an animal.

Further cases follow which under German BGB law would be considered as reasons for justification: authority conferred by law, self-defence, and necessity. Furthermore, benevolent intervention is listed. The last defence is necessary protection of values fundamental to a democratic society, in particular by dissemination of information in the media.[59]

Chapter 5 now deals with what one would have expected earlier under the heading of fault and discernment: the incapacity of adults to reason and control their actions.[60] It functions as a defence. Liability for equity is also applicable here.

It is hard to see the connection between incapacity and *unavoidable events*, which are introduced here as a further reason for exclusion of liability ('events beyond control').[61] The alternative would have been force majeure. There is no mention of legal consequences; presumably this would be the exclusion of liability. The PETL introduces both possibilities: exclusion *and* reduction of liability.[62]

There are two further points in this chapter. The first is contractual exclusion and limitation of liability.[63] Liability for causing legally relevant damage intentionally cannot be contractually limited or excluded; the same is true for the exclusion of liability for gross negligence which is connected to personal injury

56. Article 5:101.
57. Article 5:102.
58. Article 5:102 para. 4.
59. Articles 5:201-203.
60. Article 5:301.
61. Article 5:302.
62. Article 7:102 para. 1 PETL.
63. Article 5:401.

or any exclusion or limitation which would contradict good faith and fair dealing. The responsibility for slight negligence and – apart from product liability – for strict liability is negotiable. Standard contract terms are not referred to here.[64] However, it must be assumed that exclusion of liability is possible by individual contract and through standard contract terms.

The final point in this chapter, which was not included in previous drafts, involves a special case of contributory negligence and should be dealt with there. Third persons – relatives, cohabitants – have to accept that their compensation claims in fatal cases and situations of serious personal injury are affected by the contribution of the first victim in bringing about the damage.[65]

2.2.2. Chapter 6: Remedies

The primary remedy is compensation. 'Reparation' is the term selected by the Study Group as a concept, which, unlike damages, is not limited to monetary forms of compensation for damage. The important Article 6:101 governs aims and forms of compensation. The aim of non-contractual liability is to restore the previous condition, i.e., to reinstate the person suffering legally relevant damage to the position he would have been in had the damage not occurred (*restitutio in integrum*). This can take place through money payments (compensation) or through other means – which probably refers to the traditional restitution in kind. For property damage, there are two alternative forms of 'reparation' available: compensation of the loss of value or payment of the costs for repair, within the boundaries of proportionality. The explanation that the injured is free to have the repair done[66] is not given until later in the text and would be better placed here, – however with the reservation that this only applies to property damage and not to personal injuries.[67] Where this is reasonable, the surrender of profits obtained through the wrongful act can be demanded.[68] Next there are rules on equalization of benefits and multiple creditors and debtors (solidary liability). The compensation claims are transferable (and hereditary). As already emphasized, the *de minimis* rule would have been more appropriately placed within the concept of legally relevant damage.

The section on monetary compensation includes a reduction clause and the clarification that compensation could take place through lump sum or periodical payments. Article 6:204 contains the laconic statement that 'injury as such' (alias *danno biologico*) is to be compensated independently of recovery for economic or non-economic loss. The question of quantification is referred to national law.[69]

---

64. For further information, *see* DCFR, Book II, Art. 9:401 et seq. (Unfair Terms).
65. Article 5:501.
66. Article 6:201.
67. Or should this also apply in cases of personal injuries?
68. Article 6:101 para. 4.
69. In any case, this is how I interpret Art. 6:203 para. 2, although personal injury and non-economic loss are there the focal points.

While the right to prevent further threatening damages was regulated earlier in Book VI in a prominent place,[70] this preventive protection is now restricted to cases where compensation would not be an adequate alternative remedy and where it is reasonable to prevent the damage from happening.[71] Third persons who incurred reasonable expenditure or sustained other losses when they intervened in order to prevent someone from suffering impending damage or to limit the extent of the damage can claim compensation of these costs from the person who was accountable for causation of the damage.

2.2.3. Chapter 7: Ancillary Rules

The closing chapter contains five ancillary rules:[72] a general proviso is made for the respective national constitutional law. National law continues to determine the statutory provisions. State liability is exempt from regulation by Book VI. Questions of liability arising in the course of employment and between trade unions and employers' associations are excluded. This also concerns the liability of employees and business managers towards third parties, an extremely controversial question in German law.[73] Even so, it remains for the national law to determine the fate of compensation claims in tort when insurers, employers, or other third parties make payments to the injured.

Certain aspects of the law of evidence,[74] in particular the controversial and extremely important question of standard of proof, have been left out. The same is true for problems concerning the relationship of liability law and third party insurance.[75] With regard to the law of prescription, the Study Group seems to be content with the contractual provisions of the DCFR.[76]

3. CRITICISM OF THE DCFR MODEL OF LIABILITY LAW

I will restrict myself to four points of criticism, with a fifth one to be added in my closing remarks.

---

70. Article 1:102.
71. Article 6:301.
72. Articles 7:101-105.
73. In relation to employees, *see* BGH, 16.6.1987, NJW 1987, 2510; in relation to executives, *see* BGH, 5.12.1989, BGHZ 109, 297; generally, *see* Brüggemeier (n. 26 above), 151 et seq.; B. Sandmann, *Die Haftung von Arbeitnehmern, Geschäftsführern und leitenden Angestellten* (Tübingen: Mohr Siebeck, 2001).
74. For further information, *see* M. Brinkmann, *Das Beweismaß im Zivilprozess aus rechtsvergleichender Sicht* (Köln: C. Heymanns, 2005); G. Wagner, 'Europäisches Beweisrecht', *Zeitschrift für Europäisches Privatrecht* (2001): 441.
75. For further information, *see* the Swiss Draft Reform Bill on the law of non-contractual liability ('Liability and private insurance' Arts 54-54i) and for a European account, *see* G. Wagner (ed.), *Tort Law and Liability Insurance* (Wien: Springer, 2005).
76. *See* DCFR, Book III, Ch. 7: prescription.

3.1. The Basic Misconception

The Study Group had to make a fundamental decision on Book VI: should the focus be on the injury of legally protected interests – or on the causation of damage? As pointed out above, the decision was made in favour of the latter, but not without essentially modifying it.

The legally relevant (!) damage became the centre of the new concept. What is legally relevant damage?[77] It is the loss sustained through (i) the injury of a right, (ii) the injury of a protected interest, or it is (iii) determined by special rules. What are these special rules about? They deal with the injury of legally protected interests such as life, the body, health, personality interests, property, and assets. Asset protection is restricted, however. Below the limit of intentional impairment it is limited to certain damaging situations.

The conceptual fundamental decision of the Draft is a misconception in my opinion. It pretends not to do something which it then does *re vera* after all – or possibly must do: to focus on the injury of a protected interest. This is then done with an openly displayed lack of consequence in the provisions on strict liability (Articles 3:202-306: 'personal injury', 'property damage').

In other words, *the legally qualified damage is the damage resulting from the injury of a legally protected interest.*[78] The price paid for this decision is high: terminological confusion and conceptual inconsistency. Injury as a condition of non-contractual liability and damage as the content of liability are distinct categories. The draft model of Book VI uses a confusing variety of concepts: damage, loss, injury, personal injury, injury as such, violation. All concepts serve the purpose of describing one and the same thing: the objective prerequisite of liability (the latter augmented by the elements of accountability and causation.) This course of action necessarily results in the intermingling of the condition of liability and the extent of liability/remedies. Where does compensation for pain and suffering belong? Where indeed is it regulated in the Draft?[79] Where do the costs of repair belong: to the legally relevant damage at the top or to the remedies below? This indecisiveness is also apparent in the *de minimis* rule. Traditionally, it belongs to the extent of liability. If the distinction between extent of liability and condition of liability is abolished, it definitely belongs to 'legally relevant damage'.

In my opinion the difference between the condition of liability – the injury of a legally protected interest – and that of the resulting consequences – compensation/ 'reparation' of damage – is an evolutionary accomplishment of private law jurisprudence in the second half of the nineteenth century. One must not repeat, however, the mistake of the BGB legislators who felt they had to draw up, in

77. For further information, *see* above text (section 2.1.1) with references.
78. *See* for example, Art. 2:206: 'Loss caused to a person as a result of an infringement of that person's property right'.
79. In the case of legally relevant damage, a legal definition can be found at the fore (Art. 2:101 para. 4(b)). In Ch. 6, which deals with remedies, only a statement that the assessment of the compensation for injury is determined by national law, can be found.

§ 823(1), a complete catalogue of protected interests. An alternative solution is offered by the Japanese law of delict of 1898 which provides in Article 709 for a non-enumerative catalogue of protected rights and interests, whose injury triggers an obligation to compensate. 'An interest is protected if the law of delict/torts affirms an injury and if compensation in whichever form is granted for this injury'.[80] This is exactly the path taken by the DCFR in Book VI with its default rules in the important Article 2:101 b) and c). Why then all this camouflage? Why destroy this clear structure through the unproductive detour via the compromise formula of 'legally relevant damage' as the central element of the condition of liability?

3.1.1. Accountability

This section, too, displays light as well as shadow, and also the distinct tendency to avoid terminological precision. The terms fault and strict liability do not appear in the text although they alone are the subject matter. Intentional and negligent causation of damage serve as modes of accountability. As pointed out before, the Study Group has fortunately abandoned the categories of unlawfulness and breach of duty.[81] However, this does not alter the fact that unlawfulness is needed as a sub-category in the law of intentional torts, in contrast to the law of negligence liability where this sub-category is superfluous. In this respect, the Draft uses defences instead. Insofar Book VI of the DCFR ultimately and clearly repudiates the tendency emanating from the common law of torts to merge the delictous/tortious wrong in the breach of duty.[82]

One of the negative aspects is, in my opinion, that the Draft even today does not regard fault and strict liability (I use these terms to designate the subject matter) as fundamentally equivalent modes of accountability. This would imply that there is no longer a distinction between the personal and objective scope of protection. But the opposite is done here, as in accordance with, e.g., German law.

A further flaw is that the subject of *enterprise liability* is completely ignored. Many civil law regimes in Europe and nearly all national as well as transnational reform drafts on liability law provide for a quasi-strict enterprise liability for defective and inadequate processes and organization.[83] Book VI of the DCFR acknowledges only the traditional vicarious liability for employees' torts.[84] This

80. Accurate definition, *see* von Bar (n. 2 above), 521.
81. For the apparent inextricable confusion over concepts of unlawfulness and violation/breach of duty, *see* E. Deutsch, *Fahrlässigkeit und erforderliche Sorgfalt*, 2nd edn (Köln: C. Heymanns, 1995); G. Wagner, *Münchener Kommentar zum Bürgerlichen Gesetzbuch*, vol. 5, 4th edn (München: C.H. Beck, 2004), preface to § 823; as a comparative European account, *see* H. Koziol (ed.), *Unification of Tort Law: Wrongfulness* (The Hague: Kluwer Law International, 1998); *see* also Brüggemeier (n. 26 above), 42 et seq.
82. For an example, *see* H. Kötz & G. Wagner, *Deliktsrecht*, 10th edn (München: Luchterhand, 2006); Wagner (n. 81 above).
83. For evidence, *see* n. 34.
84. Including the tort liability of organs of corporations.

deficit may be due to the fact that for a long time the Study Group adhered to negligence as *the* comprehensive tort category for non-intentional (faulty) injuries. Negligence also covers cases of enterprise liability, as illustrated by the classic international example of producers' liability.[85]

Doing without the common law tort of negligence leads to a further intricate core problem of modern liability law. Is breach of duty an indispensable precondition at least with regard to liability for negligent causation of damage? The tort of negligence of common law always employs a duty of care. This may rightly be criticized as redundant. To some extent attempts have been made to break up this category of duty into three concepts: notional function in cases of accidents, threshold function in cases of remote damages and affirmative duties demanding a person to act.[86] Without the latter, there is no liability for omissions. According to its black letter rules, the liability law of the DCFR seems to follow the other extreme. It does not acknowledge any duty of care at all, e.g., the duty to ensure safe premises (*Verkehrssicherungspflicht*). The development of these duties appears to have been delegated to the judiciary.

Also missing is a general rule of strict liability as originally envisaged by the Study Group and provided for in the PETL. This is only partly balanced by the provisions on quasi-strict liability for dangerous substances and emissions.[87]

The area of governmental liability has been omitted entirely, without any reasons being offered in the current workshop reports – and this in spite of the fact that here we find established principles of a EU State liability law, elaborated by the European Court of Justice[88] which are missing in all other fields of EU-non-contractual liability law.[89] Why is the European law of product and environmental liability adopted nearly without reservation while the case law of the ECJ is completely ignored?

Furthermore, it is unacceptable that the question of employees' (and executives') liability is not dealt with, although it is of great political relevance and a very controversial issue among EU Member States.[90] France and the Scandinavian countries in particular require intentional injuries to trigger liability of employees. In Germany and elsewhere, employees and business managers are liable in any case of fault for indirect and direct damages. As far as the employee is concerned, he may be protected through an exemption claim against his employer. Considering

---

85. From *MacPherson v. Buick Motor Co.*, 111 N.E 1050 (N.Y. 1916) via *Donoghue v. Stevenson* [1932] AC 562 to BGH, 26.11.1968, BGHZ 51, 91 (Hühnerpest).
86. *See* for English and Scottish Law, K. Norrie, *Stair Memorial Encyclopaedia of the Laws of Scotland*, vol. 15 (1995), para. 265.
87. Article 3:206 as the only case of an explicit enterprise liability.
88. ECJ, 19.11.1991, case nos C-6/90 and 9/90, *Francovich*, [1991] ECR I-5357; 5.3.1996, case nos C-46/93 and 48/93, *Brasserie du Pêcheur*, [1996] ECR I-1029.
89. The EU state liability law is of prominent importance. *See* W. van Gerven et al. (eds), *Tort Law: Scope of Protection* (Oxford: Hart, 2000), 889 et seq. and C. van Dam, *European Tort Law* (Oxford: Oxford University Press, 2006), 23 et seq.; on genuine European liability law, *see* H. Koziol & R. Schulze (eds), *Tort Law of the European Community* (Wien: Springer, 2008).
90. This was also obviously provided for differently in earlier drafts. *See* von Bar (n. 2 above), 529.

the toolbox function of the CFR, one would expect proposals for harmonization of such controversial legal questions.

In other words: a modern European concept of liability law must necessarily incorporate the field of *enterprise liability for insurable damages*. This comprises three aspects: quasi-strict liability for defective processes (presumption of organizational fault), strict employers' liability for torts committed by employees and executives, and a regulation of the liability of employees, executives, and members of supervisory boards. Essentially, governmental liability follows this structural model of private enterprise liability.[91]

4. SPECIAL CASES OF PRODUCT AND ENVIRONMENTAL LIABILITY

4.1. PRODUCT LIABILITY

The regulation of product liability in the monstrous Article 3:204 leads back to the unclear EU law foundations of the work of the Study Group. What is this actually about? Is the EC law basis for the enactment of the product liability directive of 1985 also the legal basis for the Study Group when drafting rules on product liability? If it is, then it must be considered a grave technical mistake not to provide for the retention of 500 Euros. There is ECJ jurisdiction on this issue,[92] which may not be too convincing but nevertheless clearly states its point.

If it is not the case, however, if the legal basis – whatever that may be – is broader, the retention of 500 Euros can indeed be omitted. But it then makes no sense to restrict product liability for damage to corporeal things on consumer property and to exclude liability for commercial property in the law of a European civil code! Besides, if the producer is not liable for development risks, as provided for in Article 3:204 paragraph 4 e), then this gap should be filled by introducing a post-marketing duty to monitor products. Formally this involves fault liability, therefore such a rule should, according to ECJ jurisdiction, even be admissible in the field of EC product liability.

4.2. ENVIRONMENTAL LIABILITY

In product liability, the Draft incorporates European secondary law practically word for word, the attitude towards European environmental liability law is ambivalent. But admittedly in this field, the development of EC law development has not been without ruptures. First the EC Commission followed a two-track approach: strict private law enterprise liability for individual damages caused by environmental pollution, and collective compensatory systems for other

91. Exemplary the German state liability Act of 1981, BGB1. 1981 (part I), 553.
92. ECJ, 25.4.2002, case no. C-52/00, *EC Commission v. France*, [2002] ECR I-3827.

environmental damages.[93] Both approaches intended to enforce the 'polluter pays principle' (Article 174 paragraph 2 EC Treaty). Of significance for this purpose were the proposals of a waste liability directive in 1989[94] and the Green Paper on the restoration of environmental damage in 1993.[95] In the White Paper on environmental liability of 2000[96] there is a shift in focus. Regarding the traditional individual damages, Member State law was expected to adhere to a strict civil liability model. In contrast, a public law approach was now introduced for the prevention and remedying of ecological damage (impairment of biodiversity, pollution of water and land): governmental measures of restoration and cost reimbursement by the polluters, independent of fault in the case of dangerous activities and depending on fault in case of non-dangerous activities. The promised general framework directive, which was to cover civil liability and public compensation systems, has, however, not been enacted.[97] Instead, merely the administrative procedures were put into force with EC Directive 2004/35. It clearly restricts the 'polluter pays principle' in comparison with earlier drafts. Liability is no longer given in cases involving lawful typical processes and development risks.[98]

Book IV of the DCFR now attempts – contrary to given EU law and with recourse to the approach of the Lugano Convention of 1993[99] – to reunite both goals of the White Paper under the roof of a civil liability. This takes place in Article 3:206. It contains, on one hand, a quasi-strict enterprise liability for individual damages through dangerous substances and emissions. In this respect the limited liability regime of Directive 2004/35 has been adopted for private law. Liability is restricted to damages which could have been avoided through adequate

---

93. On 'ecological damage' *see* in particular, E. Rehbinder, 'Ersatz ökologischer Schäden', *Natur und Recht* (1988): 149; C. Godt, *Haftung für ökologische Schäden* (Berlin: Duncker & Humblot, 1997).
94. Proposals for a Directive on the civil law liability for damages caused through waste of 4.10.1989, OJ C 251/3 (1991), amended 1991, OJ C 192/6 (1991); for further information *see* also C. Joerges & G. Brüggemeier, 'Europäisierung des Vertrags, und Haftungsrechts', in *Gemeinsames Privatrecht in der Europäischen Gemeinschaft*, ed. P.C. Müller-Graff, 2nd edn (Baden-Baden: Nomos, 1999), 301, 341 et seq.; P. Salje, 'Umwelthaftung in Europa', *Produkthaftpflicht International* (1995): 162.
95. COM (1993) 47 final.
96. White Paper on environmental liability of 9.2.2000, COM (2000) 66 final.
97. EC Directive on environmental liability with regard to the prevention and remedying of environmental damage (2004/35/EC) of 21.4.2004, OJ L 143/56 (2004); for further information, *see* G. Winter et al., 'Weighing Up the EC Environmental Liability Directive', *Journal of Environmental Law* 20 (2008): 163; on the implementation in Germany, *see* Umweltschadengesetz of 10.5.2007, part 1, BGBI (2007), 666; for further information, *see* B. Becker, *Das neue Umweltschadensgesetz* (München: C.H. Beck, 2007).
98. For criticisms on this, *see* G. Hager, 'Der Vorschlag einer europäischen Richtlinie zur Umwelthaftung', *Juristenzeitung* (2002): 901; endorsed by L. Bergkamp, 'The Proposed EC Environmental Liability Regime and EC Law Principles', *Environmental Liability* 6 (2001): 251.
99. Convention on Civil Liability for Damage resulting from Activities Dangerous to the Environment, *Produkthaftpflicht International* (1993): 196-211.

control measures. Furthermore, compliance with national safety regulations (lawful regular processes) excludes liability.

On the other hand, attempts are made to reinstate the topic of ecological damage, without further ado, under the civil liability regime. The enterprises are liable, but, according to the Draft, not for the ecological damage they cause. Ecological damage is not a legally relevant damage. However, the costs incurred by State authorities for remedying environmental impairments should be reimbursed by the polluters responsible according to Article 3:206 under the same soft conditions. This remedy is not so much a civil liability claim for compensation of damage than a State claim in 'civilian' clothes for reimbursement of costs spent for measures in the public interest. For this remedy a legal basis outside the DCFR still had to be found,[100] and this is where Directive 2004/35 comes into play. However, the relationship to the differentiated public law system of compensation, introduced through the same Directive, remains entirely open. No reservation or reference whatsoever is made to EU law, in contrast to Chapter 7 where several such remarks are made with respect to national law.

5. THE EUROPEANIZATION OF *DANNO BIOLOGICO*

It is quite extraordinary that the interested and well-meaning reader should be left to his/her own devices when it comes to a newly introduced legal category. As has been mentioned above, the concept 'injury as such' is not explained anywhere in the whole of Book VI. One can only speculate. Article 2:201 paragraph 1[101] 'makes clear that a claim lies simply because of the fact of injury per se', says Blackie.[102] Indeed Article 2:201 and Article 2:203 plus Article 6:204 state that in cases involving personal injuries and the impairment of personality rights, the 'injury as such' besides economic and non-economic losses is to be compensated. It is a third category of damage. It appears that this way the *danno biologico* or *danno alla salute*, which has developed in Italian law since the end of the 1970s, has been adopted for European private law.[103] In Italy, this legal development served to overcome the narrow limits for the compensation of non-economic losses, which the *Codice Civile* of 1942 had introduced in Article 2059, following the German BGB-model. The starting point was the reference to the constitutionally guaranteed right to health.[104] The consequences of this legal development were three categories of damage in connection with personal injury: economic loss, non-economic loss, and injury as such/damage per se. This brought about the result

100. Or one establishes the state compensation claim as a dubious case of gestio rerum; *see* Rehbinder (n. 93 above), 162.
101. 'Loss caused to a natural person as a result of injury to his or her body or health and the injury as such are legally relevant damage'.
102. Blackie (n. 2 above), 140.
103. *See* F. Busnelli, *Il danno biologico* (Torino: Giappichelli, 2001); G. Alpa, *Il danno biologico* (Padova: Cedam, 1993).
104. Article 32 Italian Constitution.

that since 2003 there has been, beyond the area of 'biological' personal injuries, an entitlement to non-economic loss in every case of violation of a constitutionally guaranteed right of the person.[105]

Does this suffice for a European solution? Considering the very reserved stance taken with regard to enterprise and State liability, the courageous innovation and apodictic statement here must come as a surprise: 'injury as such is to be compensated independent of compensation for economic and non-economic loss' (Article 6:204). Here many points on a national and international level are still unresolved. The starting point for the Italian development was the extension of narrow confines for compensation of non-economic loss.

The present Draft, however, does not share this restriction of the Italian civil code, so this cannot be the reason for the legal innovation.[106] Is there another one? Possibly this involves nothing other than to bring about a conceptual differentiation *within* the category of non-economic loss. This could exist between the classic compensation for personal suffering as conciliation for mental distress,[107] which possibly presupposes the sensitive faculty of the victim (missing, e.g., in cases of comatose patients)[108] – and the so-called damages per se. Awards for damage per se, in the case of personal injury, compensate lasting negative impact on the person's bodily integrity, such as the loss of organs (fingers, arms, or legs) or the loss of capabilities (blindness, deafness, or stiffness) or the 'destruction of the personality' by severe medical mistakes.[109] Here, as in compensation for personal suffering, the remedy is an equitable compensation in money. Unitary treatment of comparative cases can be achieved by means of national tables and tariff systems. The statement of Article 6:204 would then be understood as follows: damages per se in personal injury cases are to be compensated, regardless of compensation for economic loss *and* personal suffering. This would be exactly in accordance with the *trias* of the Italian law of damages.

Things are different, however, regarding the impairment of personality rights. This involves mainly financial compensation solely for the injury as such, unless 'reparation' through restitution in kind (revocation and counter-statement) is considered in exceptional cases. This is hardly something new, but it has been current practice for a while. As far as personality rights are concerned, the BGH has expressly implemented the shift from compensation for pain and suffering to a financial compensation scheme *sui generis*.[110]

105. Cass. it., 31.5.2003, n. 8828, Foro it. 2003, I, 2272; Cass. 31.5.2003, n. 8827, Foro it. 2003, I, 2273; Corte const. 11.7.2003, Foro it. 2003, I, 2201.
106. Also H. Eidenmüller et al., 'Der Gemeinsame Referenzrahmen für das Europäische Privatrecht – Wertungsfragen and Kodifikationsprobleme', *Juristenzeitung* (2008): 529, at 540.
107. Article 2:101 para. 4(b): pain and suffering and impairment of the quality of life!
108. Independent of the double function-doctrine of the BGH, 6.7.1955, BGHZ (GS) 18, 149. The English courts, too, grant pain and suffering awards only in cases involving consciousness: *Wise v. Kaye* [1962] 1 QB 638.
109. *Landmark* case: BGH, 13.10.1992, BGHZ 120, 1.
110. BGH, 15.11.1994, BGHZ 128, 1 (*Caroline v. Monaco* No. 1).

6. CLOSING REMARKS: 'THE MAKING OF A HYBRID'[111]

More than a decade ago, Pierre Legrand, like Martin Luther before him in Wittenberg, nailed his theses on the virtual doors of European law faculties' lecture-halls: 'European legal systems do not converge!'.[112] One a reformer, the other a restorer? Well, the convergence of civil law and common law – and this is what it is about – can assume a range of forms.

An approximation in substance which concerns the solution of comparable cases can easily be achieved within the different national legal structures. However, can both distinct legal forms 'merge' in a third hybrid form? Admittedly mixed study groups composed of excellent civil law and common law representatives can probably not avoid coming up with this kind of compromise solution. But does this make the result better? With Book VI, the Study Group could even not agree on the name of its subject of investigation. In order to avoid the tiresome dichotomy of delict-tort, a cumbersome legal definition of liability law has been coined. The terminological problems are merely problems *in re*. The concept of fault is not used, although intent and negligence in Articles 3:101 and 3:102 have the same functions as in the law of delict in continental civil law books: abstract conditions of liability and not individual torticles. The 'legally relevant damage' enters as a substitute for the injury of a legally protected interest and of a damage resulting thereof. The common law defences have been listed in a civil law manner, although in common law they are more likely to be arranged according to individual torts.

The rules governing the incapacity of adults in Book VI can serve as a concrete illustrative example for possible consequences of this hybridization of legal forms. It is contained in Article 5:301 in the chapter on defences against liability. This chapter is clearly of a common law nature. But what is the point of including a defence against liability when it is the very prerequisite of liability that this element is missing? Misbehaviour (alias fault) is a central element of liability in the concept of the DCFR (Article 1:101 paragraph 1). It exists only if the person has discernment, i.e., is legally able to commit a tort. According to the structure of Book VI, discernment or capacity is a condition of liability for one's own misbehaviour (alias fault) – and not a defence against an existing tort. (Therefore, the capacity of minors to commit torts has been rightly dealt with before in the chapter on accountability/fault – 'intent' and 'negligence').

Neither would this be changed by a reversal of the burden of proof. It is quite an appropriate rule that an adult must rebut the presumption of his/her capacity to commit a tort. Discernment/capacity does not mutate from a prerequisite of fault to a defence against a given tort. Apparently the ostensible aspect that the capacity of

---

111. Wording taken from J. Basedow, 'Codification of Private Law in the European Union', *European Review of Private Law* (2001): 35.

112. P. Legrand, 'European Legal Systems Are Not Converging', *International and Comparative Law Quarterly* 55 (1996): 52; id., 'Against a European Civil Code', *Modern Law Review* 60 (1997): 44; id., 'AntivonBar', *Journal of Comparative Law* 1 (2006): 13.

adults presupposes, besides discernment, the ability to *control* one's actions, seeks to justify the same treatment with regard to the defence of events which are unavoidable, i.e., beyond *control* (which involves the exclusion of strict liability!).[113]

Hybridization of the legal form necessarily implies the denaturing of both civil and common law. In this respect, Legrand got it right. The harmonization of liability law in Europe should take place through a convergence in substance on parallel paths *within* the respective legal form and legal culture: through judges and statutes in common law countries and by reform of the code in civil law systems.[114]

113. Article 5:302.
114. An overview and comments on the latest national initiatives on the reform of the law of delict in Austria, France, Switzerland and Turkey can be found in B. Winiger (ed.), *Haftungsrecht von Morgen – La responsabilité civile de demain* (Genève: Schulthess, 2008).

Chapter 12

On the Economics of Good Faith Acquisition Protection in the DCFR

Arthur F. Salomons

1. INTRODUCTION

The DCFR concerns primarily contract law topics, but an important exception is Book VIII (Acquisition and loss of ownership of goods), included in the DCFR at the end of 2008. Its fifty-nine articles[1] are dedicated to 'hardcore' property law topics such as possession, transfer and commingling, with one important limitation: they relate to corporeal movables only.[2]

This contribution focuses on Article VIII.-3:101 regarding good faith acquisition. There are several reasons for this. First, good faith acquisition is an important and controversial topic, on which a staggering amount of literature is available, thereby burdening the drafters of the provision with the task of taking into account a great many aspects and making an articulate choice between the alternative manners of dealing with the topic. Second, the manner in which good faith acquisition is regulated has both social and economic consequences, making a discussion of the policy choices made by the drafters particularly suitable for a book on the politics of the DCFR. Finally, provisions on good faith acquisition like

1. Thanks go to Brigitta Lurger, one of the drafters of Book VIII DCFR, for providing the draft version from June 2008.
2. Article VIII.-1:201 DCFR.

Alessandro Somma, *The Politics of the Draft Common Frame of Reference*, pp. 199-216.

Article VIII.-3:101 can be studied separately, even though the need for them depends largely on the property law system within which they operate (e.g., in a causal system, a defective title precludes successful transfer, thereby referring the would-be acquirer to alternatives like good faith acquisition and prescription). In other words, good faith acquisition is much like an autonomous microcosm within the property law universe, as the respective elements of that microcosm can be chosen and changed independently, without hampering or altering the property law structure beyond.[3] This makes Article VIII.-3:101 an excellent single subject for examination, from which we can distil (some of) the policy goals of the drafters of Book VIII.

The fact that no *travaux préparatoires* are available[4] is not helpful, but this difficulty can be overcome. After all, the content of Article VIII.-3:101 is ample indication of the purposes of the provision. The same result can be achieved by comparing Article VIII.-3:101 with its counterpart in other jurisdictions, about which more information is available. And finally, we can take advantage from the fact that one of the drafters of Book VIII published an article in 2006 on the politics of property law, in which she devoted several pages to the politics of good faith acquisition.[5]

As will become apparent, protection of the good faith acquirer is generally justified by the economic argument that commerce would be seriously hampered if buyers, despite their good faith and the fact that they bought in a legitimate shop, would have to carry the risk that the seller was not entitled to dispose of the property, the so-called innocent purchase risk. Article VIII.-3:101 is no exception to this: its purpose is primarily to safeguard commerce against the disruptive effects of the reclaiming of property by dispossessed owners from *bona fide* acquirers. In view of this underlying goal, the appropriate method of assessing whether the provision will likely succeed in meeting that goal is to confront it with the outcome of Law & Economics research on good faith acquisition.

2. GOOD FAITH ACQUISITION IN THE DCFR: ARTICLE VIII.-3:101

Article 3:101 of Book VIII DCFR reads as follows:[6]

(1) Where the person purporting to transfer the ownership (the transferor) has no right or authority to transfer ownership of the goods, the transferee

3. Nevertheless, the scope of the good faith acquisition rule has direct consequences for the need for alternative statutory forms of protection, in particular prescription.
4. An elaborate explanation of Art. VIII.-3:101 will probably be included in B. Lurger & W. Faber (eds), *Acquisition and Loss of Ownership in Movables: Principles of European Law* (Munich: Sellier, 2009).
5. B. Lurger, 'Political Issues in Property Law', in *The Politics of a European Civil Code. Private Law in European Context Series*, ed. M. W. Hesselink, vol. 7 (The Hague: Kluwer Law International, 2006), 33-54, at 46-50.
6. Quoted so far as is relevant for present purposes.

nevertheless acquires and the former owner loses ownership provided that: (. . .)

(c) the transferee acquires the goods for value; and

(d) the transferee neither knew nor could reasonably be expected to know that the transferor had no right or authority to transfer ownership of the goods at the time ownership would pass under VIII.-2:101 (Requirements for the transfer of ownership in general). The facts from which it follows that the transferee could not reasonably be expected to know of the transferor's lack of right or authority have to be proved by the transferee.

(2) Good faith acquisition in the sense of paragraph (1) does not take place with regard to stolen goods, unless the transferee acquired the goods from a transferor acting in the ordinary course of business (. . .).

In other words, when someone acquires movable property for value from a transferor who is not entitled to transfer ownership thereof, the transfer is valid, provided all other conditions for valid transfer are met and the transferee neither knew nor could reasonably be expected to know that the transferor was not entitled to transfer, and he succeeds in proving the facts from which it follows that the last condition is met. This protection is available to the transferee of stolen objects only in case the transferor acted in the ordinary course of business.[7]

Both the condition of acquisition for value and the condition that the acquirer was not only 'subjectively' in good faith (i.e., he did not positively know that the transferor lacked authority to transfer) but also 'objectively' in good faith (i.e., could not reasonably be expected to know that) have the effect of largely restricting the good faith acquirer protection to cases of regular commercial transactions. That this is no coincidence but intention is manifested in the additional condition for cases where stolen objects are involved. In these cases, the transferee must have acted in the ordinary course of business. Even though this is not required for non-stolen objects, the condition that the acquirer should not have been able to reasonably expect that the transferor lacked title and furthermore must be able to prove so, leaves little room for cases in a non-commercial setting. The fact that donees are categorically excluded from protection (in contrast to French law) points in the same direction, as gifts are as a rule, so to speak, extra commercii (apart from Christmas hampers, promotional gifts, and bribes).

Confirmation can be found in the aforementioned article by Lurger on political issues in property law. In this article she starts by stating that economic analysis generally favours a generous approach to good faith acquisition as the more efficient solution for markets, from which even owners may profit, as the possibility of

7. This rule is also found in Austrian law; *see* § 367 ABGB, requiring purchase from an authorized professional (*befugter Gewerbsmann*), which means that the transferor must have a license to this particular trade; *see* W. Faber, 'National Report on the Transfer of Movables in Austria', in W. Faber & B. Lurger (eds), *National Reports on the Transfer of Movables in Europe* (Munich: Sellier, 2008), 1-218.

good faith acquisition generally augments the liquidation value of his property.[8] Subsequently, she discusses some of the weaknesses in the economic analyses, in particular the justification of treating lost and stolen goods differently from goods the owner had voluntarily entrusted to someone else.[9] She argues that one must be careful in placing the bar for the requirement of good faith too high; one may require a relatively high measure of good faith from regular buyers in art markets, considering their expertise and financial background, but a lower measure of good faith is appropriate for consumers buying used cars.[10] In the end, however, Lurger does not dismiss the economists' claim. On the contrary, she acknowledges the need for some kind of good faith acquisition rule by pointing to the essentially 'economic' argument that 'reasonable reliance in the honesty of your contract partner should be generally protected'.[11]

There is nothing surprising or novel in this. It is commonplace that protection of the good faith purchaser is indispensable for commerce, ever since François Bourjon, spiritual father of Article 2279 of the French *Code civil*, assured his readers in 1747 that protection of the acquirer is indispensable for *la sûreté du commerce*[12] and William Blackstone's statement in the same era that 'it is expedient that the buyer, by taking proper precautions, may at all event be secure of his purchase; otherwise all commerce between man and man must soon be at an end'.[13] In contemporary legal literature, this economic argument is regularly repeated, but rarely discussed or even problematized. Exceptions are the analyses of Law and Economics scholars, to which attention will be directed shortly. First, however, some remarks on the surprising diversity of rules on good faith acquisition in jurisdictions around the world.

3. THE DIVERSITY OF ALTERNATIVE SOLUTIONS

There are three possible responses to the purchase of a movable from an unauthorized seller: unconditional protection of the original owner, unconditional protection of the buyer, or a solution somewhere in between. To the best of this author's knowledge, *all* contemporary legal systems opt for the last solution, shunning the two extreme solutions which have, however, historic credentials. Unconditional protection of the owner in case of *bona fide* acquisition by another was the Roman law solution (*nemo plus* rule), whereas unconditional protection (at least for

8. Lurger (n. 5 above), 46-47.
9. *Ibid.*, 48-40.
10. *Ibid.*, 47, 49-50.
11. *Ibid.*, 47.
12. F. Bourjon, *Le droit commun de la France et la Coutume de Paris*, 2nd edn (Paris: Grange, 1770), 145. *See* H. Kiefner, 'Qui possidet dominus esse praesumitur. Untersuchungen zur Geschichte der Eigentumsvermutung zugunsten des Besitzers seit Placentinus', *Zeitschrift der Savigny-Stiftung* 79 (1962): 283 et seq.
13. W. Blackstone, *Commentaries on the Laws of England*, Book II (Oxford: Clarendon Press, 1765-1769), Ch. 30.

non-stolen movables) of the acquirer was the Germanic solution (*Hand wahre Hand* rule).[14]

The disappearance of these two extreme solutions was followed by the emergence of many 'in-between rules'. Within Europe, Italian and Portuguese law represent the two contemporary extremes, the former choosing for almost total protection of the good faith acquirer[15] and the latter all but completely favouring the dispossessed owner.[16] Within these two extremes, each and every legal system has its own unique set of rules on the topic.

Is it possible to explain this massive diversity, unparalleled by other legal topics? Saul Levmore has discussed the question in his 'Variety and Uniformity in the Treatment of the Good-Faith Purchaser'.[17] In his view, uniformity among different legal systems can often be explained by the fact that legal rules must control self-interested behaviour that threatens the general welfare (e.g., theft is punishable everywhere), whereas variety often arises in rules that either (a) do not matter that much (b) raise issues about which reasonable people, even in the same culture, can disagree.[18] Levmore argues, focusing on the treatment of stolen property, that the diversity with regard to the proper response to good faith acquisition can be linked to the second cause of variety, namely reasonable lawmakers can disagree regarding which alternative rule is best. Even if they would share the goal of minimizing the costs associated with theft, they may disagree with respect to the best way to achieve this. The complexity of the problem makes it hard to determine which incentives should be given to either the original owner (theft prevention, theft insurance, tracking down and reclaiming stolen property) or the good faith acquirer (inquiring after the authority of the would-be seller, title insurance) to avoid a confrontation between the two. This complexity not only explains why people may have different intuitions about which rule is most likely to have the preferred outcome, but it also makes it hard to collect helpful empirical evidence.[19]

Levmore's view that reasonable disagreement about the behavioural effects of the alternative rules is the source of the diversity is not shared by Caspar Rose. In his opinion,[20] the divergence may simply be explained by the fact that the

14. *See* with further references A. F. Salomons, 'How to Draft New Rules on the Bona Fide Acquisition of Movables for Europe? Some Remarks on Method and Content', in *Rules for the Transfer of Movables: A Candidate for European Harmonisation or National Reforms?*, eds W. Faber & B. Lurger (Munich: Sellier, 2008), 141-144. With regard to Germanic law two remarks: its unfamiliarity with the concepts of ownership and possession makes it difficult to describe and compare with Roman and contemporary private law; the text doesn't do justice to the variety and dynamic of Germanic law.
15. With an exception for movables entered in Public Registers.
16. The acquirer in good faith is entitled to restitution of the purchase price paid to a merchant and to acquisitive prescription.
17. S. Levmore, 'Variety and Uniformity in the Treatment of the Good-Faith Purchaser', *Journal of Legal Studies* 16 (1987), 43-65.
18. *Ibid.*, 44.
19. *Ibid.*, 49.
20. C. Rose, *The Transfer of Property Rights by Theft: An Economic Analysis*, American Law & Economics Association Annual Meetings Paper 32 (2005).

economic effects of the various rules have not been the subject of much attention among Law and Economics scholars. Implicitly, Rose states that with proper research on the basis of proper empirical data (which, Rose admits, are also lacking[21]) an economically sound solution would emerge which should be adopted by legislatures. Most other legal economists would challenge this view; the possibility of finding a 'best rule' is generally denied. Rose is apparently more optimistic (at least with regard to the treatment of stolen property), arguing that his game-theoretic model demonstrates that the American system of protection of the owner of stolen property *Pareto* dominates[22] the European jurisdictions which favour the *bona fide* acquirer. In this, he goes one step further than Cooter and Ulen, who also believe in the existence of a 'best rule' but admit to the difficulty of finding it: 'the lack of evidence also prevents different countries from identifying the more efficient rule and adopting it'.[23]

In my opinion, Levmore, Rose and Cooter, and Ulen pay insufficient attention to the possibility that the divergence may be explained, at least in part, by cultural and institutional differences between countries. To give only one example: the fact that law enforcement depends much more strongly on citizens' participation in the United States than is the case in Europe may well be linked to the virtual absence of protection for the good faith acquirer of stolen objects in the USA, thus giving a strong incentive to the victim of theft to go after his belongings, and thereby enabling the law enforcement authorities to catch the thief.[24] It is significant that *within* the USA, there is not much diversity in the treatment of the good faith acquirer across the different jurisdictions, a fact which seems to have puzzled Levmore, as it does not fit well in his uniformity/variety thesis. His explanation that the disappearance of diversity within the USA was the result of the formation of a national market across the separate States[25] is relevant for the harmonization of private law within Europe. This would require EU Member States to adopt a common rule to the benefit of market efficiency and to abolish rules they may prefer for cultural or institutional reasons.[26] Especially the last aspect must be taken into account:[27] harmonization of the law on good faith purchase may necessitate institutional adjustments in the field of law enforcement.

---

21. *Ibid.*, 5.
22. Situation A 'Pareto dominates' situation B if everyone's position is better or equal in A than would be the case in B.
23. R. Cooter & T. Ulen, *Law and Economics* (Boston: Addison Wesley, 2000), 141.
24. Cf. Levmore (n. 17 above), 48.
25. *Ibid.*, 60.
26. Cf. Lurger (n. 5 above), 52-53, arguing that unification of property law in the European Union should not be decided upon before the social, economic and political impacts of the differing solutions in the Member States have been analyzed thoroughly.
27. The importance of the first aspect receives sufficient attention through the *œuvre* of P. Legrand, 'Against a European Civil Code', *Modern Law Review* 60 (1997).

4. ARCHETYPICAL RULES

If it is true that the diversity owes a lot, not only to diverging intuitions, but also to institutional and cultural differences between states, it is not worth the effort to look for additional explanations, as that could no longer result in the discovery of a universally applicable 'best solution'. Furthermore, the existing diversity should not be exaggerated; most of the various rules on good faith acquisition can easily be reduced to a handful of archetypes.

The first of these archetypes may be labelled the *original owner rule.*[28] This rule resembles the ancient solution: no protection for the acquirer *a non domino;* the original owner is allowed to reclaim his property even from a *bona fide* acquirer. The rule may no longer exist in its most severe manifestation, but the USA, Portugal, and the Czech Republic are countries where protection of the original owner is emphasized.

The second archetypical rule, for the purposes of this article entitled the *good faith purchase rule*, borrows from its common Anglo-American name. It encompasses all rules which validate transfers made by an unauthorized transferor by virtue of the good faith of the transferee. Examples can be found in France (Article 2279 CC) and Germany (§ 932 BGB). The protection of the acquirer is based on the fact that he/she was justified in believing that the movable belonged to the transferor, because it was in the latter's possession.

Finally, there is the *market-overt rule*, which also protects the acquirer of a movable against a claim for recovery by its former owner, but only if an additional requirement is fulfilled: the acquisition must qualify as a regular commercial transaction, performed in a place where similar transactions usually take place. For example, the English market-overt rule (section 22, Sales of Goods Act 1979, abolished in 1995,[29] protecting purchasers at a market overt, including London shops), France (Article 2280 Cc, protecting purchasers at fairs, markets, public sales and from merchants dealing in similar things), Germany (§ 935-II BGB, protecting in case of public sale), The Netherlands (Article 3:86(3a) BW, protecting consumers purchasing stolen goods in stores).

The market-overt rule may for analytical convenience be classified as a subcategory of the good faith purchase rule.[30] Historically, however, this is

---

28. The term original owner(ship) rule is used *inter alia* by D. Öhvall, 'Economic Analysis of the Title to Stolen Personal Property', <www.emle.org/Subpages_rubric/index.php?rubric=Thesis_Archive>, Master Thesis University of Manchester 2004; S. Shavell, *Foundations of Economic Analysis of Law* (Cambridge/London: Belknap Press, 2004); D. Lueck & T. J. Miceli, 'Property Law', Arizona Legal Studies Discussion Paper no. 06-19.
29. *See* Levmore (n. 17 above), 61 et seq. and P. M. Smith, 'Valediction to Market Overt', *American Journal of Legal History* 41 (1997), 225-249.
30. In B. Medina, 'Augmenting the Value of Ownership by Protecting It Only Partially: The "Market-Overt" Rule Revisited', *Journal of Law, Economics & Organization* 19 (2003): 345 et seq., the market overt rule encompasses the good faith purchase rule; the notion 'market-overt rule' is used by Medina 'to indicate a rule under which . . . an innocent buyer is entitled to ownership right, regardless of any deficiencies in the seller's title'. Its opposite is

inaccurate,[31] and there is also an important difference with regard to the justification for the buyer's protection. For the good faith purchase rule, the emphasis is centred on reasons at a micro level, such as *culpa* on the part of the owner in entrusting his thing to an untrustworthy entrustee, justified reliance of the buyer on the control over the movable exercised by the transferee, etc. For the market-overt rule, the emphasis is centred on macro level arguments: protecting and enhancing trade and at the same time diminishing the workload of law enforcement authorities and the judiciary by obstructing recovery claims from dispossessed owners. Be that as it may, when confronted with the original owner rule, both rules are at the other side of the spectrum, and hereafter the notion 'good faith purchase rule' is meant to encompass either.

5. THE ECONOMICS OF THE GOOD FAITH PURCHASE RULE

5.1. Introduction

The economic analysis of law is involved in predicting behaviour generated by legal rules, by focusing on the incentives these rules give to people. In doing so, this science also provides legislatures with an answer to the question whether the enactment of these legal rules will lead to the policy goals behind them, usually the maximization of scarce resources (albeit 'inefficient' goals may sometimes be preferred on moral or other grounds). In fact, assessment of efficiency is the core business of Law and Economics, building upon the assumption that people generally respond in an economically rational manner to price incentives given by the law.[32]

As is well known, Law and Economics plays a far greater role in private law scholarship in the US than is the case in Europe. Without much exaggeration, one could say that American legal scholarship has become dominated by it, while it has

the absolute protection rule, 'in which the law favors the owner in case of a conflict with an innocent buyer'. The latter rule is called the 'non-negotiability rule' (referring to the fact that in the USA stolen and lost goods are not negotiable) by Weinberg and the 'lost-and-stolen rule' by Lurger. Cooter & Ulen (n. 23 above), 140-141, distinguish between an American rule and a European rule to indicate the same dichotomy with regard to stolen objects, but they make a caricature of the various European good faith purchase rules: as in the USA, non-negotiability of stolen objects is the rule, with exceptions for certain types of buyers and certain types of transactions (cf. Rose (n. 20 above), 5).

31. French law offers an example: the market-overt rule of Art. 2280 CC has its origin in medieval times, whereas Art. 2279 (*possession vaut titre*) is derived from eighteenth century Parisian case law (*see* A-.M. Patault, *Introduction historique au droit des biens* (Paris: PUF, 1989)), 291-301. D. E. Murray, 'Sale in Market Overt', *International and Comparative Law Quarterly* 9 (1960): 50 and *passim*, emphasizes that the market-overt rule was indigenous, not only to the UK but to many lands and peoples as 'a common-sense solution to a vexing problem which was bound to occur as soon as man entered into a system of exchange of goods for money'.
32. H. B. Schäfer & C. Ott, *Economic Analysis of Civil Law* (Cheltenham/Northampton: Edgar Elgar, 2004), 3-12; Cooter & Ulen (n. 23 above), 3-7.

hardly made any headway in Europe. The reasons for this 'transatlantic divergence in legal thought'[33] need not be the subject of discussion here. It suffices to remark that it seems unchallengeable that, whatever the limitations of legal economics, a sensible legislature should try to establish beforehand the feasibility of the policy goals behind its bills and that, in particular in case these policy goals are of an economic nature, a Law and Economics analysis of these bills is appropriate. A practical obstacle, however, is that this requires expertise from two disciplines: economics and law. Most private law scholars lack sufficient economic training to perform economic analyses themselves and are therefore forced to build upon existing Law and Economics literature in order to draw conclusions on specific topics. A similar problem occurs at the economists' side of Law and economics. Stefano Lombardo observed in 2002 that American corporate law professors are not actually legal scholars but rather economists whose field of research is law.[34] Testimonies of the latter are articles crammed with mathematic formulas and graphs without proper explanation of their meaning and implication for those lacking the expertise to understand them unaided. Of course, this is no excuse for legal scholars to ignore economics altogether. Interdisciplinary research will not exert any influence unless both sides make an effort.

The economic analysis of property law is still substantially less well developed than that of contract or tort law; in the words of Lueck and Miceli: 'today the economics of property law is a poor cousin to the economics of contracts, torts, and many other areas'.[35] In their opinion, this is caused both by disinterestedness among property law scholars and by the broadness of property law, 'making comprehensive analysis a daunting task'. The former explanation is more convincing than the latter: the broadness of property law does not seem to exceed that of contract and tort law, but scholars who are involved in those fields of the law do seem to be a little more open-minded towards interdisciplinary research in general.

If the economics of property law did not receive much attention over the past decades, this is even more true for the topic of good faith purchase. Posner and Landes speak of 'relatively little attention',[36] Rose even calls the issue 'almost unexplored in the Law and Economics literature'.[37] That is an exaggeration, however, since a non-negligible number of articles on the economics of good

33. *See* K. Grechenig & M. Gelter, 'The Transatlantic Divergence in Legal Thought: American Law and Economics vs. German Doctrinalism', *Hastings International and Comparative Law Review* 31 (2008), 295-360 who gives two explanations for the fact that German-speaking Europe is ill-disposed to Law and Economics: the failure of the *Freirechtschule* as compared to US Legal realism and the repudiation of utilitarianism, for long widely accepted in the US, in German philosophy.
34. *Ibid.*, § 2.1, quoting S. Lombardo, *Regulatory Competition in Company Law in the European Community* (New York: Peter Lang Publishing, 2002).
35. D. Lueck & T. Miceli, 'Property Law', in *Handbook of Law and Economic*, eds A. M. Polinsky & S. Shavell (Amsterdam: Elsevier, 2007).
36. W. M. Landes & R. A. Posner, 'The Economics of Legal Disputes over the Ownership of Works of Art and Other Collectibles', in *Economics of the Arts. Selected Essays*, eds V. A. Ginsburgh & P. M. Menger (Amsterdam: Elsevier, 1996), 177.
37. Rose (n. 20 above), 1.

faith purchase has appeared in law journals since the 1980s, and the attention has even increased in the present decade. In the following, attention will be paid to some of the most important contributions to the debate, without making a claim to be exhaustive.[38]

When studying these contributions, two things attract attention. The first is, that American authors focus primarily on the question of how to deal with unauthorized transfer of stolen objects, whereas European authors take the treatment of embezzled objects as a starting point. This in itself should not necessarily lead to different outcomes, but the second striking feature of the available literature is that the economic analyses by American authors are generally more favourable to the original ownership rule (the 'American rule' of Cooter and Ulen) whereas the analyses by their European colleagues generally lend support to the good faith purchase rule ('the European rule'). This suggests that the authors are biased towards their own legal system, but their number is not high enough to attach much importance to this observation.

All authors on the economics of unauthorized transfer take the same basic approach: assessing which of the two rules (the good faith purchase rule and the original owner rule) is the most efficient boils down to the question which of them gives the incentives that lead to the most efficient result.

It is widely acknowledged that both unconditional protection of the owner and unconditional protection of the acquirer *a non domino* is inefficient. The former rule would, e.g., discourage owners to make sufficient efforts to prevent theft (hereinafter referred to as prevention costs) and thereby lead to an increase in the number of thefts,[39] but trade would suffer as potential buyers would be discouraged to buy in view of the large risk of ownership claims. Furthermore, buyers would be forced to make excessive costs in verifying that the seller is entitled to sell (hereinafter information costs[40]).[41] Unconditional protection of the buyer, on the other hand, would have the inefficient result that owners would not be inclined to lend or hire out or even openly use their belongings themselves.[42] Therefore, efficiency is served by choosing a rule in between these two extremes, preventing excessive costs on either side and at the same time taking the effects on trade and law enforcement into account. This requires a more detailed discussion of the relevant factors.

38. References in Medina (n. 30 above), 370-372.
39. Theft in itself leads to an inefficient use of recourses, as it forces owners to spend money on prevention, theft insurance and replacement. Furthermore, taxpayers' money is needed to finance law enforcement. *See* Landes & Posner (n. 36 above), 182-183; Lueck & Miceli (n. 35 above), 37; G. Tullock, 'The Welfare Costs of Tariffs, Monopolies, and Theft', *Western Economic Journal* 5 (1967): 3, Levmore (n. 17 above), 45; O. Ben-Shahar, 'Property Rights in Stolen Goods: An Economic Analysis', Discussion Paper 99-015, <www.law.umich.edu>, 2.
40. *See*, e.g., S. E. Sterk, 'Property Rules, Liability Rules, and Uncertainty about Property Rights', *Michigan Law Review* 106 (2008), 1285-1336.
41. *See*, e.g., Schäfer & Ott (n. 32 above), 418.
42. Öhvall (n. 28 above), 33.

5.2. Theft under the Original Owner Rule

Adoption of the original owner rule discourages theft in several ways. First of all, the rule encourages owners to collect and maintain proof of their ownership right, which enhances the chances of a successful ownership claim after theft, either against the thief or against his buyers.[43] This in turn makes theft less attractive; the chances of a successful ownership claim are reflected in a decrease of the value of the stolen property.[44] However, a price decrease will – and should – make potential buyers suspicious, making them even less inclined to buy stolen property.[45] The greater number of successful ownership claims against buyers of stolen property will furthermore result in more cases in which thieves are held liable towards their customers for breach of the sales contract, which poses yet more costs to thieves.[46] Eventually, a trade-off may occur; as soon as the risk of theft is significantly diminished, owners will be inclined to spend less on theft prevention, something which is already not as important as under the good faith purchase rule (under the original owner rule, theft prevention is discouraged, but the owner will spend more on tracing and reclaiming his property after theft).[47] The result would be that theft would become less costly, causing an increase in the number of thefts.[48] We also have to consider externalities caused by adoption of the original owner rule, in particular the effect on the costs of law enforcement; enabling dispossessed owners to reclaim their stolen goods even from buyers in good faith will result in more litigation and thus in an increase of the workload of courts,[49] which is aggravated if this litigation also gives cause for more prosecution against thieves.

5.3. Probability of Tracing Stolen Property

Some authors emphasize that the aforementioned factors are mitigated by the fact that, even under the original owner rule, most stolen goods will never be successfully reclaimed, as they turn out to be untraceable.[50] Weinberg relates – referring to the situation in the USA in 1980 – that less than one-third of all stolen property is

43. Shavell (n. 28 above), 53.
44. In part, this price decrease is 'justified' by the fact that the object has less value to the owner due to the fact that he may feel forced to use it less ostentatiously, in order to hide it from a potential ownership claim (*see* Öhvall (n. 28 above), 20 with references, and Schäfer & Ott (n. 32 above), 421).
45. *See*, thus Shavell (n. 28 above), 53-54 and Öhvall (n. 28 above), 29-31. On the other hand, a price decrease could result in increased demand by certain buyers (cf. H. R. Weinberg, 'Sales Law, Economics, and the Negotiability of Goods)', *Journal of Legal Studies* 9 (1980): 576-577.
46. *Ibid.*, 580.
47. *Ibid.*, 581 and Öhvall (n. 28 above), 18-19.
48. Landes & Posner (n. 36 above), 184.
49. This litigation may be less complex than under a good faith purchase rule, as the buyer's good faith does not have to be considered; Öhvall (n. 28 above), 35.
50. Thus, e.g., Shavell (n. 28 above), 54; Landes & Posner (n. 36 above), 189.

recovered by the police.[51] This figure, which may or may not have much relevance for contemporary Europe, does not say much as to whether the recovered stolen property is returned to the owner, nor does one know how much stolen property is successfully reclaimed under threat of civil litigation, without police interference.

It is stressed by Medina that the probability of recovery of stolen property is not insignificant. Against authors who claim that the chance of recovery is negligible, he argues that it is then inconsistent to assume that the choice of the legal rule affects a buyer's incentive to take risk-prevention measures.[52] This is correct, but if it is true – as many believe – that the adoption of the good faith purchase rule would encourage theft, a small chance of recovery of stolen property is all the more relevant. Furthermore, there may be additional reasons for a buyer to be interested in the seller's entitlement than the risk of an ownership claim.[53]

5.4. Information Costs and Good Faith

Theft can be discouraged by making it more difficult for thieves to sell their stolen goods. This can be done by withholding good faith purchase protection from those who made insufficient efforts to determine whether their seller was authorized to transfer the property. However, it may be inefficient to burden potential buyers with substantial information costs, as a consequence of which trade may suffer'.[54] Registration systems have been created for certain types of movables (e.g., cars, works of art, and so forth), which can be consulted in order to determine whether a good has been reported stolen. For less expensive objects, the maintenance of such registers would not be cost justified.

The above is relevant here, as most authors assume that buyers will be less inclined to make information costs under the good faith purchase rule than is the case under the original owner rule, as the risk of a successful recovery claim is smaller.[55] This in turn makes it easier to sell stolen property, resulting in more theft. This problem is mitigated when one applies a high standard of good faith, as is in fact already common practice in many countries in Europe. Thus, mere ignorance of the fact that the transferor lacked the authority to transfer the property is insufficient for protection of the transferee ('subjective good faith'); it must be established that there were no circumstances which should have made the transferee suspicious and he was furthermore, depending on the circumstances at hand, obliged to investigate into the entitlement of the seller ('objective good faith').[56] Most authors on the economics of good faith purchase seem ignorant of this fact,

---

51. Weinberg (n. 45 above), 574.
52. Medina (n. 30 above), 345.
53. *See* Weinberg (n. 45 above), 578, on the many factors a person should consider before deciding upon concluding a 'suspicious' transaction or a 'safe' one.
54. *See*, D. Baird & T. Jackson, 'Information, Uncertainty, and the Transfer of Property', *Journal of Legal Studies* 13 (1984), 301.
55. *See*, e.g., Lueck & Miceli (n. 35 above), 25; Weinberg (n. 45 above), 576-580.
56. *See*, e.g., Arts 3:11 and 3:118 Dutch Civil Code.

as they present an assessment of the merits of the good faith purchaser rule under the assumption that subjective good faith is sufficient for application of that rule; Weinberg,[57] Landes and Posner,[58] and Rose.[59] This fact does not discredit their analyses, but it should be borne in mind that they analyze a rule that is no longer valid in much of Europe.[60] Medina[61] argues that buyers may in principle even be induced to invest *more* resources in acquiring information under the good faith purchase rule with an objective good faith requirement than is anticipated under the original owner rule. At any rate: buyers' information costs depend upon the measure of care prescribed for protection against recovery claims, which enables legislators to enhance efficiency by 'fine-tuning' the good faith requirement.

5.5. Burden of Proof

An additional fine-tuning instrument is the burden of proof. If a buyer has to prove his good faith for protection under the good faith purchase rule, he may be expected to make more efforts in gathering information on the entitlement of the seller than would be the case if his good faith would have to be disproved by the dispossessed owner. Thus, he will be less inclined to buy from an unauthorized seller (unless the latter would succeed in producing forged titles, and so forth). However, there seems to be a problem here. A buyer knows that the chance of being confronted with a dispossessed owner is very small; the likelihood that his acquisition was stolen is small to begin with, and the same goes for the likelihood that the owner will take the trouble to track it and succeed in proving his ownership right.[62] As a consequence, 'buyers will not tend to expend much effort to verify sellers' title'.[63] This means that a very large group of buyers will no longer be protected if the burden of proof with regard to good faith is shifted from the owner, as is the case in most legal systems, to the buyer, as is proposed in the DCFR. This may be considered a good thing as far as it relates to buyers who have insufficiently invested in establishing the seller's entitlement,[64] but that is not the case to the extent that protection is withheld from buyers who have incurred ample information costs, who are objectively in good faith but who, for whatever reason – e.g., because they omitted to keep receipts – fail to prove so. Such an unfortunate outcome may be

57. Weinberg (n. 45 above), 586, note 69.
58. Landes & Posner (n. 36 above), 182 (cf. 190).
59. Rose (n. 20 above), 2.
60. *See* similarly Medina (n. 30 above), 353-354, with further references.
61. *Ibid.*, 354.
62. *See*, Shavell (n. 28 above), 54.
63. *Ibid.*
64. Nevertheless, as the average buyer runs a very small risk of being confronted with a successful recovery claim by a dispossessed owner, it is inefficient if buyers in general make substantial information costs. This is different for buyers in second-hand stores, flea markets, and so forth. In other words: efficiency is enhanced by a rule which induces buyers to make research efforts depending on the circumstances.

expected to occur frequently if the rule is adopted that buyers are to bear the burden of proof. On the other hand, 'It is an almost impossible task for the original owner to show bad faith and there is an inherent risk that the purchaser manipulates evidence'.[65] Indeed, presumed good faith is hard to disprove. This may be the explanation for the phenomenon observed by Gilmore: 'As the doctrine [of good faith purchase] strikes roots in one or another field, the "good faith" component tends to atrophy and the commercial purchaser is protected with little more than lip service paid to his *bona fides*'.[66]

In view of these complications, adoption of a midway solution seems preferable; presumption of good faith of the acquirer on the condition that he provides information on the circumstances of his acquisition. Hence, buyers are induced to maintain information about former transactions and the burden of proof of the dispossessed owner is substantially lightened. An additional advantage of this rule is that it would help both the owner and the police to track down the thief.[67]

5.6. The Interests of Trade

A matter of much debate is whether the good faith purchase rule is better for trade than the original owner rule. Authors such as Murray, Medina, and Öhvall[68] argue that the former rule enhances trade because diligent buyers do not have to fear dispossessed owners reclaiming their stolen property; but according to Weinberg, there is no reason to expect commerce to be impeded by the original owner rule, as the probability of prior ownership claims actually being asserted against purchasers of movables is small.[69] The same view is taken by Levmore, who calls the claim that the good faith purchase rule is in the interest of trade or even necessary for the survival of commerce 'superficial' and 'vulnerable'. He adds that, as an empirical matter, 'commerce seems to have survived well enough in the United States with no market-overt rule'.[70]

These conflicting arguments all relate to *stolen* property. Weinberg and Levmore do not dispute that commerce is served best with application of the good faith purchase rule to non-stolen property, and indeed there are several provisions in the Uniform Commercial Code (UCC) under which only the *bona fide* acquirer of embezzled goods is protected.[71] As, in the words of Kozolchyk, the

65. Öhvall (n. 28 above), 45 (cf. 41).
66. G. Gilmore, 'The Commercial Doctrine of Good Faith Purchase', *Yale Law Journal* 63 (1954): 1057.
67. Cf. Art. 3:87(1) Dutch Civil Code.
68. Murray (n. 31 above), 25; Medina (n. 30 above), 360 et seq.; Öhvall (n. 28 above), 34.
69. Weinberg (n. 45 above), footnote 84, making an exception for commercial paper.
70. Levmore (n. 17 above), 55 and footnote 62.
71. *See* G. Gilmore (n. 66 above) and 'The Good Faith Purchase Idea and the Uniform Commercial Code: Confessions of a Repentant Draftsman', *Georgia Law Review* 15 (1980); W. D. Warren, 'Cutting Off Claims of Ownership under the Uniform Commercial Code', *University of Chicago Law Review* 30 (1963), 469-494.

UCC 'reflects trade in the most commercially active market on earth', the US ('a society whose business is business)',[72] the question should not be whether trade is hampered without good faith purchase protection, but whether trade is hampered if stolen property is excluded from that protection. This question cannot be answered for lack of empirical data. Furthermore, the implications of the introduction of either rule in a country depend strongly on other, 'institutional' factors, such as crime rates, effectiveness of law enforcement, and the extent of theft prevention efforts by owners.[73]

6. HOW TO FIND THE OPTIMAL RULE?

The factors discussed above have to be taken into account, but they do not in themselves indicate which rule is the most efficient one. Traditionally, the 'least cost avoider measure' is indicated as appropriate to determine the optimal rule. In order to understand this measure, we have to remember that we are looking for the most efficient solution to the good faith purchase problem. We want to minimize transaction costs in order to achieve an optimal use of recourses.[74] Therefore, the most efficient rule results in the lowest sum total of prevention costs spent by owners and information costs spent by buyers (assuming for a moment that the rules have equal externalities). This, in turn, means that we have to find the rule that gives the proper incentives to achieve that end. The idea is that this is achieved by ensuring that the party who can verify ownership (and thus prevent the good faith purchase problem) at the lowest cost bear the risk: the 'least cost avoider' is the superior risk bearer. For example, the *bona fide* purchaser of a used car is the superior risk bearer because it is less costly for him to examine the registration papers than it is for the owner to prevent theft (e.g., by building a solid garage).[75] However, the rule we are looking for has to be of a categorical nature: it would involve greater cost and uncertainty if the law should impose liability on the party best able to avoid the loss in the particular circumstances. The question is, therefore: who is in general the least cost avoider: owner or buyer?

The answer is probably different for stolen and for embezzled goods. For the latter category, it is argued by most authors that the owner is the least cost avoider, because he is in a better position to assess and monitor the trustworthiness of the person to whom he is to entrust his property.[76] In other words, for non-stolen property, the good faith purchase rule is economically superior. For stolen property, the problem is more complex: it comes down to issues such as 'who is the better insurer', 'who is the better self-insurer', 'what theft prevention measures and

72. B. Kozolchyk, 'Transfer of Personal Property by a Nonowner: Its Future in Light of Its Past', *Tulane Law Review* 61 (1987): 1511.
73. Cf. Rose (n. 20 above), 20.
74. Schäfer & Ott (n. 32 above), 18-20.
75. Example taken from Cooter & Ulen (n. 23 above), 421. *See* Weinberg (n. 45 above), 585.
76. *See*, e.g., Landes & Posner (n. 36 above), 216; Medina (n. 30 above), 346; Weinberg (n. 45 above), 587 et seq.; Schäfer & Ott (n. 32 above), 421.

post-theft actions can be expected from the owner',[77] 'what inquiries should the buyer make to assess the entitlement of the seller', and so forth. A detailed description of the literature on these issues can be omitted, as – probably in particular due to lack of empirical material – the authors are divided.[78]

The least cost avoider approach has been challenged by Medina on three grounds.[79] First, he argues that it is based on the premise that a party can be induced to take risk-prevention measures only by assigning him the burden of bearing the relevant risk. This premise is false as shown by the fact that under the good faith purchase rule a purchaser is induced to invest even more recourses in acquiring information than is anticipated under the original owner rule (*see* above), provided objective good faith is required for protection.[80] Second, the least cost avoider approach overlooks the fact that a buyer's willingness to pay is influenced by the choice of the legal rule. Under the original owner rule, the buyer will discount the risk of a recovery claim in his willingness to pay; this in turn will mitigate the risk of theft. The third and most important shortcoming of the least cost avoider approach, according to Medina, is that it disregards social costs caused by the fact that the choice of legal rule influences the buyer's willingness to pay. Under the original owner rule, buyers are less winning to pay, which in turn reduces the ownership right's liquidation value (alienability) and prevents efficient transactions. The underlying purpose of the law should not be merely to minimize the risk of right violation, but rather to maximize the expected value of the ownership right. The optimal rule is, therefore, the one which maximizes the expected value of the ownership right. The liquidation value of property will increase under the good faith purchase rule, but so too does the risk of right violation. Owners who are interested in a high liquidation value (e.g., owners of financial instruments) are best served by the partial protection offered to buyers under the good faith purchase rule requiring objective good faith.[81]

77. A fine example of a post-theft measure is offered by Landes & Posner (n. 36 above), 206 et seq. The owner of a stolen work of art can report the theft to the Art Loss Register; currently, this costs EUR 15 per item. There is little else the owner can do to recover his property (therefore, rules designed to encourage owners to search more are unlikely to be socially cost-justified). As for information costs: art buyers who want to see whether an object is reported stolen at the Art Loss Register have to pay EUR 50 for a single search (*see* <www.artloss.com>). The good faith purchase rule may induce the owner to trace his stolen property swiftly, before it has been acquired by a good faith purchaser. This incentive is lacking under the original owner rule (cf. Levmore (n. 17 above), 57).
78. *See*, Medina (n. 30 above), 346; Weinberg (n. 45 above), 586; Levmore (n. 17 above), 46 et seq.; and Öhvall (n. 28 above), 35 et seq.
79. Medina (n. 30 above), 346 et seq. According to Rose, another flaw of the least cost avoider approach is that it ignores the strategic interaction between the parties: buyers who know that owners spend considerable amounts on protecting their property (as is the case under the good faith purchase rule) are less likely to anticipate that the good is stolen.
80. Cf. Öhvall (n. 28 above), 18.
81. Lurger (n. 5 above), 49 calls Medina's analysis 'not of much help here because the way the owner lost control of her assets does not tell us anything about her intention to keep or rather liquidate her assets'.

In this author's opinion, Medina is correct in pointing out that, under the least cost avoider approach, some efficiency aspects are overlooked, and one of these is indeed the way in which the adopted rule affects the market price of second-hand goods. Yet, it seems that there are other important externalities involved in the choice of the optimal legal rule which are also disregarded, both in the least cost avoider measure and in Medina's 'value of ownership right measure', for the simple reason that they are not included in the model (even though their importance is generally acknowledged), namely effects on insurance premiums, costs of law enforcement, the workload of civil litigation courts, the functioning of trade, and so forth. Both measures, primarily focusing on the incentives provided by the chosen rule at a micro level (to owners, thieves, embezzlers, and buyers), have an inherent blind spot for at least some of the macro effects with external efficiency implications.

Maybe this criticism is not entirely fair. A model to assess which rule has the highest overall efficiency (taking into account both internal and external effects) would probably not only be extremely complex, but, failing sufficient and adequate empirical data, it would be also very difficult to operationalize. Be that as it may, it is clear that at present, economic analysis cannot pretend to be able to come up with an 'optimal rule'. At best, it can indicate which rule may be expected to result in the highest micro level efficiency.

7. CONCLUSIONS: THE EFFICIENCY OF GOOD FAITH PURCHASE PROTECTION IN THE DCFR

In order to assess the soundness of the policy choices made in the DCFR with regard to the problem of good faith purchase, the literature has been discussed in which this problem is analyzed from an economic perspective. Most of the Law and Economics authors regard the good faith purchase rule – under which a transfer to an acquirer in good faith is valid despite lack of authority on the part of the transferor – the most efficient rule for embezzled goods, but they are divided regarding the question of which rule is best for stolen goods: that same rule or the original owner rule. It is generally agreed that, in case of application of the good faith purchase rule, no protection should be awarded to buyers who are not objectively in good faith. Buyers must be induced to inquire whether the seller has authority to transfer the good. The burden of proof receives little attention, but according to some authors, the buyer should bear the burden of proof with regard to his good faith. A less far-reaching solution is to presume the buyer's good faith on the condition that he provides information about the circumstances of his acquisition.

As for embezzled property, the rules on good faith purchase in the DCFR (Article VIII.-3:101) are more or less in accordance with these findings. Protection is reserved for the acquirer for value who neither knew nor could reasonably be expected to know that the transferor was unauthorized to transfer. It is unclear whether the rule that the acquirer must prove the facts from which it follows that he could not reasonably be expected to know of the transferor's lack of authority is enhancing efficiency or not, as economic literature barely discusses procedural aspects like burden of proof. It is clear, however, that the rule may cause uncertainty due to its vagueness. It might be preferable to burden the acquirer merely with the duty to present information on the circumstances of the acquisition (e.g., location, date, price), on pain of not being able to invoke the protection of Article VIII.-3:101.

As for stolen property, protection is available to the transferee in case the transferor acted in the ordinary course of business. The economic rationality of this rule cannot be confirmed, as the literature is divided with regard to the efficiency of good faith purchase protection for stolen goods. Several authors, almost exclusively from the USA, firmly believe that his would be inefficient, but several others, especially European authors, have challenged this view. It may be that the drafters of Article VIII.-3:101 have tried to find a middle way in which the interests of trade are also taken into account. If so, it is worth noting that there is substantial support for the view that trade would not be hampered by adoption of the original owner rule. Efficiency considerations aside, however, the protection of the acquirer of a stolen thing in a regular business transaction has the benefit of fitting into the tradition of the market-overt rule, so strongly rooted in European legal history, both in civil and in common law. In this respect, Article VIII.-3:101 DCFR can be considered a truly European rule.

PRIVATE LAW IN EUROPEAN CONTEXT SERIES

1. Mauro Bussani & Ugo Mattei (eds), *The Common Core of European Private Law: Essays on the Project*, 2002 (ISBN 90-411-1852-7).
2. Stefan Grundmann & Jules H.V. Stuyck (eds), *An Academic Green Paper to European Contract Law*, 2002 (ISBN 90-411-1853-5).
3. Martijn W. Hesselink, *The New European Private Law: Essays on the Future of Private Law in Europe*, 2002 (ISBN 90-411-1962-0).
4. Ugo Mattei (ed.), *The European Codification Process: Cut and Paste*, 2003 (ISBN 90-411-2230-3).
5. Hugh Collins (ed.), *The Forthcoming EC Directive on Unfair Commercial Practices*, 2004 (ISBN 90-411-2224-9).
6. Stefan Grundmann & Denis Mazeaud (eds), *General Clauses and Standards in European Contract Law: Comparative Law, EC Law and Contract Law Codification*, 2005 (ISBN 90-411-2432-2).
7. Martijn W. Hesselink (ed.), *The Politics of a European Civil Code*, 2006 (ISBN 978-90-411-2410-1).
8. Stefan Grundmann & Martin Schauer (eds), *The Architecture of European Codes and Contract Law*, 2006 (ISBN 978-90-411-2530-9).
9. Fabrizio Cafaggi (ed.), *Reframing Self-Regulation in European Private Law*, 2006 (ISBN 978-90-411-2531-6).
10. Thomas Wilhelmsson, Elina Paunio & Annika Pohjolainen (eds), *Private Law and the Many Cultures of Europe*, 2007 (ISBN 978-90-411-2593-4).
11. Matthias Haentjens, *Harmonisation of Securities Law: Custody and Transfer of Securities in European Private Law*, 2007 (ISBN 978-90-411-2639-9).
12. C. Mak, *Fundamental Rights in European Contract Law*, 2008 (ISBN 978-90-411-2671-9).
13. Stefan Grundmann (ed.), *Constitutional Values and European Contract Law*, 2008 (ISBN 978-90-411-2765-5).
14. Bastiaan van Zelst, *The Politics of European Sales Law: A Legal Political Inquiry into the Drafting of the Uniform Commercial Code, the Vienna Sales Convention, the Dutch Civil Code and the European Consumer Sales Directive in the Context of the Europeanization of Contract Law*, 2008 (ISBN: 978-90-411-2752-5).
15. Hugh Collins (ed.), *Standard Contract Terms in Europe: A Basis for and a Challenge to European Contract Law*, 2008 (ISBN 978-90-411-2784-6).
16. Alessandro Somma (ed.), *The Politics of the Draft Common Frame of Reference*, 2009 (ISBN 978-90-411-3141-6).